"What have you done for me lately?"

"What have you done for me lately?"

A Benjamin Company/Rutledge Book

Prepared and produced by Rutledge Books, Inc.
Published by The Benjamin Company, Inc.
        485 Madison Avenue, New York, N.Y. 10022

Library of Congress Catalog Card Number: 79–55477
ISBN 0–87502–075–5
Printed in the United States of America
First Printing January 1980

Contents

*Dedicated to Irving Stern
and Harry Van Arsdale*

ACKNOWLEDGMENTS

Grateful acknowledgment is extended to the following for permission to reprint excerpts from copyrighted material:

Atlantic Monthly Press: From *Exploring the Dangerous Trades* by Alice Hamilton. Copyright © 1942 and 1943 by Alice Hamilton. Reprinted by permission.

A.S. Barnes & Co.: From *The Crisis of American Labor* by Sidney Lens. Copyright © 1961 by A.S. Barnes & Co. Reprinted by permission.

Cornell University Press: From *Black Workers in White Unions: Job Discrimination in the United States* by William B. Gould. Copyright © 1977 by Cornell University. Reprinted by permission of the publisher, Cornell University Press.

Delacorte Press: From *Toil and Trouble: A History of American Labor* by Thomas R. Brooks. Copyright © 1964, 1971 by Thomas R. Brooks. Reprinted by permission.

Harper & Row: From *The Organizational Revolution* by Kenneth Boulding. Copyright © 1953 by the Federal Council of Churches of Christ in America. Reprinted by permission. From *Social Responsibilities of Organized Labor* by John A. Fitch. Copyright © 1957 by the Federal Council of Churches of Christ in America. Reprinted by permission. From *Why Survive: Being Old in America* by Lawrence N. Butler. Copyright © 1975 by Lawrence N. Butler. Reprinted by permission.

Houghton Mifflin: From *Labor Today: The Triumphs and Failures of Unionism in the United States.* Copyright © 1964 by B. J. Widick. Reprinted by permission.

International Publishers: From *History of the Labor Movement in the United States.* Copyright © 1975 by International Publishers. Reprinted by permission.

Interstate Printers & Publishers: From *The Advance of American Cooperative Enterprise: 1920—1945* by Joseph Knapp. Copyright © 1973 by Interstate Printers & Publishers. Reprinted by permission.

The Macmillan Co.: From *A History of American Labor* by Joseph G. Rayback. Copyright © 1959, 1966 by Joseph G. Rayback. Reprinted by permission.

National Association of Social Workers: From *Social Work and Social Living* by Bertha Capen Reynolds. Copyright © 1951 by National Association of Social Workers. Reprinted by permission.

Pantheon Books, division of Random House: From *Work Is Dangerous to Your Health: A Handbook of Health Hazards in the Workplace and What You Can Do About Them* by Jeanne M. Stellman and Susan M. Daum. Copyright © 1971, 1973. Reprinted by permission.

Anne C. Polisar: From *History of Labor in the United States* by John R. Commons et al. Copyright © 1958 by the Macmillan Co. Reprinted by permission of Anne C. Polisar.

Princeton University Press: From *As Unions Mature: An Analysis of the Evolution of American Unionism* by Richard A. Lester. Copyright © 1958 by Princeton University Press. Princeton Paperback, 1966. Reprinted by permission.

Public Affairs Press: From *American Labor: A Bicentennial History* by M. B. Schnapper. Copyright © 1972 by M.B. Schnapper. Reprinted by permission.

Foreword

There are a few good books about working people, but there aren't many good books about the labor movement. Some are slight and most are dry as dust.

The muckrakers around the turn of the century, the Greenwich Village idealists of the 1920s, the proletarian novelists of the 1930s and a surprising number of post–World War II sociologists, economists and journalists all looked into the nature of work, the nature of the working man and the nature of the labor movement and, as one would expect in a relatively free economy and open society, came up with a variety of different conclusions based upon a variety of different perceptions. The worst of the lot were the journalists, many of whom found it easier to lecture than to report.

A rare exception was Austin Perlow, who preferred to report. For many years labor-business editor of the late *Long Island Press*, the author of this book reported all the important (and some unimportant) doings involving labor not only in Nassau and Suffolk counties, but in New York and the country as well. He never missed a beat. And even though Mr. Perlow involved himself personally in some of the activities of the Long Island labor movement, principally its community services program and the Tri-County Labor-Management Institute, which he founded, he kept his journalistic objectivity intact.

Unlike others who wrote about labor, Austin Perlow looked upon American trade unions through a wide-open lens. The result was an all-embracing view of a many-splendored movement—a movement not only concerned with union organization, collective bargaining and other seemingly parochial problems, but with a variety of activities that touch directly the very heart of the country and the very lives of its inhabitants.

To be sure, Mr. Perlow wrote his share of sensational stories about industrial relations, breakdowns, strikes, picket

lines, government intervention and even the misdeeds of falli-
ble men. But he also wrote about organized labor's involvement in community services, education, politics, the arts,
health care, rehabilitation and civil rights.

Throughout his long and successful journalistic career,
Austin Perlow saw clearly that the labor movement extends
beyond the plant gates and beyond the collective bargaining
agreement, and that the union contract is a beginning
without an end.

It is this clear perception that the author now shares with
us in this long-overdue, unusual and welcome book.

The book is long overdue because it is high time that the
interested reader was exposed to the entire labor movement
and not only to its sensational parts.

The book is unusual because there is nothing quite like it
in this country nor any other country for that matter.

And the book is welcome because it is neither slight nor
dry. In his competent journalistic fashion, Mr. Perlow has
presented us a vivid account of the less known but very important activities of a social, economic and political movement that touches the lives not only of American working
men and women but of all Americans.

LEO PERLIS
Director, AFL-CIO Department of Community Services
Washington, D.C.

Preface

After thirty-six years as a trade unionist and seventeen as a labor columnist, I am still surprised that so many American trade unionists are indifferent or hostile to their labor organizations, despite the vast array of services made available to them, in or out of the contract.

While there is a voluminous literature on the history of trade unions, the complexities of labor-management relations and the regulation of collective bargaining, there is a sparsity of data available on the extent of the services that the rank and file may obtain merely by asking for them.

It is a truism in labor that members constantly ask, "What have you done for me lately?" But my surveys indicate comparatively few union members are aware of the vast range of services they are entitled to, either directly from public or private agencies, or through the intervention of their union representatives. On the contrary, many are not even aware their unions could intervene on their behalf.

During the course of lecturing to shop stewards on means of improving communications with the rank and file, I have often suggested that a "gripe" needs as much tactful response as a grievance. But each time I have advocated that the troubled member be referred to community services, there has been the inevitable response:

A hand will be raised by a member of the shop stewards' class, and the question is always phrased: "What is community service?"

In an effort to solve the riddle of the gap between the institution and its members, but with no intention of becoming an apologist for trade unions, I have surveyed the range of services to determine the motivation for the benevolent paternalism that unions evince for their members, the response of the rank and file and the practical extent to which they are served.

While I found an appreciable degree of apathy characteristic of the "average" union member, I am convinced this reflects the apathy characteristic of society today and is not peculiar to trade unions alone.

I do not agree with Sidney Lens that union leaders fail to "rise above the narrowness and rote of their epoch" or fail to "chart a new direction."[1] It isn't labor that faces a crisis, but society. True, Lens noted this, observing that "apathy is the prevailing mood of our society," and a decade later this is, I believe, still true. Unions still reflect the attitudes of society, because they are part of society. Rather than find fault with unions and their leaders—an all-too-prevalent sport—one should look critically at what has happened to the American dream. A survey in midwinter, 1974–75, by Yankelovich, Skelly and White, Inc., revealed that 37 percent of American families may be losing faith in that dream: a home of their own, college for their children and financial security in retirement.

Nor do I foresee the dismal future B. J. Widick anticipated for labor in 1964:

> As long as [unions] are guided by business philosophy—which belongs in a business world and not in a "non-profit," "do-good" movement—they will founder and stagnate. Unions may become richer, whether smaller or larger, but they won't make the kind of contribution which is the real reason for their existence—adding dignity, stature, freedom and democracy to the lives of the men and women who work for a living in this country and who are the heart of our industrial complex.[2]

More than a decade later, it is possible to write that to a large extent unions are making "the kind of contribution which is the real reason for their existence—adding dignity, stature, freedom and democracy" to the lives of their members and the community through services not in the contract. That effort could overcome the prevailing image of organized labor as a conspiracy defrauding the consumer, chiseling the employer and circumventing the government.

In the academic mind, a distinction is unfairly drawn between "trade union" as an institution *capable* of serving its members and "trade union leadership," which more or less lives up to its obligation to serve the member.

"The question is," observed Professor Al Nash of the State School of Industrial and Labor Relations of Cornell University, "how much are labor leaders doing? And is it enough?"

I do not know how much would be enough, but I concede not enough is being done by any social institution. However, in all the research I have devoted to the services American unions do supply, it has been surprising to learn how vast an array of services is available. In one volume, however, it is possible only to sample them briefly.

The union today to a great extent is still the benevolent society it was originally in Colonial America before the development of capitalism and collective bargaining. The thought is not readily accepted, since a static corps of labor "leaders" is believed incapable of benevolence. When the topic of this book was loosely phrased as "trying to determine the extent of the services offered by unions," the reactions of prominent union officers in New York were disturbing. For instance, the president of an amalgamated local, who has a reputation for pioneering work among minority workers, commented, "Oh, a work of fiction!"

An officer of the New York Central Labor Council exclaimed, "Didn't know you wrote fiction!"

Humor, yes, but reflecting a disquieting attitude. If they were being facetious, what of the reaction of the public and the molders of public opinion? The attitude of the press may be summed up in the question a newspaper reporter asked when interviewing the director of a newly formed labor agency: "But what's in it for you?"

Clearly, the reporter was unable to understand why a union member should volunteer to help workers in distress.

This work is an effort to answer his question, as well as to examine the reasons for the poor image organized labor has. It may also help more union members answer the same questions. One community services director, asked for the rationale for helping members, lost his composure of a sudden and stammered, "But, we've always done it," and then added, "It's always been that way in my family, too. My mother was famous for helping people in Hell's Kitchen."

This work may also explain why an AFL-CIO counselor takes the following pledge:

> I pledge my services to all persons who seek my assistance on problems affecting their health and welfare.
>
> My services will extend to all my fellow union members and to my neighbors, regardless of their race, creed or color.
>
> I shall respect all personal matters confided to me and shall never betray confidence.

I shall never seek personal profit through the services I am able to give my fellow union members and to the community.

I shall do my best to support and strengthen the community services program in my own union and in the AFL-CIO as a whole.

I will always seek to increase my knowledge and understanding so that I may better serve the needs of my union and the community in which I live.[3]

It may be worth stressing that nothing in this pledge restricts the counselor to serving only AFL-CIO members. On the contrary, he serves the community.

Notes

1. Sidney Lens, *The Crisis of American Labor*, p. 25.
2. B. J. Widick, *Labor Today: The Triumphs and Failures of Unionism in the United States*, p. 210.
3. *Community Services and Rehabilitation Counselors Handbook*, p. 5.

Joe travelled up and down the country spreading the word. His message was that union organization is only a means and that collective bargaining is only a beginning—both fundamental and powerful to be sure—but first steps nonetheless; that union men and women are, after all, also citizens, consumers, parents, homeowners and taxpayers; that it is the responsibility of the union, therefore, to help meet their personal and family needs that are not covered by the union contract.

Peter Bommarito

"What have you done for me lately?"

1.
Not in the Contract

"What's a union all about, Dave?" I asked the assistant business manager. "Is it simply negotiating contracts and resolving grievances?"

"Hell, no!" he answered, then continued:

I'm not sure what the answer is, but somehow, I'm reminded of something that happened years ago when I was a business rep. I was alone on a Sunday afternoon, baby-sitting—the wife was out—when Jim Treanor called on the phone, all upset, crying about his wife, Kaye, who was in a hospital, in need of type A-positive blood or she'd die. Before I could get the story straight he hung up, without telling me what hospital she was in.

I called his home at once, but he wasn't there. His daughter told me Mrs. Treanor was in Hempstead General Hospital, about to undergo surgery and needed A-positive blood. I called the hospital, had Treanor paged and got the whole story out of him this time. It looked bad. Here it was, Sunday afternoon and nowhere to turn for help.

I took the baby to a neighbor and got to work on the phone. Called up the LILCO [Long Island Lighting] service section and ordered a radio call to all the trucks in the field with an appeal to men with type A-positive to go to Hempstead General to help Jim's wife.

Things started to pop then. Joe Turburg called his son, Ed, who took off for the hospital. Ray Jeager got a lift from Phil Boscio. Stan Lasko also went to donate blood. Jim Becher went to Charlie Keuchler's home when he remembered Charlie had A-positive. Keuchler remembered friends in the Massapequa Fire Department who could help out. So he called them.

I got into the car and dashed over to the hospital, only to find the place in an uproar. They had no technician on duty to take the blood. But we finally got it all straightened out and everybody took off to Meadowbrook to give blood there.

Well, to cut a long story short, they operated on Mrs. Treanor that day and she pulled through all right. But it was the blood that saved her.

Dave stopped for a moment and I imagined I saw a tear forming in his eyes as he remembered the drama of that distant day.

That was a long time ago, but the story ended for me just five years ago when the Treanors' girl got married and I was invited to attend. Mrs. Treanor told her daughter she was able to attend the wedding only because of what I had done.

I think that's what a union is all about. But, of course, I was only doing what I'm paid to do.

"You're a liar, Dave, and you know it," I said. "You didn't go to all that trouble because you're paid to."

"I guess you're right," he conceded. "Money doesn't have anything to do with it."

It is obvious a union is "an organization of wage earners or salaried employees for mutual aid and protection and for dealing collectively with employers."

But the dictionary definition, despite its clarity, gives no hint of the characteristic features of the American trade union—the community of interest, the fraternal spirit that motivates so many programs not covered by the contract.

To understand what impelled Dave Fabrizzio in 1966 to enlist the services of the rank and file of Local 1049, International Brotherhood of Electrical Workers, and *why they responded* to save the life of a woman probably few of them even knew, requires recognition that our contemporary trade unions are no more than an outgrowth of the first protective and benevolent societies established well over 200 years ago in the early American colonies.

Made up of masters, journeymen and apprentices, the societies were organized to help brothers either unemployed or ill, or their families when the worker died or was killed on the job. While masters are excluded today from virtually all unions (supervisors belong to public employee unions), journeymen and apprentices can still rely upon benefits during unemployment, sickness, accident or death under labor agreements negotiated by even the most corrupt of unions.

No ideology binds American trade unionists together. The unions shun syndicalism and codeterminism. Socialism is abhorrent to nearly all, except the International Longshoremen's and Warehousemen's Union (led for forty years by Harry Bridges, an avowed Marxist whose revolutionary views were tempered in time to accept peaceful, democratic change) and the Industrial Workers of the World, who still keep the faith of the Wobblies aflame. If there is any spark of ideology in labor, it is support of free enterprise. That was inevitable, as long as the poor could escape oppression as pioneers on the western frontier in preindustrial times. Today, labor is equally conservative, knowing the mixed economy can afford to meet the demands of unions through collective bargaining.

That explains why there is so little movement in the trade union movement. Ordinarily, "movement" connotes "cause," implying "aggression on the property rights or political power of others." However, since the term "labor movement" is universally accepted as synonymous with trade unionism, the term will be used here in that sense.

Unlike their European brothers, American workers have no labor philosophy beyond Samuel Gompers' exhortation to strive for "more." Certainly there are no political ties binding them together as Democrats or Republicans, nor does the wide range of alternatives—the Communist Party, the Socialists, the U. S. Labor Party, the Socialist Workers, the People's Party or even a candidate such as Senator Eugene J. McCarthy—appeal to trade unionists in significant numbers. These combined alternatives aggregated only 1,708,547 votes from all adherents, or just above 2 percent of the total Presidential vote cast in 1976.

What could be more appealing to militant trade unionists than the platform of the Socialist Workers, stressing the traditional "decline of capitalism" as rooted in the class structure of society? Its Bill of Rights calls for the right to a job, an adequate income, free education, free medical care and secure retirement. Yet, the party's candidate for President, Peter Camejo, polled only 90,109 votes in 1976.

Organized labor has been deeply involved in politics in the past, but that does not account for the dogged determination with which unions resisted every measure, from injunction to massacre, to suppress them.

Indeed, labor's political activities, from the very beginning when the Workingmen's Party named its first slate in 1828, through the National Labor Party of the 1860s, to the crest of the Socialist wave in 1912 when the party held 1,200 political offices in 340 cities, have been marked more by lobbying achievements than political representation.

There is no labor bloc to cast a vote. Certainly, trade unionists don't vote as the working class, since there is little or no awareness on the part of Americans that they belong to a "class," as there is in England, where a structured society is based on stringent class lines from which there is little chance of escape. If anything, the American worker believes he's part of the amorphous, socioeconomic middle class, a term so ill defined it has no meaning, any more than "average American" has. As for "proletariat," the term is indelibly stamped with scarlet-letter Marxist connotations.

While this may explain the positions taken by the AFL-CIO on economic questions, it does not shed light on the intrinsic nature of the labor movement that has enabled it to violate universally held labor precepts without fear of disavowal from its partisans. A few recent examples come to mind:

The AFL-CIO and the United Auto Workers collaborated with the auto industry in 1975 to bar legislation increasing fuel efficiency in autos, and two years later lobbied again to limit restrictions on auto emissions in the name of saving jobs. Nor did differences of opinion appear when ranking trade unionists voted with the heads of General Motors, General Electric, United States Steel, Alcoa, Mobil Oil and First National City Bank as members òf the President's Labor-Management Committee. There was unanimity on the issues of taxes, energy and utility expansion. A. H. Raskin of the *New York Times* observed that in any European country, spokesmen for capital and labor would have been arrayed on opposing sides of insurmountable ideological barriers.

Whether labor supports corporate enterprise because it believes in the "system" or because of its tremendous investment in union-managed pension funds (Peter F. Drucker estimated that the largest union-managed funds had $35 billion in assets at the end of 1974)[1] is not relevant, since its attitude does not impair the adversary relationship maintained through collective bargaining. (True, there are sweetheart contracts uncovered from time to time, but not to an extent that has attenuated prevailing practices of negotiation.)

But what is overlooked is organized labor's insistence on full employment and tax reform—two "radical" programs that would lead to the redistribution of wealth and a transformation of free enterprise.

The collective bargaining process does not explain the prevalence of unions; indeed, its most prominent feature, the strike, has earned far more criticism of unions than the so-called corruptness of labor leaders. The unions are a heterogeneous collection of craft and industrial organizations rarely in agreement on goals, accustomed to bargaining, with few exceptions, on a shop-by-shop basis. At the apex, the AFL-CIO, largest confederation of unions in the country, does not engage in collective bargaining for less than 100 loosely knit affiliates who function autonomously.

Autonomy is a basic feature of union structure, furnishing a clue to the essence of the trade union. Each international union—some have locals in Canada—has its own charter, constitution and bylaws, but all make common use of Robert's Rules of Order for Deliberative Assemblies, which is regarded as the Bible of unions. This may provide some insight into the violent antipathy labor has for totalitarian government, as well as the allegiance each member owes his union.

There were 16,848,000 members in the 110 AFL-CIO affiliates in 1974, or 78 percent of the total union membership. To this should be added the membership of associations that bargain collectively and the independent unions, including the International Brotherhood of Teamsters and the United Auto Workers, bringing the total to 24,200,000, or 28.6 percent of total employment in 1974. So small a number leads to the prevailing belief that "only one in four Americans belongs to a union," i.e., there's little benefit to be gained in being a union member. (The 1974–76 recession also reduced union membership by 767,000, the first loss since 1960–62, but by 1978 the total membership rose to 24,295,000 in unions and associations.)

The belief that unions fail to provide a rationale for membership is based on a fallacy; it fails to take into account the proportion of workers who can legally affiliate. Once the exclusions under the National Labor Relations Act are considered (managers, supervisors, confidential employees) plus those in the armed forces, farmers, farm managers, self-employed, unpaid family retainers, domestic workers and professionals, the proportion of union members in the labor force is no longer a disquieting one in four but better than one in three.

That doesn't take into account unaffiliated workers in open or agency shops who benefit from union contracts. Indeed, trade unionism is far more pervasive than its ardent supporters believe. And growth in membership is not only likely but inevitable among public employees and service and farm workers.

Who, after all, are the members of trade unions who find it rewarding to remain affiliated with an institution that has survived in the face of 200 years of oppression and consistently poor press and public image? Surely there must be something more to a trade union than bargaining for wages, hours and working conditions?

We have but one authoritative (but already outdated) outline of the image of the average union member in the John Kraft polling organization profile prepared for the AFL-CIO in 1967. The study was interpreted by the *Public Interest* in the winter of 1968 as tending to prove "the range and extent of the embourgeoisement of the American trade unionist," as illustrated in the "conservatism of the group and its middle-class concerns."

The judgment may appear harsh, but Alexander Barkan, director of the AFL-CIO Committee on Political Education (COPE), conceded there were "warning signals" in the lack of support for policy positions "among younger members."

As indicated by the survey,[2] the general profile of the trade union member showed:

Thirty-two percent were in the $5,000- to $7,500-a-year income range (including, in many cases, the earnings of working wives and offspring).

Forty-six percent were in the $7,500- to $15,000-a-year income range.

Twenty-five percent of union members were less than thirty years old.

Nearly 50 percent were less than forty years old.

Nearly 50 percent of all members lived in suburbs.

Nearly 75 percent of members under forty lived in suburbs.

About 20 percent of union members were women.

About 13 percent of union members were Negro and 4 percent Mexican, Oriental or other minority.

Twenty-five percent of members belonged to their union five years or less.

Fifty-four percent belonged to their unions for ten years or more.

Fifty-eight percent identified themselves as Democrats, 16 percent as Republicans, 17 percent as independents and 9 percent were not sure.

While the poll was taken in January, 1967, when President Johnson's popularity was at a low ebb, more than half the union members declared themselves emphatically for his reelection against any Republican contender. (Only those under age thirty favored Governor George Romney over Johnson.)

Strong support was shown, in varying degrees, by all age groups for the major issues of the day, including expansion of Medicare, water pollution control, truth in lending, repeal of Taft-Hartley Section 14(b), air pollution control, improved workmen's compensation, truth in packaging, higher minimum wages and federal aid to education. But open housing was coolly received, 43 percent agreeing and 46 percent disagreeing. Eleven percent responded they were "not sure."

It was only when union members were asked, "What are the big problems on your mind—the things that bother you and should be getting attention?" that the image of the American worker came into focus:

The issues clearly uppermost on their minds were those involving jobs and economic security, the war in Vietnam and civil rights.

Fifty-three percent of all members listed economic problems, ranging from the cost of living and taxes to the unemployment picture and wages. Forty-two percent listed the war in Vietnam, with the largest percentage of these supporting the President's policies there. More than 33 percent listed civil rights as a major issue. While most members supported civil rights progress in voting and public accommodations, support for open housing was slightly below the 50 percent point.[3]

Barkan's assessment appears valid although some may find the image disturbingly conservative. But why should it be disturbing? The reactions of union workers to the high cost of living and taxes are self-explanatory; they are the reactions of workers with incomes inadequate to cope with inflation, layoffs, seasonal work and a tax structure whose loopholes provide direct welfare payments to the wealthiest families and corporations in the nation.

Thus far, the average union member's profile strongly suggests there must be more involved in joining the union than merely sharing in the contract benefits. There is, since the Kraft poll did indicate that 32 percent of union families were earning only from $5,000 to $7,500 a year and another 46 percent from $7,500 to $15,000, but this often included the earnings of wives and children!

Since that survey, labor took another intensive look at the membership in 1975, when 7,506 members of forty-eight international unions returned questionnaires on housing to the AFL-CIO Department of Urban Affairs. The survey, undertaken to "provide a strategy for meeting housing goals for low- and moderate-income families," revealed something about the incomes of union members as well as their housing facilities:

Seventy-seven percent of all member households owned the homes they occupied.

The median income of surveyed households in 1974 was $14,552, compared with a median income of $11,101 for all U.S. households. [However, the survey excluded farm workers and had few elderly and one-person households. A somewhat greater percentage of households in large, industrial, higher-income states was indicated.]

Thirty-five percent of the union homeowners owned their homes free and clear, including 85 percent of all owner households whose head was sixty-five or older.

Renter households represented 23 percent of all AFL-CIO members in the survey. Their median income was $12,000. (Twenty percent of them were either one-person households or two-or-more-person households headed by females, in comparison to 7 percent of owner households.)

Over 37 percent of the rental units were more than thirty-five years old and only 11 percent of the owner-occupied units were more than thirty-five years old.

Sixty-one percent of the renters and 17 percent of the homeowners indicated their desire to move in the next five years.

The higher than U.S. median incomes may appear to indicate AFL-CIO homeowners are better off than the average American family. This, however, is an illusion, since the higher incomes were earned by more than one wage earner in a family. In fact, in those families with an income of $25,000 or more, 87 percent of the owner households had more than one worker; from $15,000 to $24,999 in income, 61 percent; $10,000 to $14,999, 31 percent; $7,000 to $9,999, 24 percent; and less than $7,000, 19 percent.[4]

The data must be treated with some caution, since 891 respondents out of 7,796 did not report their incomes. The total of 663 reporting annual incomes of $25,000 or over amounted to only 8.5 percent of the total responding.

But it should be apparent from the two profiles of the average union member that if it is wages that form the chief incentive for joining a union, clearly it must be something not in the contract that creates an intense loyalty.

It may be rightfully argued that the two profiles are sadly out of date; that the average union member of the 1970s is quite unlike the union member of a decade earlier. After all, the end of the Vietnam War (and the end of the illusion of a "peace bonus" in the form of a stimulated economy), the induced anti-inflationary recession of 1971 and the stagflation of 1974–76 had a salutary effect on the ranks of labor, undoubtedly because trade unionists had to face issues squarely as well as tighten their belts. It may well be that growing disillusionment may help promote the emergence of a new class of union member in this decade.

Thomas R. Brooks, for one, is convinced a new working class is emerging in the 1970s. Until recently, he observed,

> ethnic and religious animosities often outweighed class solidarity among working people in this country. Ethnic and religious differences help account for the lack of a working class or labor-oriented party in American politics. There are signs, however, of a change.[5]

The change is apparent in an awareness that social legislation is more productive than collective bargaining, and—its consequence—that political action is imperative, as Brooks observed. It is obvious also in the emergence of a young, educated, skeptical member who will increasingly resort to the union to have his needs satisfied, both within and out of the contract. These are the people who are loyal to the union in the face of criticism and disparagement, despite their own doubts, which are constantly nurtured by virtually daily slurs cast by the print and broadcast press. But note, if you will, that the trade unionist is not an alien, not a revolutionary, not a member of a cause determined on "aggression on the property rights or political power of others." He is an American supporting an American institution.

Why has he maintained his union membership in the face of constant discouragement? Certainly, there are reasons enough to persuade him to insist on his "right to work" without being a union member. Countless polls over the decades have made it apparent that while a large majority of Americans approve of unions *in principle* and of the right of employees to join the union of their choice, in practice they do not approve at all.

They don't approve because unions are too big. They believe unions should be more stringently regulated; that government should intervene in strikes; that unions should carry out the wishes of their leaders, not members; that unions are strike-happy and dominated by organized crime. (The Department of Justice estimated in 1978 that only 0.4 percent of the 75,000 local unions in the country were under the influence of organized crime.)[6] Overall, the public has little confidence in labor leaders. Are they unaware of what unions are and what they do aside from negotiating contracts?

Within the contract, the union carries out the basic function of negotiating agreements covering wages, hours and working conditions. Outside the contract, however, the union engages in a host of services to benefit the member and community to a greater or lesser extent, depending upon the individual union and the attitude of the immediate community. It is the extent of those services not written into the contract that ensures the prevalence of unions; otherwise they would have been legislated out of existence long ago as incompatible with free enterprise.

Those services fill a void in the social structure. No other institution furnishes them to as large and as varied a segment of the population. They include adult education, scholarships, housing, day care centers, health and medical centers, mental therapy, treatment of alcoholism, credit unions, women's rights programs, emergency assistance during fires, floods and storms, prepaid legal aid, consumer protection, job placement, assistance in applying for unemployment insurance benefits, workmen's compensation, social security, etc., as well as preretirement counseling, retirees' programs, homes for the aged and development of the arts.

Such programs, designed to keep the worker happy and able to lead a productive, satisfying life, are the very essence of the trade union movement, whose primary goal has always been to provide for the welfare of the worker, his family and the community.

We shall see not only why this is so, but the extent to which this goal is being achieved.

Notes
1. Peter F. Drucker, *The Unseen Revolution*, p. 12.

2. Alexander E. Barkan, "The Union Member: Profile and Attitudes," *American Federationist*, August 1967, pp. 1–6.
3. Ibid., p. 4.
4. *Survey of AFL-CIO Members Housing, 1975*, AFL-CIO, 1975, p. 12.
5. Thomas R. Brooks, *Toil and Trouble*, p. 375.
6. *New York Times*, 25 April 1978, p. 18.

2.

Motivation for Service

Years ago we had a young woman, a meat wrapper in one of the super-markets, who attempted suicide. Luckily, she didn't die. The shop steward called it to our attention, so we called her in and talked to her. We gave her a job in the office here. She has been working here for, let's see, about twelve years now. I feel we saved a life.

There are an untold number of public and private agencies in the United States devoted to caring for the needy, the ill, the injured, the handicapped and the victims of disasters ranging from tornadoes to earthquakes. As nonprofit enterprises, they are endlessly engaged in fund raising.

Questioning the motives—or the disposition of funds—of the American Red Cross, the National Foundation, the Y.M.C.A., the Salvation Army, Catholic Charities or Jewish Community Services appears unthinkable. Yet, they raise millions of dollars annually in contributions for their causes, without awakening a breath of suspicion.

But not so with unions; that's quite another matter!

They, too, raise funds, not only on behalf of relief agencies and charities, but for their own programs aimed at serving workers, whether union members or not. The public, indeed their own members, frequently view appeals for funds with suspicion growing out of disbelief that a union could be concerned with the community's welfare.

But unions do "give a damn" about the welfare of the worker. The motivation can be found in the purposes for which unions are formed.

Start at the top with the constitution of the AFL-CIO, which provides in Article XII, Section 1(i):

The Committee on Community Services shall stimulate the active participation by members and affiliated unions in the affairs of their communities and the development of sound relationships in such communities.

Those few words, deemed vital enough to be incorporated in the

11

constitution, created a standing committee to carry out past policy when the American Federation of Labor and the Congress of Industrial Organizations merged in 1955. The committee was an outgrowth of the CIO community service program, established in 1943 when the CIO funded the committee with $13,500 for its first year of operations.

That sum included the salaries of the director, Leo Perlis, and his secretary, and the overhead for their first office at 1776 Broadway, New York. That may have been the first national CIO community services committee, but the tradition can be traced back to the first benevolent and protective societies of masters, journeymen and apprentices—long before there was collective bargaining, before there were trade unions.

In his history of American labor, Joseph Rayback observes that the first mechanics' societies were organized ". . . in most cities along the coast after 1725. Often mistaken for guilds, they were actually 'benevolent and protective' associations, open to both masters and journeymen."[1]

The articles and regulations of the earliest societies of tradesmen made no reference to wages, hours or working conditions. (Not only would that have constituted a conspiracy, but there was no collective bargaining.) What, then, did these societies declare the purpose of organization was?

The text of the Articles and Regulations of the Friendly Society of Tradesmen, House Carpenters, in the City of New York, drawn up March 10, 1767, spelled out the purposes of the society:

VII. If any of our members fall sick, or through Age or Accidents are rendered incapable of getting his Livelihood, he shall, after Six Days Illness, give proper Notice to the President, or either of the Stewards, and the Stewards shall visit the sick Member twice in the Week, and by Order of the President, shall pay unto the impotent Member, the Sum of Ten Shillings at the End of every seven Days . . .

IX. If any of our Members should go to the Country and fall sick, or be by any other unforeseen Accident rendered incapable of supporting himself, he shall transmit to some one of our Members of this Society, a Certificate signed by two or more credible Witnesses, before a Justice of the Peace, or the Parson of the Parish, where he then resides, before he shall be entitled to Benefits resulting to him as a Member of this Society.

X. On the Death of any of our Members, there shall be allowed for his funeral Expence, the Sum of Four Pounds, to be taken out of the principal Stock; and in order to supply this Deficiency, each Member, at the next Meeting, shall pay One Shilling extraordinary. . .

XI. When any of our Members die within this City, Information thereof shall be brought to the two Stewards, and the said Stewards shall give

proper Notice to as many Members of this Society as they can, to attend
the Funeral of the deceased Member, for which the said Stewards shall
receive the Sum of Four Shillings each . . .[2]

That was at least one of the roots of trade union service to the
member, and throughout American history there has been a strong
tradition of serving the member and the community—totally apart
from the procedures of collective bargaining. Education and libraries,
for example, were early campaign goals of the workers. In the
monumental *History of Labour in the United States*, John R. Commons
pointed out early in the four-volume work:

> The mechanics and tradesmen of New York took the lead in 1821 when
> their society obtained passage of an act amending its articles of incorpora-
> tion so that they might appropriate a part of their funds to the support of a
> school . . . and also to the establishment of an apprentices's library, for the
> use of apprentices of mechanics in the City of New York.[3]

That was not, of course, as common a practice as the payment of
benefits to sick members of mutual aid societies formed by journeymen
in the early 1800s. The sick benefits, paid for out of members' dues,
were among the first benefits furnished by the predecessors of trade
unions, but they were not the only ones. In case of accident, which left
the member unable to pursue his livelihood, or death, where his widow
and children were left penniless, the society remained true to its fraternal, benevolent and protective spirit, caring for the member or his
survivors.

There was no workmen's compensation in those early days, no
Social Security, no health insurance plan, no pension or welfare program subsidized in part or wholly by the employer. On the contrary,
the employer had little or no moral obligation and no legal compulsion
to recompense the worker sickened or killed by the conditions of his
employment. There was only the benevolent society of journeymen to
turn to for help.

The constitutions of trade unions, whether written in the twentieth century or 200 years earlier, provide adequate evidence that
unions, as well as their forerunners, were organized to care for the
general welfare of the members. To cite one of the oldest examples in
the United States:

> When the funds of the (printers) society shall have amounted to $100, the
> board of directors may award such sum to sickly and distressed members,
> their widows and children, as to them may seem meet and proper. Provid-
> ed, that such sum shall not exceed $3 per week.[4]

Indeed, the practice was so firmly established that by 1827, when Philadelphia carpenters went out on strike, a committee of twelve was established, not only to negotiate with the master carpenters, but to "distribute the funds of the organization to those poor journeymen house carpenters who stand in need of assistance during the standout."[5]

While union constitutions may be skeptically regarded as self-serving, rhetorical, even bombastic, rather than mandates to the officers and members, the principles outlined in constitutions and, more specifically, in their preambles, are revealing as to the reasons why unions are organized. In 1955, when the AFL-CIO constitution was written, the preamble declared:

> We pledge ourselves to the more effective organization of working men and women; to the securing to them of full recognition and enjoyment of the rights to which they are justly entitled; to the achievement of ever higher standards of living and working conditions; to the attainment of security for all the people; to the enjoyment of the leisure which their skills make possible; and to the strengthening of our way of life and the fundamental freedoms which are the basis of our democratic society.

Written in the same decade, the constitution of the New York State AFL-CIO is equally restrained, but traces of the age-old dreams of trade unions emerge in at least two sections of the Article III Objects:

> 3. To preserve the right of working people to act in concert for mutual aid, protection and advancement . . .
>
> 7. To safeguard and strengthen civil rights and fundamental human freedoms . . .

The preamble to the constitution of the Amalgamated Meat Cutters and Butcher Workmen of North America* still reflects the militancy of its founding fathers, John F. Hart, George Byer, W. H. Schwartz and Homer D. Call. The union received its charter from the American Federation of Labor on January 27, 1897:

> Labor has no protection; the weak are devoured by the strong; all wealth and all power center in the hands of the few, and many are their victims and their bondmen.
>
> In all countries, and at all times, capital has been used to monopolize particular branches of business, until the vast and various industrial pursuits of the world are centralized under the immediate control of a comparatively small portion of mankind. Year after year the capital of the country becomes more and more concentrated in the hands of the few;

---

*Merged in June, 1979, with the Retail Clerks International Union into the United Food and Commercial Workers International Union.

and in proportion as the wealth of the country becomes centralized, its power increases and the laboring classes are more or less impoverished.

Realizing that in union there is strength, the Amalgamated Meat Cutters and Butcher Workmen of North America was founded, and must continue to enroll as members all persons engaged in the meat and allied industries. Collectively, the workers are better able to secure their fair share of the profits created as a result of their toil. United there is no wrong that may be inflicted upon us by the employers which we may not defy openly and correct.

Therefore, the butcher workmen in all places must organize and affiliate themselves with this international Union. . . . It must be the purpose of this organization always to continue to elevate the social, moral, economic, and intellectual status of each individual as well as the groups in affiliation with our international organization. . .

There is a balanced consideration apparent in the motives of the Meat Cutters which compensates for the excesses in language. But the "struggle against oppression" refrain—an echo from the past—remains not only in the Meat Cutters' constitution, but in preambles written decades later. Witness another echo in the preamble to the constitution of the Retail Clerks International Association:*

WHEREAS: The organization of workers into trade unions has been demonstrated to be and is, essential to the economic, social and political freedom of society and to the successful functioning of a democracy of, for, and by the people free from dictatorship, to the end that men and women shall live and work without discrimination; and,

WHEREAS: The history of the workers in our jurisdiction throughout the world has been the record of constant struggle against oppression; and,

WHEREAS: These troubles have arisen almost entirely from lack of unity and confidence in each other as workers, and misunderstanding the true causes of oppression; and, . . .

WHEREAS: It is necessary that [the worker] have full freedom of association, self-organization, and designation of representation of his own choosing to negotiate the terms and conditions of his employment, and that he shall be free from interference, restraint, or coercion of employers or their agents in the designation of such representatives, or in other concerted activities for the purpose of collective bargaining or other mutual aid or protection;

THEREFORE: For the purpose of promoting such unity and sentiment of action among the workers within our jurisdiction, and joining them closer

---

* Name changed January 1, 1978, to Retail Clerks International Union and now part of the new United Food and Commercial Workers International Union.

together for mutual protection, we have organized the RETAIL CLERKS IN-
TERNATIONAL ASSOCIATION . . .

Only traces remain, in a phrase here and there, of the militant
goals of workingmen who organized unions along more radical lines in
the nineteenth century. The Metal Workers Federation Union of
America, organized in 1885, said in its Declaration of Principles:

> The emancipation of labor cannot be brought about whether by regula-
> tion of hours of labor or by the schedule of wages. The demands and
> struggles for higher wages or shorter hours, if granted, would only better
> the conditions of the wage-earners for a short time. . . . The entire aboli-
> tion of the present system of society can alone emancipate the workers; be-
> ing replaced by a new system based upon cooperative organization of pro-
> duction in a free society.

More conservative unions, established in the same era, retain the
flavor of the language of the times, but are devoid of any desire to
destroy "the system." The Amalgamated Transit Union, organized in
1892 at Indianapolis, states in its preamble:

> We, the Amalgamated Transit Union, . . . in order to secure and defend
> our rights, advance our interests as working men, . . . build up an
> organization where all the working members of our craft can participate
> in the discussion of those practical problems upon the solution of which
> depends our welfare and prosperity, . . . establish order, harmony, pro-
> mote the general cause of humanity and brotherly love, and secure the
> blessings of friendship, equality and truth, do ordain and establish this
> Constitution and these laws for the government of said International
> Union.

But there is included in the "Obligation" something far more
touching. The oath of the new member requires him to solemnly promise and pledge, without reservation or evasion:

> I will be respectful in word and action to every woman, and be con-
> siderate to the widow and orphan, the weak and defenseless, and never
> discriminate against a fellow worker on account of creed, color or na-
> tionality.

Equally conservative is the preamble to the constitution of the International Brotherhood of Electrical Workers. The stated "Objects"
include the obvious aims one might expect, such as "to organize all
workers in the entire electrical industry in the United States and
Canada," and to "promote reasonable methods of work." But the
essense of brotherhood in the name of the union and in the nature of

unions is this age-old object: "*To assist each other in sickness and distress*" (emphasis added).

Nor should the last of eleven objects be slighted:

> And by legal and proper means to elevate the moral, intellectual and social conditions of our members, their families and dependents, in the interest of a higher standard of citizenship.

The constitution was adopted in November, 1891, at St. Louis. The declaration in the first cover page, which must have been added decades later, determines to ". . . continue to oppose communism, nazism or [any] other subversive 'ism.' We will support our God, our Nation, our Union."

Typical of later unions—in sharp contrast with earlier sentiments—was the purpose expressed in the constitution of the American Railway and Airway Supervisors Association, founded in 1935:

> The purpose of this organization . . . shall be to combine the interests of its members in order to gain representation consistent with that of other railroad and airway employees . . . to guard their financial interests and to promote their general welfare; to inculcate the membership with a feeling of true brotherhood and a spirit of loyalty towards employers; to aid in the cultivation of amicable relations between employers and employees; to assist in building up the standard of railroad and airway supervision to a high point of efficiency—all to the end that better service be given to the public which will insure greater returns for both employer and employees, alike.

It would be a mistake, however, to attribute such sentiments to each of the affiliates of the AFL-CIO. Indeed, what sounds, by far, like the most radical language, if not objectives, was used in writing the preamble to the constitution of the original American Federation of Labor.

But that should elicit no surprise. After all, the two principal architects of the AFL, Samuel Gompers and Peter J. McGuire, respectively first president and secretary, were radicals—at least in their youth. Although Gompers, leader of the AFL, was a socialist who advocated class struggle, he belonged to no party. But McGuire, head of the largest affiliate, the carpenters, was a lifelong socialist.[6]

It is doubtful if the delegates gave much heed to the language of the preamble, but they adopted it as presented by the committee on platform:

> Whereas, a struggle is going on in the nations of the civilized world, between oppressors and oppressed of all countries, a struggle between

capital and labor, which must grow in intensity from year to year and work disastrous results to the toiling millions of all nations if not combined for mutual protection and benefit. The history of the wage-workers of all countries is but the history of constant struggle and misery engendered by ignorance and disunion; whereas the history of the nonproducers of all ages proves that a minority, thoroughly organized, may work wonders for good or evil. It behooves the representatives of the workers . . . to adopt such measures and . . . such principles . . . as will unite them for all time to come, to secure the recognition of the rights to which they are justly entitled. Conforming to the old adage, "in union there is strength," the formation of a Federation embracing every trade and labor organization in North America, a union founded upon a basis as broad as the land we live in, is our only hope.

Despite their backgrounds, Gompers and McGuire made no effort to radicalize the AFL, but led it in a program to improve wages, hours and working conditions—in short, one which accepted the wage system and strove to improve the welfare of the member. There was no other ideology—then or now. Nor, indeed, is there any need for a new labor philosophy, not so long as collective bargaining can secure the benefits desired by the unions dominating the AFL-CIO.

A new ideology in the craft and industrial wings of the Federation will come when organized labor realizes its control of corporate equity is so large it need not continue to prop up free enterprise in a postindustrial economy which is rapidly shifting to corporate welfare.

Change comes slowly, painfully, in organized labor, as in all institutions of society. While there is little doubt that unions, which eschewed reform through social legislation until comparatively recently, have indeed achieved tremendous reforms, it was done reluctantly at times; selfishly at times; but at all times pragmatically. The record is clear on that point.

Going back two centuries, the early benevolent associations took repressive steps to curb apprenticeship, only to protect the journeymen members. Nor did the early unions organize women workers in the New England textile mills; the male member's welfare was the first priority. They did not foster child labor social legislation. They took, with few exceptions, no stand on the abolition of slavery. They opposed unemployment compensation.

But it was due to labor that the social reforms of the Roosevelt Era were adopted, and unions to this day foster passage of liberal legislation for the benefit of the community. What accomplished this aboutface? Once labor was recognized as legitimate in organizing, and freed of the constant burden of merely trying to stay alive, it could and did turn its attention to social betterment.

What must be kept in mind, in considering the change, is that equally valid reasons were behind opposing social reforms in the past and fostering them today. Labor leaders aren't usually starry-eyed visionaries, although there were some utopian dreamers. The imponderable they could not overcome was the American characteristic to aspire to power rather than conspire to confiscate the means of production. Helping the member "up the ladder" was the union's chief business.

There is a totally unwarranted denigration of organized labor in the term "business unionism," quite obviously because the term is misunderstood. Accurately defined, "business" means that with which one is principally and seriously concerned. With what are unions chiefly concerned? The welfare of their members!

Indeed, Philip Taft has pointed out that the first rationale for unions was "business unionism," which "stresses limited objectives, immediate improvements and eschews broader programs of social and political change." Understanding this critical point makes it far easier to understand why American trade union leaders for so many decades remained practical business trade unionists who avoided politics, shied away from social legislation and maintained unions could best win their goals through collective bargaining.

Gompers, for example, took a hard stand for many years against enactment of legislation to fix the hours of male workers in private employment—a stand which makes little sense now in the context of the social legislation since enacted. But when he was AFL president (from 1886 to his death in 1924, except for the year 1895), the AFL stand against political involvement made sense. The AFL knew from bitter experience that legislators, the courts and big business were a triumvirate too powerful to oppose. And what the legislature could give, it could also take away. The fear of anti-labor legislation was one of the principal concerns of the AFL, which, under Gompers' control, shied away from political activity. Gompers made that clear:

> I have some apprehension that if the legislature were allowed to establish a maximum work day, it might also compel workers to work up to the maximum allowed . . .

In expressing opposition to legislation fixing minimum wage laws, Gompers summed up the AFL position:

> I apprehend that once the state is allowed to fix a minimum rate, [it] could also take the right to compel men and women to work at that rate.

Recall that even then the elite craft unions of the AFL had already carved out for themselves—through collective bargaining—wages, hours and fringe benefits which legislated minimums could not possibly meet.

Business unionism called for trade unions to use initiative in securing economic demands, rather than becoming dependent upon government. Similarly, there was a distrust of the social reformers, who were not workers, and whose help, while freely offered, was rejected out of fear that in the long run it would destroy the initiative of the unions.

In short, Gompers was insistent upon the independence of the labor movement and the conviction that it could achieve its own goals. He made that apparent when he said, "Social insurance cannot remove or prevent poverty. It does not get at the causes of social injustice. The only agency that does get at the cause of poverty is the organized labor movement."

This attitude, which prevailed for so many decades, reflected the determination to concentrate upon the business of trade unionism: protecting the member. Business unionism persists today, even in terminology, since so many unions have business managers and business agents. The constitution of the Sheet Metal Workers International Association describes the business of these officers:

> Business managers or business representatives or both shall represent their local unions and the members thereof in matters pertaining to collective bargaining agreements, wages, hours, conditions of employment and jurisdictional matters and supervise the conduct and activities of members in connection therewith to the end that the provisions of this Constitution and the policies of this association are complied with . . .

But it would be idle to pretend that the term "business unionism" in a pejorative sense has no validity whatsoever, since all unions, quite obviously, are not cut from the same pattern. There are, indeed, unions which have become institutionalized to the extent of operating as business ventures selling services. Sidney Lens has defined this quite explicitly:

> The essence of business unionism is that it converts the union from a cooperative venture on the part of its members, in which workers collectively decide their own fate, into a service industry, in which the business agent and union leader sell a service to the membership. . . .
>
> It is this progressive emasculation of the democratic process which typifies the business union. To call it honest or dishonest is irrelevant; first, because most business unionists are personally honest, and second, because there is neither more nor less integrity in this form of business than in any other.
>
> Business unionism converts the union from an evangelical effort on the

part of the underprivileged to raise their status into a business venture. It is in that respect no more crooked than business itself and no more lamentable than the prevailing mores of the business community generally.[7]

Yet the image of unions as businesses dealing in labor as a commodity has become pervasive. B. J. Widick, after finding the union hierarchy ranking in national opinion polls down with the oil industry and business executives at the bottom of public esteem, concluded that as a "social movement of the working majority," the unions lacked "the dynamic appeal, momentum and influence generated by such mass activities as the civil rights or antiwar movements of recent times." That, obviously, is not quite fair. Labor was an integral part of both movements.

It is a matter of record that a large labor delegation joined in the march from Montgomery to Selma, Alabama, from March 21 to 25, 1965, led by Russell Cromwell (Laundry and Dry Cleaning Workers), Charles Cogen (American Federation of Teachers), Donald Slaiman (Civil Rights Department, AFL-CIO), Max Greenberg (Retail, Wholesale and Department Store Union), Dave Sullivan (Service Employees International Union), Robert Powcell (Hod Carriers), Ralph Helstein (Packing House Workers) and James B. Carey (International Union of Electrical, Radio and Machine Workers).

And as for the antiwar movement, despite the flag-waving, patriotic stand of George Meany and Co., many unions voiced their anger at the needless, mindless slaughter in Vietnam long before President Nixon made that war universally unpalatable with carpet bombing.

Labor for Peace brought together 985 representatives of organized labor in St. Louis on June 24, 1972, when they adopted a statement of policy which declared in part:

> It is self-evident that this nightmare of killing and destruction has gone on far too long, and that this war is illegal and not in our national interest.
>
> It is self-evident that this war has exacted an intolerable toll in the divisions among our people, in the alienation of our youth, the blighting of our cities and the distortion of our national priorities—and that it has triggered unprecedented strife, racism and violence. . . .
>
> It is self-evident that the overwhelming majority of Americans agree that this war is not worth one more life, one more prisoner, one more hard-earned tax dollar, or one more devastated city, whether here or in Indo-China.
>
> We are therefore resolved that the voice of American labor . . . shall not

remain silent . . . we proclaim our responsibility to harness every effort to end the Vietnam War NOW.

We demand the immediate withdrawal from Indo-China of every American soldier, every gun, every plane, every tank, every warship and every dollar.

True, there were only 985 labor representatives at the convention, and although they represented a significant portion of the trade union movement, their protest did not match the stridency of the shrill, patriotic cries of the AFL-CIO hierarchy. The war continued while President Nixon's "secret plan" for peace gathered dust months longer, and finally ended on March 29, 1973.

But can anyone flatly declare the statement of policy of Labor for Peace did not help bring about that peace?

What Professor Widick undoubtedly found lacking in American unions was a revolutionary ideology—something clearly uncharacteristic of the labor movement. He made that obvious with an attack on George Meany, in which he quoted the president of the AFL-CIO as approving of working "within the American system," and decrying any suggestion that labor should "man the barricades" or "take to the streets," or call general strikes.[8]

Is that what Widick wanted? Barricades, general strikes, violence? Of course it could arrive at that if projections of a 7 percent unemployment rate for some years in the future come to pass. But violence would be destructive, undoing all that unions are seeking to achieve for their members.

Violence has not entirely disappeared from the labor scene in the seventies, but comes to the surface infrequently—in the wildcat walkouts of the mine workers, in the bullet-pocked Essex Group auto plant in Elwood, Indiana, where Local 1663 of the United Auto Workers battled armed guards, a sheriff with a force of thirteen deputies and imported scabs, and in California's lush growing fields where the United Farm Workers of America has been contending for years with arrests for trespassing, brutal assaults by law-enforcement officers and armed Teamster "guards" and raids by shotgun-armed hoodlums who have injured or killed UFW pickets.

The man leading the California farm workers, Cesar Chavez, does not espouse violence; on the contrary, fasting, prayer and nonviolence have been typical of his leadership of *La Causa*. Why does he do it? Chavez explained:

I once said you couldn't organize farm workers in conventional ways. What we're saying is that it has to be a *movement*, it has to be an *idea*. Some labor leaders can't understand that. What happens is the people get to feel that the idea, the movement, belongs to them. It's theirs, not ours. No force on earth . . . can take that away from them. The more the people get beaten, the more they'll fight. The more persecution, the more strength they have.

Does that sound like the reasoning of a business trade unionist dealing with labor as a commodity? Is that a man concerned with power, money, influence? (He earns about $5,000 a year, including the rent value of his home in Keene, California; the standard salary of most UFW officers and staff is five dollars a week.) Virtually the only remaining frontier for organizing, the farm worker still evokes the militant, crusading spirit of the trade union. Significantly, it is not organization or wages the UFW is fighting for, but *dignidad*, the dignity of the worker. How else can he attain it if not through the union? The motivation for serving the worker is self-evident.

The fact remains unchallenged that a considerable number of unions go far beyond contract terms to serve their members' needs. But the question still remains: Why? The responses from union officers who should know the answer are varied, depending upon their experience. Consider the response of Leo Perlis:

Ask ten AFL-CIO members what Community Service is and you'll get ten answers—and they'll all be right. Strike assistance, one will say. Blood banking, another will add. Consumer counseling and debt counseling. Preparation for retirement. Unemployment relief. Disaster service. Union counseling. Rehabilitation. Programs against alcoholism and drug abuse. Legal aid. Fund raising for voluntary health and welfare agencies.

AFL-CIO Community Services is not a social work agency. Yet, it engages in what social workers call case work, group work, community organization and social action.

In one way or another . . . and at one time or another, AFL-CIO Community Services does it all—and it does it for the following purposes:

1. To meet the personal and family needs of workers not covered by the union contract.

2. To encourage citizen participation in community affairs.

3. To promote a more representative and responsive community.

In the context of these objectives, AFL-CIO Community Service activities run the whole gamut from Adoptions to Zoos, helping childless couples adopt children and helping citizens to appreciate zoos as important cultural and ecological institutions.

This is in line with the AFL-CIO Constitution which provides for the establishment of a Committee on Community Services for the purpose of stimulating "the active participation by members and affiliated unions in

the affairs of their communities and the development of sound relationships with social agencies in such communities.[9]

In discussing the question during an interview in his Washington
office, Perlis stood by these previously published thoughts, but revealed an added ingredient as well—his personal involvement:

> We're here because the people want it. People need it. If they didn't, we
> could all have stood on our heads. What is a union for, after all? Why are
> we concerned with our fellow man? I feel a union is not worth its salt if it
> is only a dues-collecting agency. A union is an instrument. You have to
> achieve power first in collective bargaining procedures. Once you achieve
> that base, you go beyond that to serve people in a larger arena. And this is
> what community service is all about. Unions have always served people.
> It's a question of degree.

Speaking of his involvement with community services over a
period of thirty years (from the time he was named director of the CIO
War Relief Committee in 1946), Perlis conceded he became involved in
community services, indeed, in the labor movement, "by accident,"
since his youthful ambition was to be a journalist. But his hopes of going to New York University were dashed when he had to go to work as a
twister in a Paterson, New Jersey, silk mill. That led to joining the
Associated Silk Workers of the United Textile Workers Union, which
led to organizing textile workers, then political activity, war relief and
ultimately to community services.

Immaculately garbed as he sat behind his orderly desk, Perlis
rambled on, radiating as much candor and informality as confidence,
while the questions became more probing.

> I've always had a feeling for the underdog. It never occurred to me that I
> got into community services, however, because I wanted to help my
> fellow man, but I am deriving a sense of inner satisfaction from what I am
> doing. I never said I was going to work for humanity. You show me a man
> who says he is dedicated to humanity and I'll show you a guy who's kick-
> ing his grandmother!

> What am I getting out of my work here? It gives me what social
> psychologists call "psychic satisfaction." I feel it fulfills me personally. I'm
> making a living, yes, but then, everyone has to earn a living. I'm exposed
> to the whole wide world. I've learned a great deal. I've had the oppor-
> tunity to know many great men, such as John L. Lewis, Sidney Hillman,
> Phil Murray, Jim Carey and others. I ought to be paying the labor move-
> ment for giving me this chance . . . I'll always be grateful to the American
> labor movement.

Does such a man devote himself to community service activities because of his personality, or does community service develop that personality? It is a question to consider soberly, since so many trade unionists have explained their devotion to their work in personal terms.

There is reason to believe that the community-of-interest factor so deeply ingrained in union membership develops the leadership of the fraternity. A prime example would be Patrick Gleeson, who retired in 1975 as president of Retail Clerks Local 1500, in New York City, after a long career as a union officer.

Cornered at a luncheon of the Retirees Club of 1500, he was asked why the union sponsored a program of activities for retired members who no longer paid dues, no longer were working and weren't even covered by contracts. Gleeson was not quite as articulate as Perlis, but he, too, had answers to the same questions:

> If you want to be a union leader, you must work at it 365 days a year. The contract is not enough. No worker can put in a day's work unless he is happy. It's our job to make him happy. We owe it to the members. They owe us nothing. If I let them down, the union is weakened.
>
> I think I'm right, because after all, we have 20,000 members and we did it without any mergers. The membership must have confidence in us.

And, he implied, how could they have confidence in us, "if we did nothing for the retirees?"

There's another view of the obligations unions have toward their members that clarifies the picture somewhat. Ewan Clague pointed out that "the basic policy of any union is the protection of its members, whether they are young or old,"[10] and also noted that unions were protecting their members long before there was an old-age insurance system or unemployment insurance, and the only pensions were "old-age public pensions provided in some states when based upon proof of need and usually amounted to about thirty dollars a month."

The point of view of labor representatives working for health insurance firms sheds some new light on the question of whether it is the union or the highly motivated union member (or officer) who tries to help his fellow man.

Frank Donovan, labor "rep" at the Greater New York Blue Cross and Blue Shield, put it this way:

> I've been exposed to this all my life in the unions, but I want to help the individual. I have an obligation to the labor movement, so I'm following a course to help the individual. What did you do to make the world a better place to live in today? I make that a joke frequently with my kids, so they should do it because of the repeated joke. It's a good feeling to do something for the other guy.

25

Charles McMahon, a vice president of Group Health Inc., New York, a member of the International Brotherhood of Electrical Workers and formerly an AFL-CIO area director for COPE, summed it up:

> I was a rank and file member of the Electrical Workers. Once an apprentice electrician in Washington and now a vice president of a health insurance firm, I still want to do something to help the rank and file. The union develops a chemistry in the person who truly cares, while the people make the trade union what it is. It's the association [between the two] that does it.

It sounded like a symbiotic relationship, not only mutually beneficial to the union and the member, but the community as well. Granted, it was but one man's opinion. However, his uncommonly apt way of describing the relationship turned out to be a view reflecting the belief of other less articulate trade unionists.

The same inquiries, put to the national community services director of the International Union of Electrical, Radio and Machine Workers, also evoked personal reactions. After recounting a story about a retired IUE member living in a small Massachusetts town, who had written to him about not being able to afford a pound of frankfurters, Edward Carlson was asked "Why did you help him, Ed?"

> No one ever asked me this before. I guess it's part of me, like getting up in the morning and shaving. I suppose it goes back to my childhood. I can remember living in the Gas House [district] on First Avenue in New York. People were always asking my mother for help. And then, there was the Knights of Columbus. They always helped out, too, and it was non-sectarian, also. I suppose if you put all those things together, that's it. There's no money in it, no glory, but there is satisfaction.

But there is an impersonal, trade union answer to the question. Clad in blue dungarees, barefoot, Anthony Mazzocchi of the Oil, Chemical and Atomic Workers International Union was quick to respond as he slouched in a chair in his shabby office in the IUE's Philip Murray Building in Washington:

> The trade union as a movement has a commitment to struggle to make things better for the worker. This is an imperative. There are fraternal aspects to trade unionism, a device which people use to secure immediate aims to improve their economic well-being.
>
> It's personal, too. I came out of World War II and went to work at Ford Motor Company. My father was active in the Amalgamated Clothing Workers and I was brought up in the climate.

There's a tendency for the individual trade union leader to confuse his own motivation for serving the membership with the union's rationale, often to the point of failing to see the concept on which unions are built. There are two aspects to reconcile: what unions profess and what non-union critics consider the motivation for serving the rank and file.

The pro-union image has been summed up by one of the more articulate and scholarly spokesmen of the labor movement, Gus Tyler, assistant president of the International Ladies Garment Workers Union. After listing some of the services the ILG provides, Tyler said:

> To answer your question, "Why do we do it?" Because we are concerned with the total life of the member. The ILG is a way of life. We opened the first health center in the United States in 1913. That union health center was the beginning of third-party medicine in the United States. We are concerned with a social wage, more than money, including unemployment insurance, Social Security, welfare, housing, consumer services, hospitalization, legislation . . . As the pastor [of a church] takes care of his flock, the union, too, takes care of its members.

> What good is an extra buck in the pay envelope if the member gets ripped off buying a two-dollar bum watch? That's why we are concerned.

> Why, we pay a member to come in for a physical checkup at the medical center. It's cheaper than paying the bills when he is sick.

Over the decades, the image of labor has changed extensively, yet in Tyler's graphic citations, an enduring picture comes through of the obligations unions have toward their members and the community.

While the AFL's constitutional preamble spoke of the need to combine the toiling millions "for mutual protection and benefit," the AFL-CIO more than half a century later stated in its preamble that one of its aims was "the attainment of security for *all the people.*"

The change in language and purpose reflected a maturing of trade unionism marked by a lessening need for labor to be truculent. Labor no longer felt a need to strut with a chip on its collective shoulder, daring the boss to knock it off. Gone was the expression, "A struggle is going on . . . between the oppressors and the oppressed," which appeared on the AFL masthead; it was replaced by the AFL-CIO's declaration:

> The establishment of this Federation . . . is an expression of the hopes and aspirations of the working people of America. We seek the fulfillment of these hopes and aspirations through democratic processes within the framework of our constitutional government and consistent with our institutions and traditions.

The dedication to the welfare of the working man and woman remained unaltered, but in the intervening years organized labor had matured, reflecting a sense of security won through the legislation of the 1930s. Without the Norris-LaGuardia Act of 1933, the National Recovery Act of 1933, amendments to the Railway Labor Act in 1934 and the Wagner Act of 1935, what direction would unions have taken? Is it inconceivable to hypothesize they might have tilted far to the left?

We need not, however, depend on the self-serving declarations of unions. We may look, instead, to more objective observers and critics of the labor movement for an understanding of the motivation unions have for serving their members. For instance, Professor Emeritus John A. Fitch of the New York School of Social Work summed up the scope of the services:

> Altogether the service rendered to their members by local and international unions outside the scope of collective bargaining is impressive. It ranges from setting up various forms of financial safeguards against industrial hazards through efforts in the direction of cooperative housing to educational activities at technical and cultural levels; finally it introduces a worldwide view with respect to problems that are of concern to men and women everywhere. Thus steps are taken in the direction of a broader understanding of the issues that confront not only the working people but society itself.[11]

But Professor Fitch goes even further in a rare assessment of labor's sense of social responsibility that's virtually unique in the vast, spleen-spattered body of labor criticism:

> The record is neither wholly positive nor wholly negative. Some of the practices here noted are to be condemned, and are increasingly condemned in labor circles as well as elsewhere. Other courses are deserving of praise. The fraternal spirit engendered by men working together for their common good is one of the finest fruits of trade unionism. I have seen organized workingmen so joined in righteous purpose as to put me in mind of what I have read of the spirit of the early Christians.

The Jewish counterpart to that early Christian spirit was exemplified by the Workmen's Circle, organized in 1882 by a handful of Jewish workers on the lower east side of New York as a mutual aid society for the immigrants who "sought a way to relate Jewish culture and life to the new trade unionism and the cause of social justice," Thomas R. Brooks wrote in a brief history of the movement.[12]

The Workmen's Circle was composed, then and now, of trade unionists, but in seventy-five years *Der Arbeiter Ring* grew from a handful of needle trades workers, typesetters, actors and writers to a nationwide chain of 325 branches with 55,000 members. Separated from the benevolent societies of colonial days not only by a century of time, but an unbridgeable ethnic gap, the Workmen's Circle retains in its purposes an uncanny resemblance to its fraternal forebears. Brooks relates:

> The order provided benefits—a five-dollar-a-week sick benefit and funeral benefits of $400 for the men and $200 for the women—that the struggling unions of the time could not secure ·in bargaining . . . The Workmen's Circle charter, for example, stated that when a member was ill and required attention through the night, the officers were required to appoint three members in alphabetical order to spend the night in the member's home. A pregnant member could call on the help of others in the branch. And it was expected that all members who were in the city at the time of death of a fellow member "would accompany the hearse to the ferry," which carried the body to the cemeteries of Long Island. The order soon built a sanitarium for tuberculosis victims and offered burial plots. The 146 victims of the Triangle Waist Company 1911 fire were buried in a common grave at the Workmen's Circle Cemetery.

But there is another motivation, unlike the spirit of the Christian or Jewish missionaries, which uses community service as a power base. Through services to the members, an ambitious, calculating community services chairman can build up enough support to become a political threat to any regime. The author can think of two instances in which trade unionists rose in the hierarchy to become powers in the labor movement. But how can one fault either one, in view of the services they unquestionably performed on the way up?

However, the underlying, impersonal motivation for the institution itself—not its adherents—to serve the membership outside the contract comes from the very nature of the trade union as a vehicle for social change. And there is the heart of the matter.

It would be pointless to single out a handful of outstanding labor leaders and ascribe to each the achievements of a particular era of labor progress, since the labor movement has always produced its own leaders for each era. And if they have been at all dissimilar in temperament or philosophy, these leaders have merely reflected the maturing of the labor movement, which, it must be conceded, has become institutionalized. But it remains committed to its purpose and is effective in the role. As Richard Lester has expressed it:

> American unions have constituted part of a movement, designed to alter existing rights and privileges for the benefit of the workers. As a vehicle for social change, organized labor in the United States has its own folklore and songs, its traditions and martyrs. Union members are "brothers."

They do not scab on one another, nor do they cross the picket lines of other unions. The "good" unionist is willing to sacrifice for the cause; unions open their treasuries to other unions suffering under the financial strain of a serious strike.

A significant part of the motive power behind organized labor stems from personal dedication to its cause. Zeal for the cause of unionism is likely to be particularly prominent during the early stages of a union's development. Personal loyalty and devotion supply much of the volunteer work, so essential to the life of a union, especially at the local level. It is the "actives," mostly unpaid for their services, who constitute the grass roots of trade unionism. They account for much of a union's vitality and moral tone. And it is in their interest to preserve the democratic tradition of American unionism against centralizing encroachment in the name of efficient administration from the top.[13]

It does not matter that unions have changed over the decades, that they have adapted to external and internal pressures; even their members are unlike those of the days of affliction. Their occupations, their education, their working conditions do not resemble those of their forebears. It does not matter that their leadership has also adapted to those pressures. Fundamentally, trade unionism has been, remains and will continue to be—in the hearts of its followers—a "cause." One need not look further to understand its humanitarian aims.

Notes

1. Joseph G. Rayback, *A History of American Labor*, p. 17.
2. M. B. Schnapper, *American Labor: A Pictorial, Social History*, p. 10.
3. John R. Commons, ed., *History of Labour in the United States*, vol. 1, p. 77.
4. Ibid., p. 124.
5. Ibid., p. 600. (N.B.: A *standout* was a strike.)
6. Sidney Lens, *The Crisis of American Labor*, p. 42.
7. Ibid., pp. 59–60.
8. B. J. Widick, "Labor 1975: The Triumph of Business Unionism," *Nation*, 6 September 1975, pp. 170–71.
9. Leo Perlis, "AFL-CIO Community Service: The Human Contract," *Journeyman Barber and Beauty Culture*, October 1972.
10. Ewan Clague, Balrag Palli and Leo Kramer, *The Aging Worker and the Union*, p. 3.
11. John A. Fitch, *Social Responsibilities of Organized Labor*, p. 131.
12. Thomas R. Brooks, "Seventy-five Years of Workers' Mutual Aid," *American Federationist*, September 1975, p. 14; vide Irving Howe, *World of Our Fathers*, (New York: Harcourt Brace Jovanovich, 1976).
13. Richard A. Lester, *As Unions Mature: An Analysis of the Evolution of American Unionism*, p. 51.

3.
The Trade Union Spirit

That is the most perfect government in which an injury to one is the concern of all.

Inscription on the seal of the Knights of Labor

What enabled American trade unions to endure despite adversity, which often reached the proportions of persecution, was, unquestionably, the fraternal nature of the institution.

A union is a fraternity, a lodge, in which members are addressed as "brothers" and "sisters." The term "brotherhood" is part of the name of countless unions. The railroad unions, in fact, are known as *the* brotherhoods—the Brotherhood of Railway Carmen, the Brotherhood of Railway, Airline and Steamship Clerks and the Brotherhood of Railroad Signalmen, to cite a few. Locals of the International Association of Machinists are known as "lodges."

But it's more than a name; it's a characteristic of the trade union indicating an ongoing tradition of association of brothers in adversity. In a colorful, effective way, Kenneth Boulding has put it all together in a single paragraph:

Behind the dirty union hall and even the shiftless or racketeering official there stands the Labor Movement, a stream of history which also has its saints and martyrs, its Mother Joneses and its Joe Hills, its songs and its stories and its traditions, giving a curious, secret strength to its often commonplace embodiment. Alongside the job-conscious business likeness there runs a stream of idealism, expressed in the concept of a "good union man." There have been many unsung sufferers for the cause—people who have suffered loss of jobs, blacklisting, tarring-and-feathering, imprisonment, and even death because they believed in the union, not as a means of personal advancement, but as a great movement in history for the betterment of the group. It is this faith which ultimately gives the labor movement its strength, and which especially gives it strength to withstand the attacks of employers and of the state in periods when they have been hostile.[1]

It is a picture which tempts one to portray its corporate counterpart—the business structure which devotes its energies to bolstering the "bottom line," i.e., net profit; which develops "good company men," breeds anthropoidal automatons garbed in "gray flannel suits" and rewards success with pay increases, stock options and gold-plated keys to the men's room; punishes failure with dismissal.

However, business has its heroes, too, and a long list it is indeed, going back over a century to such eminently successful men as Jay Gould, William H. Vanderbilt, James J. Hill, Andrew Carnegie, Jay Cooke, Philip D. Armour, John D. Rockefeller and their like; men who had one characteristic in common: a talent for amassing wealth—the American mark of success in life.

True, there is also a spirit of fraternity in business organizations, where brothers in adversity commiserate with each other over the sad state of the economy at weekly meetings of Rotary International or the Lions Club.

But there is no sense of brotherhood in the corporate structure that compares with the atmosphere of the union "lodge," which provides the members with fellowship, with a sense of being an integral part of the union—a feeling nurtured by initiation ceremonies and rituals—quite unlike the corporate atmosphere in which serving the company does not preclude ruthless rivalry for cushy posts. The concept of "dog eat dog" came out of the business world, not the labor movement.

This is readily apparent in the rituals adopted decades ago but still faithfully observed by many unions. The procedure given for the order of business by the constitution, bylaws and ritual of the United Glass and Ceramic Workers of North America, for example, opens with the following:

PROCEDURE

(Where there are female members, the word Brother and/or Sister shall be used in all appropriate places.)

1. CHAIRMAN: *(Give one rap of gavel)*. All officers of this Local will now assume their respective offices. Brother Inner Guard, you will satisfy yourself that all present are qualified to remain in this meeting.

INNER GUARD: Bro. Chairman, I am satisfied that all present are entitled to remain.

2. CHAIRMAN: Brothers, I now declare this meeting regularly opened for the transaction of such business as may lawfully come before it. *(Give two raps of gavel.)* Brothers, arise; let us now bow our heads in prayer.

Our Father, Thou great Workman, Thou who has created heaven and earth, Thou who has made all things well, we are but little workmen in this great world in which we have found ourselves, mingling our lives together, trying to help one another to find how we can live on this earth, serve Thee and be to one another as brothers should be.

We ask Thy divine blessing on this meeting and the brothers here assembled and we pray that every action taken by them will work for the good of our membership. We ask it in the name of Jesus. Amen.

3. CHAIRMAN: We will remain standing and pledge allegiance to our flag. *(American members only.)*

"I pledge allegiance to the flag of the United States of America, and to the Republic for which it stands—one Nation, under God, indivisible, with Liberty and Justice for all."

4. CHAIRMAN: We will remain standing for "Thirty Seconds of silence in honor of any member that has passed away (died) since the last meeting."

Some unions have even more elaborate rituals. The International Brotherhood of Painters and Allied Trades has a burial service "to be used at the graves of deceased members of the Brotherhood. Officers of Local Unions must consult the relatives or friends of the deceased before using this ceremony as it is not obligatory. (After the body is deposited in the grave.)"

The burial ritual points up the fraternal aspect of trade unions far better than any self-serving declarations:

LEADING PALL BEARER: Brothers, we have discharged our trust and laid in its place of final rest the body of our departed brother, by you committed to our care.

PRESIDENT: In the presence of death all heads should bow, all voices soften with sympathy, all hearts be filled with awe; we stand in that solemn presence today. It has pleased the All-Wise Father to remove our brother from this scene of toil to "That Undiscovered Country, from Whose Bourne No Traveler Returns." He is beyond the reach of any helping hand or cheering word from us. There is nothing left for us to do but to render him our last sad tribute of respect and memory and love. While he wrought as one of us he covered many an unsightly blot left by other hands, turning into beauty and delight what, otherwise, had been ugly and deformed. So, let us hope, the infinite tenderness and skill of the All-Wise and All-Loving Artist of the earth and sky may cover those failings which he possessed in common with us all, and present him in immortal beauty. Of his brief labor with us here the end has come, and what shall we say?

RECORDING SECRETARY: His record is finished.

FINANCIAL SECRETARY: His account is closed.

TREASURER: His last debt is paid.

VICE PRESIDENT: So let him rest in peace.

(Then shall the President, or someone appointed by him, offer the following prayer):

Oh, Thou, first and greatest of all workers; Thou, who has spread out the earth in beauty; Thou, who hast painted over it the starry canopy of the sky and curtained it with clouds, help us to learn from Thee to decorate and adorn our souls so that, when our time shall come to quit this earthly sphere, we may be found worthy of a place in Thy Glorious Temple, the "House Not Made with Hands, Eternal in the Heavens." Amen.

BROTHERHOOD: So let it be.

(If the officiating minister be present, let him then dismiss the people.)

It may not be sophisticated, but the Painters' burial service has an authentic, folklore air about it that undoubtedly takes it back to the founding year of 1887; however, its text still appeared in the 1975 edition of the constitution.

The form of the opening and closing ceremonies of local unions ordinarily appears in the constitutions of the internationals, as well as the oath of allegiance taken by new members. Much of the ritual, especially the rites of the century-old (or older) unions, appears to have been modeled on patterns established by fraternal orders of days gone by.

The initiation ceremony of the International Union, Allied Industrial Workers of America, appears to bear this out:

The President shall say to the Guide: "You will now place the applicant before me for the obligation."

The Guide advances with the applicant and places him in front of the President's station. All newly elected members, before being admitted to full membership, shall subscribe to the following obligation:

PRESIDENT: You will now recite the following obligation, using your name when I use mine.

I, ———, pledge my honor to faithfully observe the Constitution and laws of this Union; to comply with all the rules and regulations for the government thereof; not to divulge or make known any private proceedings of this Union; to faithfully perform all the duties assigned to me to the best of my ability and skill; to so conduct myself at all times as not to bring reproach upon my Union; and at all times to bear true and faithful allegiance to the International Union, Allied Industrial Workers of America.

PRESIDENT: I charge you to educate yourself (selves) and your fellow workers in the history of the Labor Movement and to defend to the best of your ability, the Trade Union principle which guards its autonomy, recognizing that capital is the product of past labor, and that wages can never be regarded as the full equivalent for labor performed.

I further charge you, in your own interests and in the interests of your fellow man, to resist the competition of cheap labor by purchasing only Union-made goods wherever and whenever possible.

You are now members of the International Union, Allied Industrial Workers of America and Local Union No.———.

The full implications of the secret fraternal nature of trade unions became apparent to the author when several members of a class in communications refused to do a homework assignment, which called for them to write the minutes of a meeting of their union. They were members of the United Transportation Union and they were under oath, they maintained, not to reveal what had gone on during the business session of their local.

The element of secrecy, however, is far from being unique with the UTU. Among other promises, the new members sworn into the International Union of Journeymen Horseshoers must pledge "that I will never divulge the workings of this Union or any password that may be issued from its National Executive Committee, to any person except a clergyman."

The need for secrecy, aside from an assurance that no "fink" will reveal to management the union's position on collective bargaining issues, disappeared when trade unions were legitimized by the Wagner Act. But there was a time when secrecy was essential—to the survival of the union and physical well-being of its leaders. During the depression of 1873 to 1879, when the ranks of unions were decimated not only by unemployment but employers' lockouts, blacklists and legal prosecution, union leaders met in secret to adopt rituals, signs, grips and passwords so that the brotherhood could not be betrayed by any spy. The essential aim of the union at that time was not collective bargaining, but survival!

Among the secret orders of the times were such peaceful groups as the Knights of Labor, the Sovereign Sons of Industry, the Industrial Brotherhood and the Junior Sons of '76, and the violent Mollie Maguires, who organized in the anthracite coal mines and were crushed within a few years after a "reign of terror" ended with the conviction of twenty-four of its criminal leaders. A century later, enough doubt had been aroused by research to undermine that "reign of terror" concept. In fact, John (Black Jack) Kehoe, leader of the Workmen's Benevolent Association, was granted a state pardon 100 years after he was hanged for the murder of a mine official.

There is no need for all the trappings of the lodge ritual today, beyond the purely emotional satisfaction derived from the rites, but there is no question that the traditional forms are still maintained, passed on, not only in the written word, but from father to son in the closed circle of membership which has persisted in so many craft unions. There is a strong hunger in American men for the mummery, the mysticism, the sharing of esoteric runes unknown to the outsider. It may well be an atavistic longing for the pageantry of royalty that has been denied to Americans. One wonders why unions have not adopted gilt-encrusted and braided uniforms to give voice to this yearning; one wonders what the rising influence of women will do to this tendency.

But there is no doubt of the intimate relationship between a significant proportion of rank and file members and their union. It was well illustrated on many an occasion for the author when a trade unionist, heading for home after a long, hard day, voiced the thought, "My wife's going to cite the union as corespondent when she sues for divorce."

The intimate involvement with the union frequently goes to such lengths that men become alienated from their families. A young man, in writing his homework for one of the author's classes, put it this way:

> In August, 1968, I finally got the chance to get into Local 25. Ah, finally, a career in a booming industry with four years of training. Being an electrician in Local 25 is a proud profession and you get self-satisfaction out of your job.
>
> Local 25 is my life. I go to union meetings religiously, and even my wife seems to wonder at times who comes first. I believe in the union and I'm grateful for the comfortable living the electrical industry provides me.

There's no point in pretending this attitude is typical of union members, but first-hand knowledge indicates it is prevalent to such an extent that it accounts for the enduring and persistent strength of the trade union movement in the face of equally persistent deterrents.

The colorful history of trade unions in the United States appears to remain unknown to most young trade unionists. Those who have gone back to school seem, for the most part, to be unaware that organizing a shop was not always a simple matter of collecting and presenting representation cards to the regional office of the National Labor Relations Board. But that is the way it has been in their lifetime.

Organized labor has an honor roll of martyrs who gave their lives to organizing the unorganized. It has its martyrs, traditions, songs, struggles, pain, hunger and heartbreak. The martyrs' number is legion.

On May 3, 1886, for example, 1,400 locked-out workers, members of the Knights of Labor, who were seeking an eight-hour day and a two-dollar-a-day wage, demonstrated at the McCormick Harvester factory in Chicago. Three hundred scabs were brought in under the protection of a guard of 500 police. The police fired without warning, killing at least four and wounding many others.[2]

That was not the massacre. The massacre came the next day, when a peaceful mass meeting, called to protest the previous day's police brutality, was nearing its end in Haymarket Square.

The police appeared. Armed and marching in military fashion, 180 strong, they came on the scene, a few minutes after the mayor [Carter H. Harrison] was out of sight, under the command of Captain John Bonfield, hated throughout the city for his extreme brutality. Captain Ward, on Bonfield's order, commanded the dwindling crowd to disperse. [Samuel] Fielden cried out that it was a peaceable meeting. As though by a signal a bomb was thrown toward the police, and its explosion killed one policeman instantly, wounded five others so severely that they died later, and inflicted less serious wounds on some half hundred more. The police immediately opened fire on the crowd, chasing, clubbing and shooting down workers. Several [were] killed (how many is unknown) and at least 200 were wounded.[3]

In an interview three years later the Chicago chief of police, Captain Frederick Ebersold, admitted that the police, led by Captain Michael J. Schaak, deliberately organized anarchist societies and planted bombs and ammunition at meetings of these organizations.

But the damage had been done; the public linked the drive for the eight-hour day to anarchy. Eight men were tried for murder and seven of them were condemned to be hanged. One was sentenced to fifteen years in prison. When court appeals proved vain, worldwide demonstrations followed, convincing the governor of Illinois to commute the sentences of two defendants to life imprisonment. Another committed suicide—or was murdered by police guards. Three men were hanged. The remainder were finally pardoned in 1893 by Governor John Peter Altgeld, who said, "The defendants were not proven guilty of the crime."

Who were the martyrs of Haymarket Square? Albert Parsons, August Spies, Samuel J. Fielden, Eugene Schwab, Adolph Fischer, George Engel, Louis Lingg and Oscar Neebe. Their only memorial: a few lines in a few history books, few of which even list their names.

The Homestead, Pennsylvania, strike in 1892 had its martyrs, too: members of six lodges of the Amalgamated Association of Iron and Steel Workers, who were locked out of the Carnegie, Phipps & Co. steel mill on June 29, before the contract expired. Three hundred Pinkerton Detective Agency guards, armed with Winchesters, were called in to protect strikebreakers who had been recruited through a newspaper campaign.

A battle followed on the Monongahela River when an effort was made to sneak the Pinkertons in on barges. The strikers and guards exchanged fire.

Who fired the first shot is not known, both sides later claiming the other fired first. But it was the Pinkertons who fired into the crowd of women and children and brought down several . . . The battle lasted from 4 o'clock in the morning of July 6 until 5 o'clock that afternoon. At least nine workers were killed and three of the Pinkertons paid with their lives for their attempt to take over the mill.

An eight-foot stone shaft was erected at a street intersection in Homestead to commemorate the battle. The inscription reads:

Erected by the members of the Steel Workers Organizing Committee Local Unions in memory of the iron and steel workers who were killed in Homestead, Pa., on July 6, 1892, while striking against the Carnegie Steel Company in defense of their American rights.[4]

The name *Pinkerton* became for trade unionists, including many who never heard of the Battle of the Monongahela, an obscenity. The battle, however, did not end the strike, which continued while the strikers' Advisory Committee maintained law and order, resulting in charges of "revolution, treason and anarchy" being levied against the committee. Eight thousand national guardsmen were called out by the governor to protect the recruited strikebreakers.

While the strike was broken, as much by the national guard's guns as by the strikebreakers, the treason charge, as explained by Supreme Court Justice Edward Paxson, shed some light on the attitude of the public toward workers at that time. Speaking of the "addition of large numbers of foreigners to our labouring population," Justice Paxson said:

Many of them are densely ignorant, as well as brutal in their dispositions. They have false ideas of the kind of liberty we enjoy in this country. It is needed that all such persons should be taught this lesson that our liberty is the liberty of law and not the liberty of license.

Despite this invocation, not a single striker was found guilty.[5]

The Pullman strike of 1894 was another blood-stained blot on the pages of labor history. Attorney General Richard Olney, who had been a railroad attorney and had sizable investments in railroads, sent federal troops (without a request from the legislature or governor to do so) on Independence Day to the Pullman Corporation in Chicago, determined to make full use of the federal government's machinery to destroy the American Railway Union's boycott of Pullman cars.

As Philip S. Foner relates, "Among the crowd were hoodlums who remained in Chicago after the close of the Columbian Exposition, a semi-criminal element, not a few of whom were hired by the railroads for the purpose," and they and "the U.S. deputy marshals assigned to strike duty, were largely responsible for the violence and destruction of railroad property during the four days following the arrival of the federal troops."

The public reaction, not to the use of federal troops, which was illegal since it was done without the consent of the state government, but to the strike, can best be summed up in the words of Dr. Herrick Johnson, who was a professor at the Presbyterian Theological Seminary in Chicago: "The soldiers must use their guns. They must shoot to kill."

The soldiers did use their guns. They killed twenty-five workers and injured sixty others.

The United Mine Workers felt the brunt of government and business wrath in 1914 in Colorado when the union dared to organize miners of the Colorado Fuel & Iron Co., controlled by the Rockefeller family. The workers, seeking the right to bargain collectively and enforcement of state labor laws ignored by the Rockefellers, called for a conference with mine operators. This was refused.

When the strike was called, the operators hired several hundred Baldwin-Felts Agency guards.

(They) cruised the area in armored automobiles. They attacked the tent colony which evicted miners set up at Forbes and a strikers' mass meeting at Walsenburg. The governor sent General Chase of Cripple Creek fame to impose martial law. Chase promptly began breaking up picket lines, arresting strikers, and deporting strike leaders. The climax came in April, 1914, when a detachment of militia attacked the strikers' tent village at Ludlow. The fight, in which two strikers and a boy were killed, ended with the troops capturing the camp and setting it afire. The main tragedy was discovered the next day: Two women and eleven children, seeking escape from the militia, had been smothered to death in a cave. The "Ludlow Massacre" turned the striking miners into furious avengers. They attacked and destroyed a half-dozen mine properties, attacked mine guard encampments and the militia. For a week southern Colorado was a battlefield. The governor called for federal troops. With their arrival peace was restored.[6]

It might be argued that these examples were exceptions, not typical of the times. On the contrary, these examples provide a model of the reactions unions could expect from the business world, the police, the courts, the federal government and the clergy until passage of the National Labor Relations Act.

It would be fallacious to assume there have been no similar incidents in labor history since passage of the NLRA. On the contrary, bloody massacres of workers not only preceded its passage—as in the battle of San Francisco police and longshoremen which left two dead and 100 injured on Bloody Thursday, July 5, 1934—but followed enactment, as on Memorial Day of 1937, when ten workers were slain and 100 injured as 150 South Chicago police attacked an impromptu parade of Republic Steel strikers and their families. Seven of the ten who died were found to have bullet holes in their backs.

In the same year, the United Auto Workers encountered the same inhumane, labor-busting tactics at the hands of the service department of the Ford Motor Company, when Walter Reuther attempted to organize the River Rouge plant. A peaceful attempt to distribute leaflets to workers under a permit granted by Dearborn, Michigan, turned into a bloody confrontation with the service department's hired thugs, in which Reuther and Richard Frankensteen, leading the organizing drive, were mercilessly mauled, punched, kicked and routed from the scene with all of their followers.[7]

Again, it would be erroneous to assume such violence has had no parallel in the decade of the seventies. To the contrary, organized labor believes it has a martyr in Karen G. Silkwood.

Miss Silkwood was on her way to meet Steven Wodka, legislative assistant to the Oil, Chemical and Atomic Workers International Union, and David Burnham, reporter for the *New York Times*, when her white 1973 Honda smashed into the culvert on the left side of the road a few miles south of Crescent, Oklahoma. The Oklahoma Highway Patrol described the crash as an accident, but Anthony Mazzocchi, Washington representative of OCAW, in calling upon the Justice Department and the Atomic Energy Commission to investigate the tragedy, said an investigator hired by the union had found evidence to "suggest that Miss Silkwood's car was hit from behind by another vehicle, causing her to leave the road and hit the concrete culvert."

A laboratory technician employed in the Kerr-McGee plutonium plant located near Crescent, Miss Silkwood was known to have a brown paper envelope with her in the Honda, containing "the documentation of her allegations of health and safety hazards in the plant and falsification of quality control records."

The envelope was never seen again. Also, Miss Silkwood had been under treatment in the week before her death for exposure to plutonium radiation. Charges made by the lab technician, who had been active in the drive to have OCAW Local 5-283 continue to represent workers in the plant, were investigated by the AEC (now the Nuclear Regulatory Agency). Enough evidence was found within two months by the AEC to order a five-man panel to review the manufacturing and inspection practices of Kerr-McGee. The panel substantiated or partly substantiated twenty of the thirty-nine allegations made by the union concerning worker health.[8]

Miss Silkwood's death provided labor with a modern martyr. In Mazzocchi's mind, there was no room for doubt she was murdered, although this has not been established. But a federal court jury in 1979 ordered Kerr-McGee to pay $10,505,000 to her estate for its negligence in her plutonium contamination.

The circumstances of Miss Silkwood's death will probably never be established, any more than the slaying of Norman Rayford— another martyr of the 1970s — will be solved. An organizer for the National Union of Hospital and Nursing Home Employees, Rayford was shot and killed August 28, 1972, by a private guard at Philadelphia's Metropolitan Hospital. The guard claimed Rayford threatened him with a knife and that he shot in self-defense.

Rayford's associates said this was not possible; that Rayford never carried a knife and that such an action would be completely out of character. No one was ever charged with the murder. But the union is convinced that "Norman Rayford, 1199C organizer, was murdered in Philadelphia." The *1199 News* said of him: "Killed in action in the service of his union."

Miss Silkwood and Mr. Rayford were only two in a long line of martyrs, whose deaths have given solidarity to the brotherhood of trade unionists. Traditions, rituals, oppression, martyrs and a community of interests created a social institution which richly deserves to be considered unique.

That's what makes the dearth of trade union songs so startling in a land where the folk song is so highly regarded. There are, indeed, songs of workers, as there are innumerable songs about woodsmen, slaves, farmers, soldiers, sailors, pioneers and hoboes. But the bulk of the workers' songs not only do not mention unions, but can easily be traced back to their origin in hymns, folk songs and the songs of persuasion written by radicals who were not representative of the trade union movement.

The flood of workers' songs which smote the air in the 1930s can be attributed to the left wing. According to R. Serge Denisoff:

> The few spontaneous songs that did emerge from urban strike situations were of short duration and put to popular tunes. Despite these social facts, Stalinists were convinced that folk material was, in fact, the music of the industrial proletariat. The major issue of the song of persuasion took place, not in the labor movement, but during the period called the proletarian renaissance of the late 1930's and early 1940's.[9]

Indeed, so few songs of the workers have the union label on them today that the Amalgamated Clothing Workers of America was hard pressed to find enough to fill a forty-eight page booklet in 1968, the

Amalgamated Songbook. The *AFL-CIO Song Book*, in the edition revised in 1974, shows the same shortcoming.

But among such tunes as "Auld Lang Syne," "My Wild Irish Rose" and "O Susanna," there are union songs, the mixture based, presumably, on the premise that once the songs most people know are sung, the others will be more acceptable. And the others include "Solidarity Forever":

> Solidarity forever,
> Solidarity forever,
> Solidarity forever,
> For the Union makes us strong!

The chorus, whose music and lyrics are so simple anyone can join in, will raise the temperature in any union hall and solidify the spirit of fraternal brotherhood among even the stodgiest of prim and proper professionals. Solidarity is respectable now. Solidarity House is the name of the UAW headquarters. There's another workers' song, "Joe Hill," which not only appears in the Amalgamated and AFL-CIO songbooks, but was used to close the funeral services for Walter Reuther, killed in an airplane crash on May 9, 1970. "Joe Hill," hymn to a Wobbly martyr, was one of Reuther's favorite songs. It must be conceded that many trade unionists who lift their voices in praise of Joe Hill haven't the vaguest idea who he was, and probably little faith that he never died, but remains "standing there as big as life" at the side of workingmen who organize or are out on strike. Yet his spirit lives on, because "Joe Hill ain't never died."

But who remembers that Joe Hill's name was Joel Emanuel Hagglund? Or that he was an organizer for the Industrial Workers of the World and was executed November 19, 1915, on a framed-up murder charge so blatant that the American Federation of Labor, which had no love for the Wobblies, protested he had not had a fair and impartial trial?

The workers' songs were songs of persuasion that were widely sung and wisely used, each of them reflecting the conviction that in union there is strength. One of the early workers' songs, "Storm the Fort, Ye Knights of Labor," dates back to the 1880s:

> Toiling millions now are waking,
> See them marching on;
> All the tyrants now are shaking,
> Ere their power is gone.
>
> Storm the fort, ye Knights of Labor,
> Battle for your cause;
> Equal rights for every neighbor,
> Down with tyrant laws.

There are other songs which have endured, preserving the legends of personalities now regarded as myths, but of whose existence there should be no doubt, each of them adding to the stature of the archetypical American worker. The "Ballad of John Henry," who constantly lamented, "Hammer's gonna be the death of me, Lord, Lord," enshrines the memory of a man who outdrilled a Burleigh steam drill fourteen feet to nine in the red shale of the Big Bend Tunnel of Summers County, West Virginia, over a hundred years ago. As Jeffrey M. Miller pointed out in the *Laborer* in February, 1973:

> John Henry has become a prime symbol of man's struggle with the elements of nature and with the dominance of his own technology. Today, the true sons of John Henry are found, more than anywhere else, among the ranks of the Laborers International Union—in the men who work underground, as he did, and in the laboring men who perform the hard work of the world.

John Henry, however, is not the only symbol of the worker's struggle; another in the ranks of the legendary heroes, Casey Jones, is probably better known—but as an engineer, not as a trade unionist. The legend tells the story of John Luther "Casey" Jones, "a brave engineer," who sacrificed his life to slow down the No. 382 on the Illinois Central, saving the lives of his passengers and crew when the Cannonball Express ploughed into the rear of a freight near Vaughan, Massachusetts. But the name of Casey Jones has also survived in trade union annals as a strikebreaker:

> Casey Jones got a job in heaven;
> Casey Jones was doing mighty fine;
> Casey Jones went scabbing on the angels,
> Just like he did to workers on the S.P. line.

It's doubtful the legend of the brave engineer will ever be forgotten. The Brotherhood of Locomotive Engineers retold the story in the *Locomotive Engineer* in August, 1975—but without mentioning the hero as a Southern Pacific Railroad strikebreaker.

Workers' songs haven't disappeared but have changed with the times, as might be expected. The International Ladies Garment Workers Union, which produced the musical *Pins and Needles* in the 1930s, carries on the tradition. Forty years ago, the ILG was singing a song of social significance, in which meaning was shining from every line. *Pins and Needles*, Denisoff noted,

> accomplished more than all of Will Geer's "raggedy-assed" folksingers in the thirties. The musical succeeded in finding that broad audience that

43

the Communist Party and its associated leagues were seeking in vain for during the entire decade of the thirties. The play was produced for over a thousand performances in New York and made one road trip.[10]

There was nothing else quite like *Pins and Needles* until 1976, when *I Paid My Dues* was staged as a bicentennial celebration of the American worker's contributions. The musical ran for two weeks, courtesy of District Council 37, American Federation of State, County and Municipal Employees, which bought out the house, and then for one more night at the annual National AFL-CIO Conference on Community Services in Ford's Theatre in Washington, D.C.

But it is doubtful that either its songs or message made the wide impact the ILG achieved with a singing commercial that has been performed on television and radio and seen in print. In an ILG institutional advertisement, a women's chorus sings the words:

Look for the union label
When you're buying a coat,
Dress or blouse.
Remember somewhere
Our union's sewing,
Our wages going
To feed the kids and
Run the house.

We work hard
But who's complaining?
Thanks to the ILG
We're paying our way.
So always look for
The union label,
It says we're able
To make it in the U.S.A.*

That may be far removed from the blood and guts of the not-so-distant past, but in the vernacular of its own times and the context of the conditions of the age, the ILG's union-label song expresses the way members feel about their union. Still, it's a long way from miners singing "Sixteen Tons."

That Kentucky lament, seemingly forgotten, but periodically revived because it seems to reflect an ache in the hearts even of workers who are not coal miners, recites the trials of the miner who loads sixteen tons of coal, but has only age and more debts to show for his labor because he owes his soul to the company store. "Company store" will

---

* © 1975 ILGWU

require definition for the American worker, it is feared.

The American worker has come a long way since "Sixteen Tons," but only because of the trade union movement, not only in improved working conditions, better wages and fringe benefits undreamt of a generation ago, but in scores of benefits outside the contract.

Notes

1. Kenneth E. Boulding, *The Organizational Revolution*, p. 97.
2. Philip S. Foner, *History of the Labor Movement in the United States*, p. 105.
3. Ibid., p. 106.
4. Ibid., p. 210.
5. Ibid., p. 215.
6. Joseph G. Rayback, *A History of American Labor*, pp. 257–58.
7. The story is told in detail in *Reuther* by Frank Cormier and William J. Eaton (Englewood Cliffs, N. J.: Prentice-Hall, 1970), pp. 103–7.
8. *New York Times*, 8 January 1975, p. 17.
9. R. Serge Denisoff, *Great Day Coming: Folk Music and the American Left*, p. 67.
10. Ibid.

4.
Beyond
Collective Bargaining

Why do we do it? Because we are comrades in struggle. The members are not strangers. We are fellow strugglers. We are friends. We are comrades in the struggle for a better life for everybody.

Sol Molofsky

Wages, hours and working conditions are terms of employment in contracts arrived at through collective bargaining. Because of government regulations, enacted under social pressures, there are minimum wage standards, at least ostensibly safe working conditions, workmen's compensation, unemployment insurance, Social Security and similar benefits.

But what of the unions' contributions to the welfare of the worker and his family, attained beyond collective bargaining, through the unions' own initiative, with their own manpower and funds? The fringe benefits introduced by the union invariably become part of the contract, apparently paid for by the employer because of a sense of social responsibility, whether the "noneconomic" fringe benefits may be the monitoring of toxic fumes in the plant, furnishing of first-aid equipment or providing periodic health examinations.

But what is overlooked all too often is the decisive role the union plays, either in launching a fringe benefit at its own expense with its own personnel or in inducing the employer to do so. It is overlooked because in the course of time through collective bargaining a past practice, even in an area not covered by a labor agreement, becomes as valid and binding as a contract term. By the time the benefit is being funded by the employer, an industry trust fund or joint labor-management welfare fund, who can remember that it was the union that initiated the benefit?

One example provides a framework for a pattern frequently followed. A news report appeared in the *New York Times* on July 10, 1975, under a six-column headline, "Hypertension Detection and Treatment Program at Gimbels Is Successful." The story opened:

A novel medical program in which Gimbel's workers with high blood pressure were treated at the department store has achieved such favorable results that it is viewed as holding promise as a practical way of treating larger groups of patients all over the world.

Throughout the story, which ran 23.5 inches long, there was but one mention of the union involved—nine inches down in the first column—but all it said was, *"the Gimbel's program,* which was *supported* primarily by the United Storeworkers Union, has been expanded to include 1,000 workers at Bloomingdale's and District Council 37 of the Municipal Employees Union" (emphasis added).

True, the practice of examining Gimbel's employees to determine whether or not they're subject to hypertension *is* supported by the United Storeworkers Union, but an hour's probing uncovered the story that the union initiated the program, which is supported by Gimbel's. Indeed, the hypertension program could not have been successful on any other basis, since the workers were apprehensive lest Gimbel's learn any one of them was ill.

The initiative for the hypertension program came from William Michelson, president of the union, and Dr. Eugene McCarthy, the union's medical adviser, in 1973.

With the cooperation of Dr. Michael Alderman of the Department of Public Health at Cornell University Medical College (Dr. McCarthy is on the same staff), the union obtained a grant to underwrite the cost of the examinations—and treatment, when indicated. A copy of Dr. Alderman's "Proposal for Hypertension Control Through Medical Outreach," dated March 9, 1974, reveals it was the union which initiated the program:

> At Gimbel's 34th Street, 1401 (76%) of the total 1,850 employees were screened at the union headquarters, and 234 (25%) were found to be hypertensive . . .[1]

The results, in Dr. Alderman's word, were "gratifying," not to him alone, but to the union members and Gimbel's as well, for hypertension takes a dreadful toll "through its cardiovascular, cerebrovascular and renal complications, substantial morbidity and mortality results." Hypertension affects 20 million Americans and the economic costs of hypertensive disease has been estimated to be over $9 billion annually, of which $7.6 billion were due to the complications of high blood pressure.

The success of the United Storeworkers Union's program was estimated early in 1976 in the following terms:

> 1,401 Gimbel's members screened for Hypertension
> 234 were discovered as having Hypertension

96 Gimbel's members now under treatment . . . in union program
1,386 Bloomingdale members screened for Hypertension,
277 determined to be Hypertensive
199 Bloomingdale members now under treatment
Note: Gimbel people in treatment program for eight months. Of those in
this treatment program, 76 (79.2%) no longer hypertensive. Their blood
pressure down to normal. In similar program at New York Hospital
Hypertension Clinic, only 24% of people being treated for Hypertension
have been brought under normal pressures. Conclusion: Union program
for treatment of Hypertension has been the most effective one that the
medical profession has yet seen.

That, of course, is the union's report on the program. Dr. Alderman's view was that a satisfactory and economical way had been found
to treat hypertension by bringing "detection and treatment programs
directly to physically clustered population groups."

The point of this care program is to treat patients with hypertension
where they work, thus removing the impediments to health care caused
by cost, travel, lost work time, and inconvenient appointment hours.
Nurse-clinicians supervised by a physician, are the primary providers of
care. Under these circumstances, one physician markedly increases the
number of patients under his effective care. Diagnostic tests are mini-
mized and therapy follows a predetermined protocol.

Follow-up is close and the few patients with uncontrolled blood pressures
(determined in the first six months) are referred to more sophisticated
backup facilities for subsequent management. Patients are encouraged to
maintain their source of general medical care, and full cooperation with
private physicians is assured.

The value of this program is its ability to provide more effective and complete care of hypertensives than alternative care systems. It is less expensive for each patient today, and minimizes the greater expense of a heart
attack, kidney failure or stroke tomorrow.[2]

The hypertension screening program continued so that by
mid-1976 over 100 department store workers were under treatment.
Both the screening and treatment remained in the union office at 101
West 31st Street, New York, not far from Gimbel's 34th Street. There
was always a union officer or shop steward present, but no one from
Gimbel's management. Local 3 members employed at Bloomingdale's
were also enrolled, as were Gimbel's employees in Westchester County
and Paramus, New Jersey.

It is a program subsidized and conducted by the union and its
medical staff. Has it been worthwhile? The answers can be found in the
number of lives saved, healthier members, fewer instances of hospitalization, fewer disabled workers, and less work time lost.

Why did the union become involved in such a program? Executive vice president Sol Molofsky, balding, cherubic, bubbling with enthusiasm, looked incredulous, undoubtedly wondering why anyone would question something so obvious: "We did it because we are comrades in struggle."

In time, like so many other union programs, hypertension detection and treatment could become just one more benefit under the union's Store Workers Security Plan, which is jointly administered by labor and management trustees. It could become just one more benefit covered by collective bargaining agreement and funded by an employer contribution equal to 5.5 percent of the payroll. And, like the accident and sick benefits, hospitalization, "fee-for-service" medical and surgical benefits, podiatry, prescription drug and optical plan, physical examinations and death benefits, it could be considered (by the employee and the public) to be a contribution made by the employer.

But seemingly aware of this eventuality, the United Storeworkers Union informs its members who's responsible for the program.

In explaining the employer contributions funding the plan, Bill Michelson, president of the union and chairman of the Store Workers Security Plan, told the members:

> These contributions are derived from those portions of negotiated wage increases which members of the union decided to set aside to pay for their health care benefits. Thus in a real sense, the plan and its funds represent accumulated savings of the members.[3]

A second factor is equally pertinent. The hypertension screening program will remain a purely union function administered by the union officers and staff. The members can be confident their medical records will be kept confidential.

The United Storeworkers Union has convinced its members the union is concerned about their health. But this is not generally true in many other unions. Consider, for example, hospitalization insurance plans. Originally, Blue Cross policies were sold to employers, "which was fine with us," said Frank Donovan at Greater New York's Blue Cross and Blue Shield, "since the employer did all the work for us with payroll deductions."

> The rank and file attitude was expressed in, "The boss is paying for me, not the union." But since World War II, when unions could not get wage increases, but bargained for fringe benefits, Blue Cross has shown the greatest growth. Now, with the deferred wage concept and the employer giving his "contribution" to the union pension and welfare plan, it is the union, through the trust fund, which serves the members. Now, it's the union, not the boss, "who is paying for me."

Donovan estimated that 70 percent of the Blue Cross business handled in Greater New York was the result of labor contracts. It is a point worth stressing, since the union rarely is credited with winning any benefits beyond wages, or even with being concerned with the member's welfare. The weight of the evidence, however, is to the contrary, once more pointing up the failure of labor organizations to tell their story effectively to their members—or the public.

This failure is exemplified by the practices followed by the 50,000-member United Federation of Teachers, which is Local 2 of the American Federation of Teachers. Three staff members of the local appeared dazed when questioned about the UFT community service program. Their groping efforts to understand the questions mirrored the reactions of two editors of *New York Teacher*, official publication of the New York State United Teachers.

The reason for the staff's bewilderment soon came to light: The UFT has no "community service program," per se, and does not use the term, because whatever the union does on behalf of either the member or community is considered to be part of carrying out the contract with the Board of Education. One example uncovers the distinction and flaw in reasoning.

Each year the UFT gives a million dollars in scholarships to high school seniors from low-income families. Each year 300 young people, who are selected on the basis of potential, scholastic achievement and financial need, are each awarded $1,000 a year for four years of college. (Payments on scholarships awarded in prior years bring the annual cost up to a million dollars.) Where does the UFT get a million dollars to give away annually as a community service? In 1971 the union elected to make that sacrifice by giving up a million dollars worth of welfare benefits in the contract negotiated with the Board of Education.

So the scholarship program is "merely part of the contract."

While the UFT has taken pride in its scholarship program and has even extended it to provide $1,500 a year for graduate scholarships, there has been little or no public recognition of the community service rendered. Failing to win acclaim, or even newspaper coverage of the annual scholarship awards, the union, until recently, paid for a costly two-page advertisement in the *New York Times* to announce the awards. But with the Board of Education under fire for its vast budget, the advertisement no longer appears for fear that the reaction of the public would be a demand for a million-dollar cut in the budget.

Similarly, the UFT has brought into the school system thousands of minority members with low incomes to serve as paraprofessionals or teachers' assistants. The union won a representation election and negotiated a contract for the paraprofessionals, many of whom have gone on to college to become teachers themselves. The service to the community and to the paraprofessional is obvious, but unrecognized.

The UFT may have no community service program, but it can and does handle the personal problems of its members, since chapter chairmen and field representatives are trained to cope with those problems. There's an overriding reason for keeping this aspect of the union's functions low-keyed: A teacher in distress quickly comes under community pressure to resign as unfit to teach.

But New York City's financial woes are forcing the UFT to revise its thinking. Because of the extensive layoffs in the school system, the UFT for the first time in September, 1976, distributed a kit to members, including instructions for collecting unemployment insurance benefits and preparing a job resume, along with a list of the eligibility requirements for food stamps. This dismayed some teachers, but thousands more called on the union for more information. Apparently, it is not true that all teachers are well equipped to handle their own problems because they are accustomed to helping their students and the children's parents.

No one doubts that the UFT and its parent organization, the AFT—Albert Shanker is president of both—are devoted to serving the member and community, yet the teacher unions have far from a favorable public image.

That may be because of public hostility toward teacher strikes which affect family life directly, but it may also be attributed to public ignorance of the intense involvement of the union in community affairs. The AFT will have to give more thought to improving its public image by publicizing its community services. But that will require a reorientation in thinking, as may be seen in the response Shanker made to the question, "Why does a union go beyond the letter of the contract to help its members?"

There is no one answer to your question. There are a number of answers which depend upon the philosophy of the union leadership and the relative security of the union. There are limits to what can be accomplished within the contract and frequently the agreement is undone by other forces. For example: A union negotiates health and medical benefits and, let us say, the member gets a ten-dollar visit to the dentist, but that's not enough if the dentist doubles his price. We must go beyond it and make arrangements with the dentist to set a fee schedule; or, to go further, we in the AFT have a panel which examines every dental bill over ten dollars. The panel must see the X-rays and okay the action.

Another instance: Here in New York we do not have the usual security of an agency shop and, at the moment, the UFT doesn't have a dues checkoff [a penalty invoked by the New York State Public Employment Relations Board for engaging in a strike in violation of the Taylor Law].

But we are offering services to the member. After all, how convenient is it to pay dues of $200 a year? You could really use the money yourself for other purposes. In a sense, we are performing government service for all of the members. We are running a governmental voluntary system of taxation. How does a union continue? It develops things to tie the member to the union, since membership is voluntary. Those unions which have no union shop or agency shop must develop programs which serve the members.

An even more negative attitude is shown by Actors Equity Association, which regards service to the member—and there are extensive services—as "not beyond the contract." Frederick O'Neal, president emeritus, could well be proud of the social services department, which stands ready eight hours a day to help any member in distress, and is prepared, if its own resources prove inadequate, to refer him to the Central Labor Council's more adequate facilities. The concept of "not beyond the contract" stems from the fact that Equity's welfare fund is based on the receipts of performances specifically staged for the benefit of Actors Equity under contract provisions. The arrangement is a cooperative one, since the actors perform in the benefits without pay. "The Theatre Authority," O'Neal said, "which authorizes members to appear in benefits, apportions the receipts to the union to be used for welfare purposes exclusively."

The same practice is followed by the Actors Fund and the Catholic, Jewish, Negro, Episcopal and Actors guilds. "In this way," O'Neal added, "the unions carry out their responsibility and function of caring for the welfare of the member."

The responsibility covers the actor's welfare from the day he enters the union to his retirement and later, too. O'Neal can be very determined in arguing that a would-be actor should not be assessed union dues and initiation fee until he has a job—a point of view not shared by unions concerned with revenues. The retired actor can find shelter in the Actors Home in Englewood, New Jersey, or the Screen Actors Guild home in Woodland Hills, California. "We take care of each other," O'Neal commented. "In many ways, actors are a microcosm of society. We may fight each other, but when the showdown comes, we'll give each other the shirts off our backs."

That's an admirable spirit but the overall approach of considering the member's welfare a contract function appears to be self-defeating. Similarly, one of the most recent benefits being sought by many unions—prepaid legal services—will also become before long an employer-subsidized contract provision.

Prepaid group legal services plans, much like group medical plans, have become not only "the wave of the future," to quote one observer, but essential to the middle-income wage earner who cannot afford the exorbitant fees of attorneys or qualify for free legal service. The plans, which already cover more than 2 million people nationwide, were not initiated by the organized bar, but unions—and not in the past decade, but closer to half a century ago, when the union attorney came to the union hall on a scheduled evening, to be available for consultation for any troubled rank and filer.

It is amusing to read the comment of Copal Mintz, president of the New York County Legal Services Corporation:

> The organized bar (if not the legal profession), spearheaded by the American Bar Association, in recent years has recognized the inaccessability to nonbusiness-middle-income-Americans of legal services at affordable cost. That concern and agitation of bar leaders gave rise to the concept of prepaid legal services.[4]

The concern and agitation of union leaders gave rise to the concept of prepaid legal services over the opposition of the American Bar Association, which contested the use of closed panel programs (wherein the client may go only to the lawyers specified by the insurer).

The first legal services program was initiated by Laborers Local 229 in Shreveport, Louisiana, in January, 1971, with the cooperation of the state bar association and with assistance from the Ford Foundation. Other pioneer programs were mounted by District Council 37, American Federation of State, County and Municipal Employees, and by Teamsters Local 237 (which represents 15,000 public employees in New York).

Of the 6,000 legal plans organized in recent years, about one-third of them were labor sponsored. But they are not all financed by "employer contributions"; on the contrary, direct payment from union treasuries pay lawyers who help members without fee, or in some instances (i.e., District Council 37) the union members allocate a portion of their cost-of-living adjustments to finance the program.

Now that changes in the Taft-Hartley Act and the Internal Revenue Code permit unions to negotiate tax-exempt employer contributions to prepaid group legal plans, "Legal Blue Cross" is likely to become just one more fringe benefit widely enjoyed by union members. But the employer deserves no more credit for the benefit than does the American Bar Association.

It should be kept in mind that legislative action which helped make these prepaid legal plans feasible was sparked by the National Consumer Center for Legal Services, which is sponsored by the National Council of Senior Citizens, the National Association for the Advancement of Colored People, the National Education Association and the AFL-CIO. But that is not generally recognized and organized labor has failed to appreciate the value of publicizing its contributions to the welfare of the community and the member in areas beyond collective bargaining.

Notes

1. Michael H. Alderman, *A Proposal for Hypertension Control Through Medical Outreach* (Ithaca, N.Y.: Department of Public Health, Cornell University Medical College, 9 March 1974), p. 3.
2. Ibid., pp. 2–3.
3. *Store Workers Security Plan*, no. 11, September 1971, p. 6.
4. *New York Times*, letter to the editor, 22 March 1976.

5.
Expendable Workers

WASHINGTON—Millions of workers are being exposed to toxic substances on the job but often don't know it because manufacturers keep the ingredients a secret, federal officials warned.

Newly analyzed data indicates that "more than seven million workers" are exposed to Labor Department-regulated toxic substances in products sold under trade names, Dr. John Finklea, director of the National Institute for Occupational Safety and Health, told a House subcommittee.

The number of exposed workers could be as large as 14 million or 15 million, he added, noting that the institute so far has been able to identify the ingredients in only half of the 86,000 trade-name products it has located in work places . . .

Wall Street Journal, April 28, 1977

One of the great tragedies in the history of industry has yet to be brought forcefully to the attention of the public; if it were, the reaction would be cataclysmic. It is the annual death toll of American workers from industrial diseases and accidents.

More than 14,000 deaths on the job and about 2.2 million disabling injuries are reported annually, according to Dr. Jeanne M. Stellman and Dr. Susan M. Daum. But they add:

Those are probably minimal figures, for every worker knows the devices by which industry hides or disguises accidents on the job and pads its safety records. A recent report has estimated that the actual numbers may run as high as 25,000 deaths and 20 to 25 million job-related injuries annually.[1]

There is reason to accept these estimates skeptically—particularly in light of the 3,000 new chemicals introduced annually by industry into the environment. Chemicals, there is reason to believe, are killing an unknown number of workers by virtually imperceptible stages. They are workers who may not die for twenty or more years after they have first been exposed to the toxic effects of the fumes, powders and dusts.

And so little is known about the effects that standards for only a small fraction of them can be introduced annually.

It is tragic, indeed, since the dangers were known ages ago. The literature teems with references to toxic substances workers were exposed to 400 or more years ago.

But a distinction must be drawn between twentieth-century synthetics and the natural substances used in earlier centuries. As for the new poisons, vinyl chloride provides the best example of how little is known of their dangers. In a handbook published as recently as 1973, the properties of vinyl chloride were described:

> Vinyl chloride, or some other chemicals used in the synthesis of polyvinyl chloride, occasionally causes a peculiar reaction on the hands of workers who handle these chemicals. It affects the blood vessels of the fingers, causing decreased circulation, especially when the fingers are cold. They become blue, numb and painful ... Because of the loss of circulation, the skin over the fingertips may become thickened and hard. Changes in the bones and arthritis may develop . . .[2]

But it is now recognized that vinyl chloride is a killer of workers on a large scale, through angiosarcoma of the liver, a cancer that is slow to appear, but fatal. However, it was not until late in 1974 that the Labor Department's Occupational Safety and Health Administration (OSHA) issued a standard limiting worker exposure to vinyl chloride.

The new limit, stalled by industry appeals until May 1, 1975, requires a drastically reduced exposure level of no more than one part vinyl chloride to one million parts of air over an eight-hour period. It may not average more than five ppm in any fifteen-minute period.

Organized labor fought for the new standards, but lost the battle for protection for another million workers who fabricate or handle VC products. Nor was a more stringent "no detectable level" enacted, although labor argued all available medical evidence precluded any exposure to vinyl chloride.

How many workers have died from exposure to PVC? Seventeen deaths were attributed to angiosarcoma of the liver by the time the standards went into effect, but how many more already stricken will die? The answer will not be known for many years. Nor is there any reliable data on the death toll among workers fabricating VC products, ranging from fireproof coating for electrical wiring to containers, phonograph records, curtains, floor tile, shower curtains, etc. (Eighteen billion pounds of PVC are produced worldwide annually by 2.2 million workers to fill the demand.)

When B. F. Goodrich Company disclosed in January, 1974, that it was investigating whether the cancer deaths of three workers in Louisville, Kentucky, were job related, the effect was shattering.

"I look at this as the dropping of a bomb," said Louis Beliczky, industrial hygienist on the staff of the United Rubber Workers Union. "It opens up the possibility of a whole new occupational disease." And so it was. By the time the OSHA exposure level went into effect fifteen months later, seventeen deaths had been attributed to angiosarcoma of the liver in the United States. Worldwide, the death toll was forty-five. But it was not the number of deaths tracked down in so short a time which moved unions to fight for a zero exposure level; it was the realization that PVC workers were going to die for years to come because of their exposure to PVC in the past! This was confirmed by Goodrich:

> Dr. Maurice Johnson, Goodrich's medical director, told a news conference that in light of the long latent period between first exposure to vinyl chloride and the development of cancer (a maximum thus far of 30 years), the company expects to continue seeing new angiosarcoma cases up to the turn of the century as a result of earlier worker exposure to higher levels of vinyl chloride than currently prevail in Goodrich plants.[3]

Goodrich does not expect any of its employees to develop angiosarcoma at the present exposure levels, which were bitterly contested by the plastics industry. As for the "no-detectable" exposure level proposed by the unions, the Society of the Plastics Industry, a trade group, contended the technology did not exist to attain it. Ralph Harding Jr., society president, said the standard was

> technologically infeasible to achieve, even with the highly sophisticated methods of in-plant control that have been developed by the industry over the years. If the proposed "no-detectable level" standard is adopted, the vinyl chloride and polyvinyl chloride resin producing industries will be forced to close down immediately.

The adoption of the one ppm tolerance level did not close down the industry; even though the difference between one ppm and zero is so minute, the industry had to aim for a "no-exposure" level because it was not feasible to develop a system providing for the difference between zero and one ppm. The doomsday prediction proved to be far from accurate, the *New York Times* reported on December 28, 1975. One small plant had closed its doors, but four new ones were "coming on stream." Supplies of PVC were plentiful and the price of PVC was "running about 10 percent below 1974 highs."

Before the one ppm level was adopted, unions were doing something about the "newfound" industrial hazard. Local 8–277 of the Oil, Chemical and Atomic Workers, for example, called on Dr. Irving Selikoff of the Mount Sinai School of Medicine to send fourteen members of his environmental medicine research team to examine 401 workers in the Goodyear Tire and Rubber Company plant at Niagara Falls, New York, for possible effects of VC poisoning. It was, wrote Jane E. Brody of the *New York Times* on March 13, 1974, "the most intensive mass medical examination in the history of occupational health."

Frank Micale, father of five and president of Local 8–277, revealed how worried his members were after eleven cases of angiosarcoma of the liver had been linked to occupational exposure to vinyl chloride within seven weeks.

"Cancer, it's so final, we had to do something," Micale said.

Note: It was the union, not the plant, that initiated the program in the union hall, and it was not for union members only, but also for "salaried personnel and former Goodyear workers." And it was the unions that disseminated information on the perils of VC, alerting members to the need to press for safety precautions and to lobby for legislation.

The *AFL-CIO News* kept up a constant stream of news stories on OSHA developments in 1974, concentrating on VC. It is a fair estimate to say the weekly paper ran an OSHA story in at least every other issue in 1974 and 1975. The *American Federationist*, published monthly, did a thorough review of the "Continuing Fight for Job Safety" in its June, 1974, issue.

AFL-CIO Legislative Director Andrew J. Biemiller went before Congress in July, 1974, to oppose as "callous and inhumane" an amendment to exempt establishments with up to 25 workers from coverage of OSHA. The amendment would have excluded 30 percent of all workers and 90 percent of the work sites covered by the law.

When the *Wall Street Journal* in mid-1974 surveyed the PVC picture, Walter Mossberg opened the first of two lengthy articles with a synopsis of what one union was doing to alert its members:

Recently Nello Morbidelli, a local union leader from Connecticut, came to [Washington] to attend a seminar that, he says, "was the greatest thing ever."

The conference concerned safety and health in the workplace. And not long after returning to his duties as head of a United Rubber Workers local at a small rubber products plant in Connecticut, Mr. Morbidelli was able to put the seminar's lessons to work. "I found that while I was away, two women workers were taken to the hospital with aplastic anemia, a bone-marrow disease we had learned a lot about at the seminar. I started looking around the plant, and I realized we were using a benzene solution, which they had explained in Washington can cause aplastic anemia."

So he called his union's industrial hygienist, who flew in from Ohio, surveyed the plant and confirmed Mr. Morbidelli's fears. They met with management and worked out a health-improvement plan. Soon the benzene solution was gone, and consultants were brought in to recommend further changes.[4]

(But it was not until April 29, 1977, that the Labor Department issued an emergency order reducing permissible worker exposure to benzene from ten parts per million to one part per million over an eight-hour average, effective May 21, 1977, for 150,000 workers in 1,200 plants. Yes, the petroleum industry *did* ask for a permanent stay of the standard and the AFL-CIO Industrial Department and the Rubber Workers *did* file a joint brief challenging the request.)

OCAW has been holding conferences for district councils for several years to help make workers aware of the hazards and how to correct them. OCAW's District 8 went even further, publishing *Industrial Hazards, a Worker's Manual for Controlling the Work Environment* in 1971 for use in a course at Rutgers University's Labor Center. Written by the Scientists Committee for Occupational Health, the manual was useful for identifying hazards. But no manual can possibly remain timely, for every day revelations of previously unsuspected hazards come to light.

Some six years before the toxic effects of VC were uncovered, Local 342 of the Amalgamated Meat Cutters and Butcher Workmen began sifting through complaints of "meat cutters' syndrome" made by meat wrappers in supermarkets who were using a 600-degree F. wire to cut and wrap PVC film around meat and cheese products. Ralph Quattrocchi, safety chairman, and Thelma King, his assistant, explained that this new industrial disease, which involved respiratory ailments and asthma, is not attributable to vinyl chloride fumes but "hydrochloric acid, traces of benzene, a number of plasticizers and phosgene." The last item, Quattrocchi recalled, "is a deadly chemical banned after World War I." But what does a local union know about chemicals or their toxic effects?

When members complained of labored breathing, wheezing, coughing and eye irritation, the union undertook its own research—research in which the safety committee called upon not only its consultant, Dr. Selikoff, but also the Midwest Research Institute of Kansas and the National Institute for Occupational Safety and Health, for information and guidance. The union had an established safety committee, which had already proven that cut fingers, hands lost entirely, broken backs and "all the rest" could be prevented; that work "did not have to be hazardous, if we could learn how to work safely."

Acting at the initiative of the union's officers, the committee tackled the PVC problem, which had national implications. Local 342's success in compelling 60 percent of the supermarket industry in its jurisdiction to replace the 600-degree wire with a low-temperature wire, and a commitment from the other supermarkets to follow suit quickly, led the international union to name the local's president, Nickolas Abondolo, as national safety chairman.

The industry has been cooperative and a joint labor-management committee was formed to sponsor a health study by the Harvard School of Public Health on the effects of the fumes emitted by heat-activated price labels. But what was intriguing was the union's motivation for the PVC research.

In a taped interview, Quattrocchi and King responded to the question hesitantly, as so many union people have, giving the impression they had not previously articulated the rationale for safety, but had accepted the responsibility intuitively.

QUATTROCCHI: It's just another program beyond collective bargaining.
KING: Injuries concern the member and his family, their pocketbook.
QUATTROCCHI: It's a program so the member can improve his life, maintain his income and, as Thelma says, it stretches out to include his family . . . We have no alternative. The industry has insurance and compensation; they have all the other hidden costs that go with an accident. You can understand their motives. We have none of those things. The only motive we have for helping the members is to help people.

But when they were asked, "Why should you show any concern for members?" King replied, "That's what a union is all about. We don't call each other sister and brother for nothing!"

It was pointed out to them that earlier Alice Hasler, self-termed "grandmother of the union," had said, "A union is a family." Responded Quattrocchi, "I can't put it any better than that. It's dealing with people and their problems."

Local 342 produced a safety film, *I've Never Had an Accident in My Life*, under an OSHA grant. Copies are constantly being mailed out to unions and companies requesting "the shocking picture," Quattrocchi said. "That's what it's all about, shocking people, when they see the right and wrong ways to work."

Vinyl chloride provides a dramatic account of discovery, reaction and resolution of a problem that's unlikely to be soon repeated. But PVC is only one in a virtually endless series of toxic substances being used industrially. The extent of the danger is still unknown, as Rachel Scott, author of *Muscle and Bone*, has pointed out, because no one knows what the results will be of exposure to any one of 500,000 chemicals used in industry.

The tragedy is that nothing was done to protect workers for so many years. How did the death toll escape notice? One factor is the insidious nature of occupational diseases, claiming victims slowly over a span of two or three decades. But imagine the shock wave which would sweep the nation if all victims of PVC died on the same day? And what if all the victims of asbestosis, pneumonoconiosis, mesotheliomas, byssinosis or cancer of the lungs, pleura, trachea and bronchi also died the same day? The sheer weight of the numbers of simultaneous deaths would produce such a shock of revulsion, anguish and horror that effective precautions would be taken at once.

But the deaths do occur . . . from day to day . . . year to year . . . and the anguish is a private burden, borne only by the family of the "mugged" American worker.

"Mugged" is the term used by Anthony Mazzocchi, then legislative director of the Oil, Chemical and Atomic Workers International Union, to describe the slaughter of expendable workers:

This is the mugging of the American worker. You are far safer today on a dark street than in a factory. Crime in the factory is not being addressed. A cop's job is child's play compared with a factory job. Seventeen thousand workers are killed each year by occupational diseases. And we don't even know the full extent of the danger; we only have a recognition of the dangers which may be involved. But it's safe to say that the occupationally induced deaths annually are more than the casualties suffered in any war the United States has been involved in.

Mazzocchi was not indulging in emotional hyperbole. There were 45,937 U.S. personnel killed in action in Vietnam; 33,629 killed in Korea; 292,131 in World War II and 53,513 in World War I. Admittedly, the total casualty rolls were higher, but each of the wars lasted over a year. (A comparison might also be made with the death toll attributed to crime. The Federal Bureau of Investigation claims 19,120 people were murdered in the U.S. in 1977, but "crime in the streets" aroused a disproportionate resentment in "law and order" circles.)

Considering how little is known of the extent of industrial health hazards, it would be foolhardy to dismiss Mazzocchi's comparison as rash. Since OSHA set standards (threshold limit values, or TLVs) for less than 500 of the 19,000 toxic substances in common industrial use by 1979, and TLVs for only sixteen of the 2,400 chemicals believed to be carcinogens, the problem can't be quickly solved, nor the casualties yet to come be accurately estimated.

The overall problem of industrial safety antedates by centuries the introduction of synthetic substances, having been known since the times of the Roman Empire, when slaves succumbed to lead poisoning.

In her autobiography, *Exploring the Dangerous Trades*, Dr. Alice Hamilton wrote that in 1910

63

the American Medical Association had never held a meeting on the subject [of occupational disease], and while European journals were full of articles on industrial poisoning, the number published in American medical journals up to 1910 could be counted on one's fingers.[5]

Ignorance and indifference, Dr. Hamilton wrote, were not unique to the medical profession, but were shared by employers and workers alike. The opposition of industry to any standards to protect the workers' health is understandable if not admirable: it is a cost item which erodes profits. So it is not surprising when Dr. Hamilton states:

> But the truth is that the National Association of Manufacturers has fought the passage of occupational disease compensation as it has fought laws against child labor, laws establishing a minimum wage for women and a maximum working day.[6]

But what of the trade unions? Why didn't they clamor for protection for the workers? Dr. Hamilton spent her career investigating the causes of industrial diseases, including white or yellow phosphorus, lead, arsenic, carbon monoxide, the cyanides, turpentine, aniline dyes, mercury, benzol, carbon disulphide, hydrogen sulphide, tetraethyl lead, etc., but she does not dwell on the subject of union intervention in her autobiography. That, however, is understandable, considering that she spent most of her lifetime on the industrial scene long before unions won legitimacy in the United States. While she was crusading for safety, unions were devoting their energies to the struggle for the right to exist. Moreover, it was an age in which the efforts made to organize industrial workers were sporadic, precarious and often doomed to failure. Further, there were no government requirements providing compensation for industrial disease or injury—not until Illinois passed such a law in 1911.

The factory may be a mug's game for the worker today, but at the turn of the century the factory was a slaughterhouse, and so, too, were the railroads. Philip S. Foner has observed:

> The absence of standards of safety was typical throughout most of the industry. In the single year of 1901, one out of every 399 railroad employees was killed and one out of 26 was injured. Among engineers, conductors, brakemen, trainmen, the figures for the year showed that one out of every 137 was killed. Colorado mines took an average of 6.2 lives for every one thousand employed in 1901; the average rose in 1905 to 8.15. In one year it was found that over 50,000 accidents had taken place in New York factories alone, in which 167 workers had been killed.[7]

It was the slaughter on the railroads which led to the formation of the railroad brotherhoods, since insurance companies refused to insure the lives of men on train service. The brotherhoods were formed to provide insurance policies. But the workers were not alone in being aware of the death toll. The public, as well as businessmen, was aware of the butchery going on in industry. The dangerous trades had been identified. Foner has outlined the extent of the carnage:

In 1904 a corps of expert statisticians compiled figures showing the mortality in trades and occupations commonly classed as dangerous. Of the 19,659,440 workers in various parts of the country whose records were examined, the mortality due to conditions on the job in manufacturing industries was 15,136, and in the transportation and agricultural industries, 12,005. Of these workers, also 643.07 hat and cap makers per 10,000 succumbed to pulmonary and respiratory diseases; cigar and tobacco workers, 454.45, and marble and stone workers, 398.73.

Other occupations in which the mortality was very high were those of quarrymen, masons, carpenters (one carpenter in every 1,212 was killed in the single year 1903), bricklayers, railroad workers, glass polishers, bottlers, garment workers, iron workers, painters, dyers, printers, enamelers, miners—in short, a pretty fair cross-section of the American working class.

In the pottery factories where the air was filled all day with choking dust clouds, asthma took a huge toll; in the glass factories, lead poisoning produced a large mortality year after year (the carriage builder, the plumber, the painter, the dyer and enameler were also prey to it). In the lithographic printing trades, arsenic poisoning claimed its annual victims; in the bottling establishments, serious injuries were caused by the explosion of bottles of aerated water, and many an eye was blown out; in the sweatshops of New York, where hundreds of thousands of garment workers were huddled together in a few, filthy East Side garrets, the mortality rate from a wide variety of diseases was incredibly high.

It is an undeniable fact, the report concluded, "that several millions of men and women in the United States are today engaged in occupations that yearly take their toll of human life and health as inevitably, as inexorably, as the seasons roll in their grooves." *The Cleveland Citizen* put it more tersely when it called the United States "the industrial slaughter house."[8]

The first workmen's compensation laws were enacted as early as 1884, not in the United States, but in Germany; England followed suit in 1897. But it was not until 1902 that the first such measures were enacted here, in Maryland—only to be declared unconstitutional. Similar laws met the same fate in 1909 in Montana and 1910 in New York on the grounds that they deprived employers of their property without due process of law. There was, apparently, merit to the AFL belief that legislators, the courts and big business were more concerned with profits than the workers' welfare.

But there was another, equally important factor, apart from ignorance, which kept the worker from mounting protests against the slaughterhouses: a primary concern with jobs. Work was more important than cleaning up the workplace. Industry's threats to close down rather than reform were as convincing fifty years ago as now.

Nor, it should be added, has labor's attitude changed to any considerable extent. Workers are not being persuaded by their unions to abandon the short-term view of "jobs now, safety later," to consider not only their own lives and deaths but those of their children and grandchildren. But it should be recalled the battle has barely begun. Labor did not have the power, let alone the technology, to mount an effective campaign for the health and safety of the worker until the past four decades. And it has been an even shorter span of time in which modern chemistry has transformed the environment and the workplace into death traps. Only in the past decade has the term *ecology* come into common usage.

There are unions conscious of the obligation to go beyond collective bargaining to protect their members from injury, disease and death on the job, "but they are all too few," Mazzocchi sadly conceded. But, few as they may be, they have made significant strides, working against the reluctance of the employer to take safety precautions, the reluctance of the government to set or enforce standards and the reluctance of the worker to risk his job to avoid the insidious infection which may wipe out his life twenty or thirty years in the future.

It is the fear of job loss that impels rank and file union members to be hostile to the philosophy of the "ecology set" and to the Environmental Protection Agency's regulations. It is an understandable fear, for the loss of one's own job far outweighs such considerations as the creation of other jobs in the new industries fighting water and air pollution. Robert Hamrin, staff economist of the Joint Economic Committee of Congress, estimated pollution controls forced the closing of sixty-nine plants and the loss of 12,000 jobs between January, 1971, and June, 1974. But tens of thousands of new jobs were created by the 300 firms in the air equipment business and 400 firms in water treatment and water pollution control. The Bureau of Labor Statistics maintains 20,000 jobs are created for every billion dollars spent on sewage treatment projects.

Employment for one's self alone outweighs employment prospects for others, far more than occupational safety and health. News reports frequently illustrate this.

ATLANTIC CITY, N.J., Jan. 29, 1976 (UPI)—Unemployed construction workers and oil company spokesmen clashed with naturalists yesterday over the probable effects of drilling for oil and natural gas off the New Jersey coast.

About 150 operating engineers heckled opponents of offshore drilling who said further study was needed on the impact drilling would have on beaches and marine life. They cheered industry representatives who said the nation needs jobs and new energy sources.

The workers carried signs reading, "Support off-shore leasing" and "Independence from foreign oil blackmail."

"We're here to show our support for leasing because it means a decade or more of work for us," said Tom Greer of Margate, N.J., one of the union spokesmen.

And again, in the *New York Times:*

BUCHANAN, N.Y., Feb. 29, 1976—Demonstrators calling for the closing of the Indian Point nuclear power plant were outnumbered and outshouted today by union members threatened with the loss of their jobs.

About 200 supporters of the Citizens Committee for the Protection of the Environment and the Westchester Peoples Action Committee gathered early this afternoon near the entrance of the plant, on the banks of the Hudson, which houses three nuclear generators owned by the Consolidated Edison Company and the State Power Authority. The environmentalists stood in small clusters, waiting for the arrival of their speakers . . . Across the road, separated from [them] by wooden barricades and lines of policemen, well over 1,000 members of Utility Workers Union Local 1-2, some with wives and children, crowded together, carrying signs that read, "[Representative Bella] Abzug Aids Arab Oil," and "These employees have families, too."

Today's demonstration was planned in response to the resignation of Robert D. Pollard, a Federal safety engineer, who three weeks ago left his position as project manager for the United States Nuclear Regulatory Commission, charging that the Indian Point No. 2 reactor was "an accident waiting to happen," and calling for its immediate closing . . .

"That plant is as safe as being in your bathtub," said Jim Joy, business manager of the union. "There's a bigger chance of the George Washington Bridge falling down."

While that may be true, what Joy and other utility workers are reluctant to consider is the totally inadequate safety precautions taken for storing nuclear waste, the danger of nuclear materials being diverted for weapons production and the risk of nuclear accident, in which not one person, but as many as 120,000 might be killed—sixteen times the number of casualties the Atomic Energy Commission blithely estimated in 1973, to the dismay of the Union of Concerned Scientists.

Workers are reluctant to risk the loss of employment by supporting any consumer or environmental program to curb the use of carcinogens or to clean up the environment. This can lead to untenable positions with an element of humor in the posture. For example, one might cite the attitude of the Tobacco Workers Union* in regard to smoking: "'No smoking' ordinances adopted in a number of cities to ban smoking in public places divert attention from basic reform and 'delay cleaning up the work environment,' Homer Cole, secretary of the Tobacco Workers, charged. The new ordinances are 'unneeded and unenforceable,' he said, and help created 'another class of lawbreakers.'"

But the real problem is that the controversy over smoking in public places is diverting attention from industrial pollution to which millions of workers—smokers and nonsmokers—are exposed, Cole declared in the *AFL-CIO News* on March 8, 1975. "The TWIU firmly maintains," Cole said, "that the question of what is causing disease among the working population can only be resolved through intensive, objective research, not by scapegoating tobacco. 'No smoking' ordinances which set smoker against nonsmoker and delay cleaning up the work environment are not the solution."

Is Cole's attitude typical of union leaders? Have they shown any inclination to spearhead the fight to protect the lives of their members? Some have, too many have not. And that is deplorable, since half the workers on asbestos have asbestosis; 100 out of 145 in lead plants have lead poisoning; men around coke ovens are three times as prone to cancer as other steel workers; and textile workers run a 12 to 30 percent risk of suffering from byssinosis. Around nickel refining, the cancer rate is five times that of the population at large; around chromates, it is twenty-five times as high. But little is done about it, as Gus Tyler has observed, because "it is death without drama."

In recent years, unions have been calling attention to the menace of industrial hazards with stories in the labor press designed to alert members to the dangers. But why did they delay so long in recognizing the hazards? Arnold Miller, president of the United Mine Workers, spelled it out in an address:

> I worked for a total of 24 years in the coal mines of my native state of West Virginia until 1970 when I was forced to quit because of my health. I was just 47 years old at the time, and I couldn't qualify for a pension for another eight years. But I had no choice. My lungs were filled with coal dust. And my bones were stiff and numb from arthritis, brought on by years of work in knee-deep water and the cool, damp mine air.

---

* Since merged into the Bakery, Confectionery and Tobacco Workers International Union.

My experience was not unique. If a roof fall or an explosion didn't get them first, coal miners in my day could count on having their health destroyed as a price for working in the mines. It was the miner's lot, and nobody really thought that anything could be done about it.

It wasn't that miners lacked the will or the courage to try to change their condition. Hundreds of miners endured long and bitter strikes and many died organizing our union. What we lacked was an understanding of what was destroying our health.

During my years in the mines, the bosses always told me that coal dust wasn't harmful. Company doctors said the same thing. In fact, several claimed that coal dust was good for us. And they always threw in some four-syllable scientific mumbo-jumbo to support their claims.

Silicosis was the only lung disease miners suffered, we were instructed, and it was mainly found among hard coal miners in the anthracite region of eastern Pennsylvania and a few hard rock drillers. All we soft coal miners needed was a good chew of tobacco, the doctors said, and we didn't have a thing in the world to fear from coal dust.

Miners who complained of shortness of breath were regularly diagnosed as having "anxiety" problems or psychological disorders. Or they were accused of trying to get out of working by winning a disability award. The company mockingly called it "compensationitis."

We didn't know at the time we were being fed this medical snake oil that 3,000 miles away in Britain the National Coal Board had identified black lung as a major occupational disease. We didn't know that in the early forties the British had set up a program of compensation awards for black lung victims and rigid dust standards in the mines.[9]

If the UMW didn't know it, it should have. Obviously, it would have come to light had there been a UMW industrial hygiene department worth its salt. (There's a remarkable parallel between black lung and brown lung, or byssinosis, the cotton-dust disease which has disabled, even killed, textile mill workers. But the lung disease was recognized in Britain in 1932 and five years later the Factory Act mandated medical inspections of workplaces, compulsory reporting of industrial diseases and compensation of diseased and disabled workers. However, the British cotton mill workers were strongly organized, contrasting with the low level of organization by the Textile Workers Union in the South, where the American Textile Manufacturers Institute, abetted by the U.S. Public Health Service and the U.S. Labor Department, contended until 1968 that byssinosis was not a problem in cotton mills.)

In the same year, three West Virginia doctors, alarmed at the death rate among miners from respiratory disorders five times the population's rate, told the miners coal dust was to blame. The word was spread through the coal fields despite the heated objections of the county medical associations, which threatened the doctors with disciplinary action. The West Virginia Black Lung Association was formed a year later by miners, who asked the state legislature to recognize black lung as a compensable occupational disease. Passage of the act was blocked by the coal-dominated legislators. Forty thousand miners walked out of the pits and many of them marched on the state capitol, demanding passage of the bill. They went back to work only after the bill was passed and signed by the governor. Miller has termed the strike "probably the largest strike over occupational health issues by American workers." The effects were far-reaching. Congress passed a federal black lung benefits program as part of the 1969 Coal Mine Health and Safety Act. Unfortunately, the Interior Department was less than vigorous in enforcing its provisions, as the annual death toll of miners, from accidents and disease, amply indicates. The UMW lobbied for legislation providing for the Bureau of Mines to be transferred to the Labor Department and sought full black lung benefits without medical examinations for every miner with thirty years in bituminous or twenty-five years in anthracite mining.

The UMW under the leadership of Arnold Miller, himself a black lung victim, has made some strides in safeguarding the health of miners, but still has a long way to go. It is a union which has shown concern for the community. For example, the UMW is on record as opposing construction of a hydroelectric power project on the New River in western Virginia and North Carolina. That came a day after the AFL-CIO joined hands with the American Electric Power System to oppose a bill in Congress placing the river in the wildlife and scenic system. The federation's reasoning was that the project would create jobs for electrical workers and operating engineers.

The UMW can differ with the AFL-CIO on policy; it is an independent union, out of the AFL since 1936 and out of the CIO since 1942.

The AFL-CIO's endorsement of the New River hydroelectric power project is typical of its major pursuit—employment for members—and rightly so, but it is not a goal which entirely blinds the federation to the dangers of industrial disease, injury or death. The federation is aware of the need to promote effective enforcement of the Occupational Safety and Health Act, since concern over the health, welfare and safety of the member, at least in historical perspective, has always been a union priority.

That there is an Occupational Safety and Health Act is unquestionably due to the intensive political action undertaken by the AFL-CIO, its affiliates and independent unions. One need not go to self-serving labor sources for confirmation; the Chamber of Commerce of the United States has testified to this in a vitriolic attack on OSHA, which saw "labor union leaders extolling the safety act," not because of concern over worker safety, but in the expectation of such "windfalls" as larger work crews, designation as "unsafe" or "unhealthy" of automated equipment and the concentration of bargaining powers "on the juicier aims of bigger wages and shorter hours."[10]

Certainly, it was not American industry which trudged to Capitol Hill to urge enactment of H.R. 14816 and S. 2864. On the contrary, the Chamber of Commerce, despite a posture of not quarreling with the expressed purpose of the bills—"to make working safer and healthier"—maintained American businessmen had achieved "the world's finest safety record," motivated by a sense of compassion toward the welfare of the employees and "strong money reasons for promoting safety."[11]

If businessmen did not clamor for passage of OSHA, who did? The names are revealing and so are the organizations represented.

The "big guns" of the AFL-CIO turned out en masse to testify on behalf of OSHA, including President George Meany; Sheldon Samuels, director of the AFL-CIO Department of Occupational Health and Safety; Andrew J. Biemiller, director, AFL-CIO Department of Legislation; Jacob Clayman, administrative director, AFL-CIO Industrial Union Department; John A. McCart, operations director, AFL-CIO Government Employees Council; and George Taylor, economist, AFL-CIO Research Department.*

But also in the line-up of labor witnesses were officers of international unions, including the International Chemical Workers Union, the United Mine Workers of America, the Transport Workers Union, Service Employes International Union, the Brotherhood of Teamsters, International Longshoremen's Association and the Oil, Chemical and Atomic Workers International Union.

What was significant in the parade of labor witnesses, however, was the large number of local union officials, legislative directors, research directors and even grievance committee chairmen of district councils and local unions, reflecting a mass movement on behalf of a life and death issue.

To cite one example, the Senate Subcommittee on Labor of the Committee on Labor and Public Welfare heard from the following Steelworkers' representatives during a five-month period in 1968:

John J. Sheehan, legislative director; John Proto, education and

---

* Samuels has since been named job safety director of the AFL-CIO Industrial Union Department; Biemiller retired in 1979; Clayman was president of IUD until September 1979; and Taylor was named director of the Occupational Health and Safety Department.

legislative director, District 9; William Morton, staff representative; Anthony Cascone, education chairman, Local 837; Michael Romanko, president, Local 7036; Abbott Richardson, negotiations committee member, Local 4985; James Wiggers, president, Local 1482; Steven Cadena, staff assistant, Hillside, New Jersey; Charles Lema, safety chairman, Jersey City; Frank Sass, safety chairman, Ingersoll-Rand, Phillipsburg, New Jersey; Anthony Lemeraro, safety chairman, Fairless Works; Henry Robinson, grievance committee chairman, Local 2954, Bucks County, Pennsylvania; John J. Seman, safety and health coordinator, District 15; Dan Hannan, president, Local 1575, U.S. Steel, Clairton Works; Bernard Novak, president, Local 2227, Irwin Works, U.S. Steel, West Mifflin, Pennsylvania; William Petrisko, president, Local 1256, U.S. Steel, Duquesne Works; John McManigal, president, Local 1397, U.S. Steel, Homestead Works; and George Cope, Jones & Laughlin Steel Corporation.

Equally large delegations from other unions appeared before the same committee. But as with one voice, they urged enactment of OSHA. Speaking on their behalf, Meany had this to say:

> Every year thousands of workers die slow, often agonizing deaths from the effects of coal dust, asbestos, beryllium, lead, cotton dust, carbon monoxide, cancer-causing chemicals, dyes, radiation, pesticides and exotic fuels. Others suffer long illnesses. Thousands suffer from employment in artificially created harmful environments.

Meany wound up his testimony with a plea for enactment of the legislation, but shrewdly called for amendments to extend the act to cover 2.8 million federal employees and workers in small privately owned business firms. The AFL-CIO's other suggestions were to create a statutory Center for Occupational Health; to use only qualified inspectors; to take "firm, decisive action, not arbitrary, nor capricious"; and to delegate the Secretary of Labor's authority to states only if their standards were comparable to the federal standards. "Organized labor considers this bill as an historic milestone in the evolution of humanitarian concern for the welfare of American workers," Meany said in winding up his testimony before the House Education and Labor subcommittee.

The AFL-CIO Industrial Union Department (IUD), directed by Jacob Clayman, administrator, and its Legislative Department, directed by Biemiller, worked indefatigably to push OSHA through Congress against the determined opposition of industry and its trade associations and chambers of commerce but was unsuccessful in obtaining protection for federal workers. While OSHA guarantees "a safe and healthful workplace" for all working people, that's far from reality. Section 2 states the purpose is "to assure so far as possible every working man and woman in the nation safe and healthful working conditions," but the act does not cover over 13.5 million public employees.

Lobbying on behalf of OSHA was not a one-time thrust. Clayman, Biemiller and Samuels, a career environmentalist and director of the IUD's Department of Health, Safety and Environmental Affairs, went back to Congress time and again to testify in opposition to attempts to weaken the act with amendments providing for variances, on-site consultations rather than citations or penalties, exemption of small business firms from provisions of the act, priorities for economic impact rather than safety and diversion of funds from inspections to education.

The AFL-CIO went even further, citing the U.S. Labor Department in court twice within as many years for failures to properly enforce the act.

On the day the law became effective, IUD set up its health, safety and environmental affairs division to inform its fifty-nine affiliates on effective use of the act through research, educational materials and information. Samuels became editor of the IUD *Spotlight on Health and Safety*; a quarterly publication which keeps affiliates informed of labor's activism in job safety and health.

Samuels once recounted an experience he had while serving as an air pollution control expert. A group of workers, impatient with his discussion on community air pollution, turned the topic to plant conditions. When he finally asked one worker just what he wanted, the reply was terse: "Work without fear." That became the title of the IUD pamphlet explaining what OSHA means to the worker. It also convinced Samuels that "we can no longer distinguish between what goes on in the community and what goes on in the shop."

The IUD went further, sponsoring a half dozen workshops, courses and evening sessions in the months after OSHA became law. And within a year, IUD President I. W. Abel sent out an invitation to IUD affiliates to send union safety and health representatives to a basic four-day training program being offered by the Labor Studies Center in ten universities throughout the nation.

The institutes were held—and so were subsequent ones in later years. *Job Safety and Health*, a monthly publication of the U.S. Labor Department, said of these courses in January, 1973:

> Through these courses, 290 union officials learned about inspection procedures and employee rights under the law, industrial hygiene, general job safety, and labor's role in safety and health. Regular IUD mailings and field conferences supplement the course material. Training this cadre of officials has had the desired snowball effect. Many trainees have become safety and health directors of their unions and are launching their own programs.

The Utility Workers Union, for example, now has workshops on job safety and health in all its regions. The United Cement, Lime and Gypsum Workers International Union has trained officials in nearly half of its 250 U.S. locals. The 10 participating universities also have received numerous requests for additional programs. In Ohio, the most active state, Ohio State University and the Ohio AFL-CIO already have offered a total of at least 60 courses in every major Ohio city since the first institute at the university a year ago.[12]

And yet, labor is given poor grades for its concern about safety, in complete disregard of the scope of safety programs routinely provided for in years past. The familiar sight of the hard hats worn by construction workers to avoid skull-shattering impacts from falling tools and rivets should point up the concern of the building trades. A second example comes to mind: The boast of Local 25, International Brotherhood of Electrical Workers is that only once since 1932 has a brother been electrocuted on the job!

If Rachel Scott found "unions haven't done much" to protect the lives and health of their members, Ralph Nader, who recognizes no boundaries for outraged dissent, has been scathing in denouncing unions. His argument:

Most of the large unions have few or no safety engineers, industrial hygienists, physicians and lawyers specializing in advancing the workers' rights to a safe working environment. The United Mine Workers' leadership disgraced themselves on the black lung disease that was eroding half their members' health. The International Brotherhood of Teamsters has nobody in Washington working full time to achieve safer working conditions and safety equipment for truck drivers. The United Auto Workers have only four full-time health and safety staff members at their national headquarters . . . The labor press only recently began to report much news about job safety developments, but still does virtually no investigations, nor by and large, do they poll their enormous readership . . . to collect data from the workers directly about their complaints and knowledge. The few unions who are beginning to do this, such as the Oil, Chemical and Atomic Workers and the Amalgamated Clothing Workers, receive much useful information as well as suggested initiatives from the rank and file.[13]

Industry's attitude, as may easily be imagined, comes in for an equally severe drubbing from Nader: "As long as it costs less to permit casualties than to prevent them, the motivational direction of the company is not to invest in new equipment and procedures."

Government's reactions to the hazards can be viewed cynically. When public pressure outweighs campaign contributions, safety regulations are enacted by Congress, but enforcement is not prosecuted and staffs are not funded. Political tampering has rendered OSHA ineffective. This is illustrated by Assistant Secretary of Labor George C. Guenther's infamous "Watergate Memorandum" to Under Secretary of Labor Laurence H. Silberman in 1974, proposing that the Republican National Committee and the Committee to Re-elect the President recruit applicants for the OSHA staff. President Ford was blatantly obvious in instructing OSHA to start dealing "with citizens as friends, not enemies." (Eula Bingham, named to run OSHA in 1977, was shocked by what she found there. She was the choice of the Nader health advocate groups and was expected to improve the agency's effectiveness.)

But unions are not monolithic and do not react as a coherent body. One can only judge what some unions have done. The union which has undoubtedly done the most to safeguard its members, OCAW, has a commitment to the problem. But its legislative director recognized how much more remains to be done. "There's not enough excitement over the problem," said Tony Mazzocchi, "and it's already an international problem. I used to think radiation was the worst hazard, but obviously it isn't."

The dangers of radiation, at least in some quarters, are recognized and appreciated. The extent of the hazards of toxic chemicals is not.

> The workers don't know, either, [Mazzocchi continued]. No one knows about the toxicity of the chemicals we work with. The medical community doesn't know. OCAW has made it one of our main concerns. We have held conferences and made environmental safety one of our bargaining demands. That's why we struck Shell Oil. We worked hard for OSHA, presenting testimony. We lobbied with the Industrial Union Department (of the AFL-CIO). It was important to tie in with the concern of the environmentalists to form a broad coalition. We built up a professional staff. We have a doctor in Denver and a legal staff in Washington. We want to know the generic names of the chemicals we work with. We've taken it to arbitration and won the right to know. We teach our members to take blood tests and we monitor the worker, too.

Mazzocchi leapt from one topic to another, rarely stopping to amplify or explain his observations. But if he spoke rapidly, it was clear his mind was forging ahead even more rapidly. There had been a clear signal from OCAW President A. F. Grospiron to press ahead on industrial safety. This was the union that in 1973 struck five Shell Oil refineries and chemical plants to win the right to monitor industrial hygiene and company data on the workers' health status. In other words, it was the first environmental strike in labor history.

If he was discouraged about union activity in the past, Mazzocchi was not discouraged by current developments, since "unions are starting to move." Seeing in this a "wave of the future," Mazzocchi said:

Unions will hire professionals who are anxious to work for scientific institutes. The new worker is young, better educated and he will see the light and be more responsive. I've been involved in this for 10 years and I know, it's here and can't be buried. Automation and productivity make the workplace deteriorate. Maintenance is cut to the bone. Safeguards are circumvented. The dilemma of the modern industrial state is that it is incompatible with health. Man won't survive unless we restructure society, because management won't do anything. It can only be done by the struggle of the union. If we wait for the federal government to act, it won't get done. They vacillate, make dilatory moves.

OCAW, however, is not the only union concerned with the workers' health. The United Steel Workers of America is engaged in a running battle with the steel industry over regulations for controlling emissions from coke ovens, in particular, benzo (A) pyrene, a carcinogen, but found to its dismay the Ford Administration favored recommendations "acceptable to the industry," according to I.W. Abel.

Joint action by the AFL-CIO, the United Rubber Workers and the Health Research Group compelled the Labor Department to set emergency health standards for asbestos, vinyl chloride and fourteen other carcinogens since 1971. But the labor petitions do not always meet with success. Petitions seeking a zero exposure standard for asbestos ran into a stone wall in 1973 when OSHA set a standard of five fibers per cubic centimeter of air, but the standard referred to particles above five microns in length. These, however, are not the most harmful particles which cause asbestosis. The harm is done by fibers so small they can be seen only in electronic microscopes so sophisticated regular sampling would be impractical.

The tolerance level, however, reduced to 2 million fibers per cubic meter of air in July, 1976, covers 50,000 workers involved in the manufacture of asbestos-containing products and about 50,000 field insulation workers exposed to asbestos dust. It does not cover millions of workers in the construction industry, where three-fourths of all asbestos products are used. "Separate standards" are to be set for them, OSHA announced, because they are usually employed in non-fixed workplaces and tend to be highly transient.

The United Rubber Workers, whose president is Peter Bommarito, long ago recognized the risks its members faced in working for rubber products manufacturing firms, and took steps to inform them of the risks when it started to study the health experience of those exposed to carcinogens in the course of their work. By 1970 its master contracts provided for joint occupational health programs with six major rubber companies. The agreements provide for establishment at a school of public health of an occupational health research group to implement the occupational health research program.

Bommarito and the URW confronted a new nightmare just two years after the hazards of PVC came to light. The leukemia deaths of some rubber workers prompted the National Institute of Occupational Safety and Health (NIOSH) to conduct a major investigation of the potential health hazards of synthetic rubber operations. Bernard Wysocki Jr. wrote in the *Wall Street Journal*:

> B.F. Goodrich Co. surprised industrial health officials earlier this year when it reported five relatively recent cases of leukemia among its workers at a synthetic rubber plant in Texas.
>
> Since then, initial surprise has given way to deep worry. At similar plants in Ohio, Texas, Kentucky and Louisiana, recent studies have revealed nearly two dozen worker deaths from leukemia, a progressively malignant cancer of the blood-forming organs, and other closely related illnesses. Several other employees at the plants are undergoing treatment. Officials fear that further investigations now underway will bring many more cases to light.
>
> Says Louis Beliczky, an industrial hygienist with the United Rubber Workers Union: "I'm sure we will find a lot more (employees with leukemia) when we look closely at the operations."

Nine months later, NIOSH recommended strict safety standards for worker exposure to benzene, based on findings which "demonstrated overwhelmingly an increased risk of leukemia in workers exposed to benzene." (Yes, industry did go to court and did obtain a delay in effecting the emergency standard!)

Bommarito presided when trade unionists of sixteen countries, including the United States, met in October, 1974, in Geneva for a three-day international occupational health conference. The International Chemical and General Workers Federation (ICGWF), of which Charles Levinson is secretary-general, sponsored the sessions. It was a historic first, Levinson wrote:

> For the first time trade unionists with representation in the plants producing and utilizing hazardous industrial chemicals sat down in common discussions with key scientists and specialists in occupational health from across the globe. These international trade unionists and scientists exchanged information and experiences on this vital concern of working people and created a mechanism for achieving major breakthroughs in protecting workers from their use as industrial guinea pigs for chemical testing.

The conference heard scientific papers presented by a roster of distinguished scientists including Dr. Selikoff, Dr. M. El Batawai of the World Health Organization, Dr. Cesare Maltoni of the Intituto di

Oncologia e Centro Tunori, Dr. Samuel Epstein of Case Western Reserve, Dr. Joseph Wagoner of the National Institute of Occupational Safety and Health, Dr. John Peters of the Harvard School of Public Health, Dr. Robert Harris of the University of North Carolina and many others. The exchange of ideas and the formation of an international labor forum led Bommarito to say at the close of the conference:

> This conference has established a new international force in occupational health, the collective strength of all the labor unions throughout the world, united and dedicated in purpose for the recognition and resolution of the hazards of the chemical environment, for the protection of this generation and all generations to follow for every country of the world.

It was more than rhetoric, for Bommarito took note of the proposal made at the conference that an international clearinghouse for information on health and safety had to be established, so that "our collective experiences should be made available immediately to other international unions around the world." His concluding words reflected the militancy of an aroused labor movement:

> We want . . . every delegate to know that you have helped to create a new, unified, international force on occupational health—that you are no longer alone. The multinational companies must abide by the law, they must carry out their moral and social responsibilities to the workers. The government must be responsive to the occupational health needs of the workers. There must be social justice for the worker and his family. We are of one purpose—the right to live. We must and we will provide the collective strength of all international unions throughout the world. Our cause is just.[14]

Notes

1. Jeanne M. Stellman and Susan M. Daum, *Work Is Dangerous to Your Health*, p. xiii.
2. Ibid., p. 232.
3. *New York Times*, 7 December 1975, p. 57.
4. *Wall Street Journal*, 19 August 1974, p. 1.
5. Alice Hamilton, *Exploring the Dangerous Trades*, p. 3.
6. Ibid., p. 12.
7. Philip S. Foner, *History of the Labor Movement in the United States*, p. 20.
8. Ibid., pp. 21–22.
9. Arnold Miller, "The Wages of Neglect," Walter Reuther Memorial Lecture (National Conference on Social Welfare, San Francisco, 15 May 1975), pp. 1–2.
10. "Life or Death for Your Business?" *Nation's Business*, April 1968, p. 38.
11. Ibid., p. 39.
12. Phyllis Lehmann, "Work Without Fear," *Job Safety and Health*, January 1973, p. 4.
13. *Occupational Epidemic*, pp. vi–vii.
14. Charles Levinson, ed., *The New Multinational Health Hazards*, pp. 297–98.

6.
The Redundant Worker

Ralph told the story of the elderly telephone operator who lived two blocks away from the union office, but was unable to walk even that short distance because she had emphysema. So she was driven in a car to and from the union to take over the switchboard during the regular operator's luncheon break. The old woman had been an employee of the local for more than ten years, "but Nick won't hear of getting rid of her."

Reacting to my comment, "No corporation would be that generous," Ralph curtly replied, "But we are not in business."

There were about 150 elderly men and women seated around the tables in the union hall at the monthly luncheon for retirees of Retail Clerks Local 1500, Queens Village, New York.

Each of them, obviously dressed in Sunday best, had been in younger days a food store employee, a dues-paying member of Local 1500, which has well over 20,000 members. The atmosphere was bright, cheerful; these were people whose lives had not been cut short by retirement. The comments of the Retirees Club of 1500 testified to that.

"What does the club mean to me?" Al Krasner repeated the question. "It means I am alive. This club has awakened people who were ready to die. This is utopia for them."

"I come to the meetings to meet people," said another. "I live in Washington, New Jersey. And that's a 100-mile trip. And I don't miss many meetings, except, of course, if there's snow and ice on the ground. There's fellowship here."

Three women eating lunch nearby responded quickly to similar questions. Said one of them, "I come here to meet other people. They give us a nice lunch and we play bingo; we take trips which are very nice. You meet nice people here."

The second agreed, "The social gets you out of the house. And if you need help, all you have to do is call up the union. Everyone here is so nice."

But the third woman summed it up in fewer words: "This is one big family. It's love."

And that's what counts for the retiree; that's what keeps him alive when the routine of the job is over and the problems begin to pile up, as inevitably they do for the aged. Local 1500 organized its Retirees Club in 1972 to meet those problems. It now has over 300 members, virtually all of them pensioners, who pay five dollars a year in dues as club members. Said Tony Peres:

> No other union does for its retirees what we do. We're the number one retirees club in the country. Each year we hold a dance and the union gives us the hall free, helps us to finance the dance. We hold outings for the members, including trips to Washington, and the union subsidizes the buses. We also hold a luncheon once a month.
>
> Anthony Peres, that's me, is president. We have 312 members now and are the leading AFL-CIO club. We have a citation, No. 1, most active in the country.
>
> Sure, the retirees help out the union, too. They assist us in the blood banks and help out when the union holds affairs, like the annual party for kids. They're active in politics and get involved in the elections.

The trips to Washington are far more than sightseeing, as the area's Congressional bloc could testify. A busload of retirees clamoring for legislative relief usually gets a hearing. Congressmen know they vote.

"The club preserves a feeling of good fellowship," Al Krasner said. "Some of them still work part-time. The union pays for our Medicaid with refunds. There are 150 at the lunch today and some of them come from far away. One is from the Catskills."

The social events, as important as they are in maintaining morale, are no indication of the services Local 1500 offers its retirees. They receive free legal advice on request from the union's counsel. Those who are doing part-time work remain active members, paying dues commensurate with their earnings.

Local 1500 pays Blue Cross premiums for its members until both husband and wife reach age sixty-five. (The premiums are funded by the union's welfare trust fund, based on employers' contributions to the fund, but the member feels, "It's the union that's taking care of me.") Retirees can and do attend membership meetings, where they have both a voice and a vote.

It is true that the retirees of Local 1500 are pensioners whose benefits are paid by employers' contributions (as deferred wages) under contracts negotiated by the union. But it's equally obvious that past President Pat Gleeson and Arthur Wolfson, who succeeded him, have gone far beyond their collective bargaining responsibilities to preserve the morale (and thus the lives) of the retired members. In this, Local 1500 is neither unique, nor, alas, representative of most trade unions. But there is a long and honorable tradition in the labor movement recognizing the union's responsibility for the redundant worker which preceded either the community's or the employer's recognition of the problem.

"Redundant," used in the American sense, to mean "being in excess," and not in the British sense, "unemployed," accurately describes the worker who is of no further use to his employer or the economy, except as a consumer—if he has the means to avoid becoming a public charge. The American trade union was the first agency to provide him with compassionate care, Derek C. Bok and John T. Dunlop observed:

> Under these circumstances (in which the community took little or no responsibility to assist), unions were a natural agency to provide protection against such losses. In fact, so many labor organizations began as benefit societies that it is hardly an exaggeration to say that trade unionism in America arose almost as much from a desire to band together for mutual insurance as from a desire to bargain collectively.[1]

Or, one might say, "before there was a need to bargain collectively." The early needs were for cash benefits, which came out of union dues for the disabled or sick worker, or for his family if he was killed on the job or died. There were no provisions for social insurance because there were few aged, retired workers in the preindustrial economy. Due to the brevity of life, they were not even a factor to be considered in the census.

Longer life expectancy and social insurance were inevitable concommitants of the twentieth century. And the span of life is increasing. According to Howard Fullerton and James Byrne:

> Over this entire century, life expectancy at birth for men has climbed by almost 20 years, while work-life expectancy has increased by less than half of that. Thus, average time not in the labor force has risen dramatically. Practically all of the nonwork activity of men at the turn of the century occurred before entrance into the labor force. Now a large proportion of the nonwork years are spent in retirement, though an extended period of education has also delayed labor force entry for many men.[2]

A Census Bureau report in 1976 estimated that as of 1974, women could expect to live an average of 75.9 years and men an average of 68.2 years.

With an over-sixty-five population of more than 23 million persons, the elderly account for 10.5 percent of the nation (17 percent by the year 2030, the Census Bureau estimated), but more than a quarter of the working population—high enough to cry out for measures by the community as well as unions. But unions were involved with the problem before there was a social insurance system in the U.S., when only old-age public pensions were provided by some states, and then only based upon a needs test, paying only starvation benefits.

The Granite Cutters established the first pension plan for trade unionists in 1905. Brother Cornelius Justin, P.S.C., and Mario E. Impellizeri give this account:

> The members, usually of their own free will, participated in these pension plans and paid their contributions or dues directly to the fund. Actuarial guidance was not of the highest and these pay-as-you-go funds resorted to special assessments when the fund needed more money . . . These early plans were organized in the craft and railroad unions where, traditionally, job-turnover has been, through the years, very low.[3]

Workers' pensions are now funded by contributions of the employee and/or employer in response to the demands of the growing segment of older workers in the population. But even those pensions won in lieu of wage increases were achieved through union initiative.

The unions also played a major role in lobbying for social insurance benefits under government auspices. But it was not until 1935 that the Social Security Act was legislated, reflecting an awareness of the growing number of aged in the population (in response, at least in part, to the highly publicized Townsend Movement), a response to the growing number of bankruptcies in employer-funded benefit plans and a shift in strategy by the CIO, whose industrial unions could not make effective provision for seniority protection or restriction of membership. Social Security provided benefits for 34,083,000 retired workers to the tune of $48,134,000 in monthly payments in 1977.

Pensions, however, aren't the exclusive concern of unions. Business, eager to retain trained, skilled workers, offered pensions for "long and faithful service" from the turn of the century, but chiefly for executives and white collar workers, leaving employees at the bottom of the wage scale to shift for themselves on retirement, armed only with gold watches. Paul P. Harbrecht relates:

> By 1925 an estimated 4 million employees were covered by approximately 400 plans. These figures do not indicate very wide coverage of private pension plans, however, since over half of the workers covered were employed by 13 corporations, each of which had at least 50,000 employees, and more than 40 per cent worked for railroad corporations. Further analysis shows that a third of the covered employees were in four corporations, the U.S. Steel Corporation, the American Telephone & Telegraph Co., the Pennsylvania System and the New York Central Lines.[4]

Pension plans for employees in private industry are provided for in contracts initiated by unions on behalf of hourly paid workers. The United Mine Workers, led by John L. Lewis, negotiated the first pension plan financed by employer contributions in 1947. Joseph E. Finley, who has not been loathe to chastise the UMW, waxed rhapsodic in recounting the story of the first miners' Welfare and Retirement Fund:

> It stands above all the great efforts of Lewis because of its essential humanity, its alleviation of suffering, its kindling of light in the souls of torn and warped people. This judgment must remain, despite the sadness of the later days of the Fund, despite the callousness that later crept into it, despite the afflictions of weary bureaucracy that brought it to humiliation in a courtroom and deposited bitterness among its beneficiaries . . .
>
> It was a product of the finest hours of John L. Lewis . . . Coal operators had always paid attention to their machinery. They oiled it, repaired it, replaced it, cared for it. The care and feeding of equipment was fundamental; men came and went and died. Human beings were entitled to the same treatment as machines, said Lewis. The time had come for the operators to pay attention to the body of man as well. The thought processes of industrial America had never grasped the point before; the Lewis demand was bold and startling. "There must be a trust fund established," said Lewis, "to provide medical care, disability benefits and pensions for coal miners . . . financed by royalties on every ton of coal produced."[5]

The fund made its first payments in 1947, but they were death benefits paid the widows of ninety-nine miners killed in a mine blast in Centralia, Illinois. The first pensions of $100 a month were paid to retired miners at the age of sixty-two, but only after considerable resistance from the operators, a strike, a Taft-Hartley injunction and massive fines levied against Lewis and the UMW. But the federal district court judge who had levied the fine, T. Alan Goldsborough, was moved to say from the bench that the $100 pension " . . . is just enough to keep them from being objects of charity in their old age; it is just enough to give them a little dignity; it is something to make them able to hold their heads up."[6]

The welfare and retirement fund, however, was not funded, and ran into difficulties which forced a cutback in pension benefits in 1953. Another pioneer pension plan, negotiated in 1949 by the United Steelworkers, was also unfunded, but is noteworthy for several reasons. It was fought for by the union in response to rank and file desire for security as monitored by USWA President Philip Murray; it took a forty-two-day strike before U.S. Steel capitulated, and led to a landmark decision of the National Labor Relations Board, upheld by the U.S. Circuit Court of Appeals, bringing pensions within the scope of collective bargaining for the first time.

It is doubtful whether the auto industry's pension plans (or for that matter, those of any other industry), which came to the fore some two years later, would ever have been achieved without the spadework of the Steelworkers.

In 1949 the United Auto Workers obtained its first employer-funded pension plan from Ford Motor Company, under threat of a strike. Walter Reuther's slogan, "Too old to work and too young to die," inspired Joe Glazer, then education director of the United Rubber Workers, to write a song based on that slogan. The song lives on to inspire other workers to fight for pension plans, haunted as they are by the question of how to get by when they're too old to work and too young to die.

The UAW's concern for the retired member was expressed by Reuther in testimony before the Senate Special Committee on Aging in 1969, when he declared the nation would be judged and found wanting unless it bestowed a measure of dignity and self-respect upon its senior citizens.

The UAW has sought to protect its older members, not only through contracts assuring them of seniority, improvement of skills, transfers to lighter jobs and antidiscrimination clauses ensuring employment of older workers, but has gone beyond to sponsor preretirement and postretirement programs on its own initiative.

Another international union which has gone to great lengths to protect its senior members is the International Union of Electrical, Radio and Machine Workers, which has actively protected the interests of its older members since the international was chartered by the CIO.

The IUE, an AFL-CIO affiliate, with some 350,000 members, has both a Community Services and Retired Members Department, both of which are headed by Edward J. Carlson. The two departments have a paid staff of fifty, including regional chairmen. The two services have been intertwined since their inception, because union counselors were trained to assist the retired workers to serve as liaison for the community service program. "Based on their knowledge, they are well informed," Carlson said.

The IUE has formed 120 retirees' clubs, with 27,000 to 30,000 members now enrolled, but Carlson estimated there's a potential for as many as 80,000. The clubs, however, merely provide a structure for involving the retired member in the union; they are not an end in themselves.

Paul Jennings, who retired in 1976 as IUE president, described that union's approach: "You may be retired from work, but you are not retired from the union."

Carlson amplified the theme, explaining:

You don't put people on the shelf. It was their experience that built the union. They are the last of those who remember the Great Depression. They are responsible and should not be discarded, but used. They are experienced citizens, not senior citizens. In fact, they resent the title, "senior citizen." We want to utilize them and their experience. We don't want to see the retirees' clubs turned into social clubs.

The IUE's retired members, who are assured of pensions with built-in cost of living escalator clauses, remain active in the union as organizers ("they know the people in the plant"), pickets, clerical aides, manpower to handle telephones in an emergency, distributors of leaflets—in short, as active union members, a factor which unquestionably instills morale and prolongs life.

The Retired Workers Department of the IUE is an arm of the Social Action Department headed by William Gary. While the department is also involved with civil rights, women's rights, on-the-job training and educational advancement, its concern with retirees can be understood from the resolution adopted by the 1976 IUE convention:

Accompanying the contract gains won in retirement benefits, including earlier retirement and larger pensions, has been an increasing interest among IUE retirees in continuing to play a role in their unions and in the community. The IUE Retired Workers Department and Retired Workers Clubs help make it possible for our retired brothers and sisters to find such meaningful roles. Resolved:

That local unions work closely with the Retired Workers Department, and if they have not already done so, establish Retired Workers Clubs.

That the clubs and individual retirees affiliate with the National Council of Senior Citizens; IUE reaffirms its support to the council . . .

That the Retired Workers Department and the clubs enlist our retirees in COPE drives, community-fund-raising, as representatives of labor on community boards and in other areas.[7]

The Amalgamated Clothing Workers of America (merged with the Textile Workers Union in July, 1976, into the Amalgamated Clothing and Textile Workers Union) has a program for retirees which is administrated by the union's Social Services Department, under the direction of Joyce D. Miller, vice president.

The philosophy behind the program was expressed by Mrs. Miller with considerable emotion when the author played devil's advocate with her in her office at 15 Union Square, New York City. I asked her, "Why bother with retired members? They're not working, paying dues or party to contracts. They can't be anything but a nuisance!" Her answer reflects the attitude of the union:

We have an obligation and responsibility to the people who built this union and gave their lives for it. A pension is not enough reward for that kind of service to the union. We have an obligation to enrich the lives of our retired members. They're not a problem to us. Our philosophy is to help them, to do something to recognize them, to make contributions to their lives.

While the retirees may not be a problem, they are numerous. The Amalgamated Clothing Workers, which had 350,000 members prior to the merger, counted 53,000 retirees, or over 15 percent of its membership, on its rolls in 1976.

The General Executive Board formed the Retired Members Department in March, 1973, "to aid in the development and expansion of new programs and social services which will allow Amalgamated retirees as individuals to pursue a more meaningful life in their communities." For a union organized in 1914, this was not a radical departure; it merely marked an administrative change, putting direction of the retiree programs into the hands of the Social Services Department. Joint boards and locals traditionally had been concerned with retirees for decades. (The first retirement fund was established in the men's clothing industry in 1945.)

The retiree program is concerned with the following goals:

Fostering fraternal ties of members during retirement.

Keeping retired members informed of ACWA programs, policies and objectives.

Enlisting the support of retired members for union objectives.

Providing retirees with useful social and recreational facilities and opportunities.

Helping retired members secure housing, medical care, drugs and other consumer goods and services at prices they can afford to pay.

How well have these goals been met? Mrs. Miller, in a report to the General Executive Board of the union in 1974, said in part:

There are now 13 programs which meet monthly or semi-monthly. There are four centers—the New York Joint Board, the Charles Weinstein Geriatric Center in Philadelphia, Samuel Levin Center for Retirees in Chicago and Hyman Blumberg Retired Members Center in Baltimore—all are open five days a week. A new center which has opened since our last Board meeting, the Amalgamated Genis Golden Age Club, in Virginia, Minnesota—established by the Minnesota Joint Board, operates two days a week.

We have a growing response to our monthly *Retired Members Newsletter*, where we provide general information of interest to retirees concerning the Amalgamated's activities and other programs and resources to look for in their community. Most importantly, we have included information that we feel will help them to enrich their lives on an individual basis (for example on consumer questions, food buying and how to stretch their individual dollars). Information is included on government programs from which they might be able to benefit, such as Supplemental Security Income and food stamps.

The *Retired Members Newsletter* appears to have three purposes: to assist the retiree with practical advice on extending his buying power; to assure him, "The union has not forgotten you"; and to provide him with a communications link to the union. ("We answer every letter," Mrs. Miller said. "If they have problems, we help them.")

What puts a stamp of effectiveness upon the *Newsletter* is the regular feature, "Letters from our Retirees," indicating the publication is accepted by the readers as their representative. (Any publication which does not draw letters to the editor routinely may be considered ineffectual.) To encourage more feedback from the retirees, the Social Services Department, with the aid of students at the Columbia University Graduate School of Social Work, develops questionnaires for retirees, while the *Newsletter* occasionally publishes a coupon seeking information; for example, on the use of food stamps, the data to be used in testimony before the Senate Agriculture Research and General Legislation Subcommittee.

In addition to the national office staff, there are eight full-time field directors in the U.S. and Canada concerned with the retirees' welfare, indicating a commitment on the part of the union's officers. Surely, it was no coincidence that Mrs. Miller came to New York to head the department when Murray H. Finley was elected ACWA president. Both had been in Chicago previously; he, as Chicago manager, and she, as education director.

It was in Chicago in the 1960s that the social services program got under way, opening a day care center for children, setting up scholarship grants for members' children, organizing a cooperative housing project, a prepaid legal services plan, a health center for members and a retired members center. Why was it done? It would be simplistic to ascribe the motivation for these programs to Finley's (or Mrs. Miller's) personal philosophy alone. After all, the Amalgamated has a history of concern for the members' welfare. Without detracting one iota from Finley's contributions, his aphorism, "Community service is the heart and soul of trade unionism," reflects the collective attitude of the Amalgamated; indeed, of the entire trade union movement.

Mrs. Miller made that apparent with the offhand remark that "in the early days the union business agent was acting as a social worker" when members came to him with their problems. What Finley did in Chicago when the first retirees center was opened in March, 1962, was to hire a professional social worker to respond to members' problems. And while the service was publicized, problems of the individual were kept confidential.

Few other institutions of society have offered similar services on as broad a range to as heterogeneous a mass of people. One which comes to mind—and this should not be dismissed lightly—is the Tammany Hall district leader who took care of the problems of the voters in his election district. Another, of course, is the church—a parallel which Gus Tyler, assistant president of the International Ladies Garment Workers Union, cited in outlining the concern the ILG has for its "flock" of 80,000 retired members.

While he conceded the ILG does little in the way of preretirement training, and that the average pension is no more than $100 a month, Tyler pointed to the Golden Rule Clubs for retirees which provide them with a program of activities including trips, outings, concerts and theaters.

More critical needs are met with a segregated fund made available to retirees with financial emergencies and a drug prescription program which enables them to obtain virtually any drug for a one-dollar fee. That's important, since, as Tyler wryly noted, "They live on drugs." Equally important to the retiree is the availability of professional counseling as part of the community services activities program.

The Friendly Visitors are just that, visiting retirees who are shut-ins, ill or otherwise disabled and in need, not only of cheering up, but advice, which the "visitors" can offer, since they have been trained by social workers. The ILG has been offering such counseling for the past twenty-five years.

District 65, Distributive Workers of America, has a two-pronged program which reassures its retirees they have not been forgotten. A retired volunteer and a student social worker pay regular calls on retirees who are isolated, shut in and in need of help. They also make house calls when a retiree fails to keep in touch with the union. There is also a Dial 65 program in which telephone calls are made to retirees to assure them the union is concerned about them.

Other major unions which have extensive programs concerned with helping retirees cope with their problems include the International Association of Machinists, the United Steelworkers, the International Brotherhood of Electrical Workers, the Communications Workers of America (CWA) and the Service Employees International Union.

The Steelworkers, for example, do not leave to chance the essential preretirement training for its members, but offer to locals a *USWA*

Action Guide: When You Quit Work, A Pre-Retirement Course for Steelworkers. The USWA Education Department's publication instructs local unions how to plan and present preretirement courses. What is impressive in the action guide is the detailed scope of the planning for a five-course session, including suggestions on how to select and introduce appropriate speakers. The guide, however, is not unique. The International Union, Allied Industrial Workers of America, does much the same thing in its *Guide for Organizing AIW Retiree Clubs.*

The CWA conceded it hadn't done much for the retired member in the past, but President Glenn Watts has been insistent that retired members clubs be established by locals in keeping with a new Article V, Section 5, of the constitution, adopted in June, 1975:

> All associate members of the Union who are and may be retired by reasons of age or disability shall be members of the Retired Members Clubs, with such rights and prerogatives as may be granted by the Convention or Executive Board. Such members may attend the Convention, shall be issued appropriate credentials, be seated in space reserved for such members and may have a spokesman address the Convention for a predetermined time when considered appropriate by the Convention.

To assist locals in setting up the clubs so that pensioners need not spend their time "sitting around the house watching TV," CWA has published a guide outlining the benefits to be gained by the locals and retirees, as well as directions for club programs and organization. The purpose of having such clubs, the guide says, is to

> provide activities that will make the retirement years of our members more meaningful. Through such clubs they can find new interests and develop a program of satisfying activities. Involvement in their club and the affairs of their communities will give them a feeling of greater usefulness and a sense of accomplishment.

But CWA will also benefit from these activities, the *CWA Retired Members Club Guide* pointed out, since the retirees, if they remain active politically, can assist the union through political and legislative action in securing many of the goals "we seek in health care, housing, employment and better education."

A significant benefit for retirees came in 1977 when the CWA served a contract demand on the Bell System seeking a cost of living adjustment for pensions paid by the Bell System. The issue was regarded as so important during negotiations that Watts said if there were a strike, it could be touched off by the pension demand.

There was no strike, but the three-year agreement arrived at on

August 6 provided for a 25 to 30 percent increase for workers who have already retired, while for workers retiring after 1980, the pensions will be increased by 28 percent. In addition, a supplemental pension plan for workers who are forced out because of technology will add up to $250 a month for four years, or until Social Security payments start.

Considering that Bell System pensions are noncontributory and that the AT&T pension trust fund—the largest in the country—was established long before there was a CWA, those contract demands indicated a commitment to retired members far outstripping the union's community services policy. But at least one CWA officer, Morton Bahr, vice president and district director for District 1, encompassing 165 locals in eight states, explained it briefly:

> We help improve the life of all the people in the community because we are an institution made up of human beings who want to make a contribution to the living standards of society. Industry and labor are the only real forces in society, but industry looks to the bottom line, profits, while we are not a bottom-line institution. We want a better life for all and that includes pensions and dignity.

However, it is conceded CWA is generally regarded (like so many other unions, incidentally) as an "exception," for there are still too many other unions which do not prepare the worker for retirement or help him adjust to a new way of life, despite having pension plans. But the AFL-CIO has tried to broaden participation in retiree programs by its affiliates through constant pleading, adoption of resolutions and setting an example with its national Community Services Department—all of which show a commitment undeserving of the constant reproaches of labor's critics.

Resolutions adopted by the AFL-CIO conventions in 1963, 1965 and 1969, for example, outlined specific ways in which affiliates could better protect the interests of the aged worker, providing direction in the following three areas, among others: establishing retirees' clubs affiliated with the National Council of Senior Citizens; supporting legislation barring discrimination in hiring older workers; planning preretirement training programs and opening up new opportunities for greater involvement of the aged worker in community activities. These resolutions, of course, come atop considerably earlier positions implementing retraining programs, Social Security, early retirement plans and health insurance for the older worker. Probably the earliest—and yet one of the most important—features of any labor contract was the seniority clause protecting the older worker against layoffs.

There is an AFL-CIO community services program for the aged, which has been set forth in a booklet with specific instructions for local unions and central labor bodies to follow concerning the setting up of the committee, the committee's function, developing a practical program and cooperating with other labor bodies in developing community-wide programs. Pointedly, the publication advises:

> While many needs of older and retired workers are being met by federal and state-supported programs, there are many needs which can be met best in the local community.
>
> Action in the community on behalf of programs for older and retired workers may be carried forward through labor as well as community channels. While the local union is a natural focal point, the central labor body can and should play a large role in developing and promoting programs for the aging and retired worker. The Community Services Committee in the local union and the central labor body is the appropriate committee to initiate such programs.
>
> It should be clear, however, that there are some activities which are best carried out in the local union, while others are best carried out in and through the central labor body . . .[8]

What practical programs are recommended? The same publication spells out the basic functions of the Community Services Committee or the CSC subcommittee on aging and retired workers:

> 1. To maintain close and continuing contact with retired members both at the point of retirement and throughout their retirement years.
>
> 2. To familiarize retired members with the activities and programs of the union and the community, and to encourage their participation in such activities.
>
> 3. To determine problems, interests and needs of retired members and to see that these needs are met, either by the local union or by community-wide programs.
>
> 4. To develop and promote educational programs on retirement preparation for members who have not yet retired.
>
> 5. To provide representation and leadership from local unions to serve on community committees and to act as the means of communication between the community programs and the local union and its membership.

Printed instructions and resolutions are not the equivalent of action, but action is being taken by many unions, especially in the area of preretirement training—a crucial area, since retirement usually means a sharp break with a long, continuous rhythm of work, producing distressing emotional responses. This can be so unnerving that efforts are being made to keep the older worker on the job so long as he or she remains physically able.

In considering this problem, Leo Perlis has taken note of the conflicting views within organized labor. Opposed to mandatory retirement, he is convinced preretirement counseling calls for long-term preparation, even as early as age forty-five—something that commonly meets with resistance.

Nor is Perlis unaware of the supportive nature of work, not intrinsically, but in contrast to the pressures exerted by "the uncertainties about the American dream, the loss of an anchor . . . the international situation, the bomb, the economy."[9]

Quite clearly, preparation for retirement requires reorientation so that the worker can accept his new status and cope with financial, housing, health, nutritional and leisure-time problems. There is a thirty-year (or longer) history of such preretirement programs in the United States, reflecting an awareness of the expanding life expectancy rates. The earliest programs were sponsored principally by management representatives who worked with individual employees. Group programs followed in pioneering efforts by the most socially conscious unions at a pace which paralleled the growth of the senior citizen population.

Action is also being taken on another front—to provide housing for the retired worker. Over 150 federally assisted housing projects for low- and moderate-income families and the elderly have been sponsored by AFL-CIO central labor bodies and affiliates. Housing for senior citizens has been sponsored by the United Federation of Postal Clerks and the Sheet Metal Workers International Association in East Lake Wales, Florida, while in nearby Lake Wales the retirement, education, security and training foundation of the National Association of Letter Carriers sponsored an equally large, 500-unit senior citizens housing project. However, this is not a recent development reflecting an awakening of trade unions to a long-standing problem. As far back as 1964, Boris Shishkin reviewed the extent of union-sponsored housing for senior citizens and found it widespread.

Shishkin noted that the Four Freedoms program organized by William R. Steinberg, president of the American Radio Association, had already sponsored senior citizen housing projects in Miami Beach, Seattle, Gratiot Park in Detroit, and Germantown, Pennsylvania, and was planning similar projects in Pittsburgh, San Francisco, Los Angeles, Boston, New York City and Baltimore.

But the Four Freedoms program was not alone, even in the 1960s. The Mid-Columbia Building and Construction Trades Council, AFL-CIO, had sponsored a 170-unit cooperative housing project for the elderly in Vancouver, Washington; Local 858 of the International Association of Fire Fighters, undertook a fifteen-story apartment building in Denver, and Local 31 of the International Brotherhood of

Electrical Workers was the spearhead of a nonprofit organization which put up a sixty-five-unit building in Duluth for applicants over sixty-two.[10]

For five years, senior citizen housing languished under a "moratorium" imposed by President Nixon, but was revived in 1977 when the Section 202 low-interest loans to nonprofit organizations were restored to the Housing and Community Development Act of 1974. The union-dominated National Council of Senior Citizens led the drive.

But one problem yet to be confronted by the nation boasting of "the highest standard of living in the world," is how to assure the retired workers they need not live in poverty. Despite Social Security benefits, pensions and Medicare, 6.1 percent of all families with heads of households aged sixty-five or older were living below the poverty level in 1976.

That made it essential for unions to stress preretirement education, retiree clubs and senior citizen housing. But problems of the aging are not restricted to persons sixty-five or older, since early retirement has become fairly common. Social Security began paying actuarially reduced benefits in 1961 to those taking early retirement at age sixty-two and the proportion retiring early a decade later was more than sixty percent.

(Mandatory retirement at 65 was repealed by Congress in 1978 for most federal employees. Retirement at age 70 became effective for them in September, 1978; for state and local government employees and workers in the private sector, January 1, 1979; for union-contract-required retirements, January 1, 1980.)

The reasons for early retirement are, in order of importance, health, voluntary retirement, loss of job and compulsory retirement, according to a Social Security study published in 1971, with poor health by far the major reason, accounting for 54 percent of the total retirements.

Early retirements, however, create job opportunities for younger workers—a factor which creates in its turn a crushing social pressure on the older worker to quit, even if he is addicted to work, as most men tend to be after decades of punching a time clock. The prejudice against the older worker, which places "ageism" on a par with "sexism," is one that trade unions clearly exhibit, dividing their loyalties between the old and young. And as life expectancy increases, adding to the number of over-sixty-fivers in the population, the burden will become increasingly difficult for unions.

Despite divided loyalties, it is absurd to say organized labor does nothing whatever for the aging worker; yet there is a persistent notion that unions don't give a damn about the senior citizen. This creeps into even so authoritative a study as the Pulitzer Prize–winning *Why Survive? Being Old in America*:

> The union movement is hardly a movement of social responsibility any longer, doing little for those presently low on the socioeconomic ladder—the poor, the minority workers, and the elderly. "They collaborate with employers to maintain the status quo," said Herbert Hill, national labor director of the National Association for the Advancement of Colored People. Of the 80 million Americans in the United States work force, 20 million—one in four—are union members who earn from $4 to $5 per hour. Thus they do not number the poor people of America among their ranks nor do they necessarily sympathize with them.[11]

Dr. Lawrence N. Butler, the author, a gerontologist and psychiatrist, presents that stereotyped image of the labor movement, replete with the libel of "one in four," despite numerous references in his own work to union-initiated or -inspired programs for the aged. One might cite the guarded praise he gives to the National Council of Senior Citizens:

> The National Council of Senior Citizens was first organized by some of the conferees attending the 1961 White House Conference on Aging. It developed, in part, through labor leader Walter Reuther's support of Medicare. The long-range goal of NCSC, which was to be nonpartisan, was to represent "the views of older persons on major issues confronting the nation"; but in the past it was supported largely by labor and is still strongly Democratic. NCSC was first led by Amie J. Forsand (D.-R.I.), who gave up his congressional seat in order to run NCSC effectively and to lead the fight for Medicare. Its second president, until 1969, was John Edelman, long associated with the trade-union movement. He was followed by Nelson Cruikshank . . .

> By 1973 the NCSC has some 3 million members, mainly from the ranks of organized labor, in 3,500 affiliated clubs across the United States. Many of its members are poor, and anybody of any age can join. There are no mandatory dues and it gains no financial benefits from its services, which include supplemental insurance for Medicare, low-cost travel and discount drugs. Nonetheless it has been increasingly more able to be self-sustaining through its growth in membership, and accepts less and less funding from labor unions . . .

> One of the offshoots of NCSC is the Concerned Citizens for Better Government, begun in 1968. It was chaired by Matthew DeMore and served to encourage Senior Citizens Clubs to become active in presidential and congressional primary elections.[12]

Dr. Butler refers to Matthew DeMore as a former general secretary-treasurer of the International Association of Machinists, but fails to mention that Cruikshank was a former director of the AFL-CIO Social Security Department. Nor does he indicate the full extent of labor's involvement with NCSC—an oversight which was corrected by Rudolph T. Danstedt, assistant to the president of NCSC:

> The Council has had, over close to 15 years of its existence, a close working relationship with organized labor. As a matter of fact, we were organized in 1961 by representatives of the United Auto Workers and the Steelworkers to help bring about the enactment of Medicare. This was our first significant legislative achievement.
>
> We look upon ourselves as the national service agency for union retirees, and as a consequence thereof, we receive modest subsidies from the AFL-CIO,[13] and a number of international unions. The unions most actively affiliated with us began with the AFL-CIO and include the UAW, the Machinists, the Operating Engineers, the Steelworkers, the Painters, the IUE, CWA and, to a more limited degree, the Brotherhood of Railway and Airline Clerks and some units of the Teamsters.
>
> It would be my guess that close to half of the board members—at large and regional—of the Council are union retirees or have active union affiliation. It does not follow, however, that our membership is exclusively composed of union retirees, since my guess is that probably less than a half fall in this category. The rest are persons affiliated with church groups, senior citizen centers and independently organized groups of older individuals.[14]

It is difficult to equate these authoritative estimates with the prejudice-laden image of the labor movement as "hardly a movement of social responsibility," in view of Dr. Butler's other concessions. He acknowledged labor has lent its support to a national health insurance plan, that the AFL-CIO's Social Security Department has lobbied on behalf of social legislation, that the Federation supports a federal consumer protection agency and he even lists the AFL-CIO as among the "other national organizations with programs in the field of the aging," noting that the AFL-CIO:

> Provides assistance to older members and affiliates ranging from social security legislation to individual counseling on the local level. However, the role of the AFL-CIO in direct programs in these areas is to primarily assist affiliated unions in these tasks by providing supplementary manpower and guidance. Generally available only to members, but cooperative efforts with other groups are frequent.[15]

Dr. Butler's begrudging recognition that labor does show some concern for the aged does not dispel the stereotyped image of unions he has adopted and, unfortunately, disseminated in an award-winning book which frequently underlines "the genuine tragedy of old age in

America [in] a society which is extremely harsh to live in when one is old."

It is an image of unions clearly based upon prejudice or ignorance. One need only cite Dr. Butler's claim that there is a critical need for information and referral services to illustrate his bias:

> Centralized information and referral services for the elderly are especially needed so they and their families may know the nature and availability of specific services. People should be able to find out by telephone whether they are eligible for a service, and what the costs are, how to make appointments, where services are located, how to get there, and other simple and important facts. Skilled personnel should be able to assist the older caller (or his family) in deciding what help is appropriate and in gaining access for him by direct referral.[16]

While that is a suggestion to create information and referral services, it is also, unbeknownst to Dr. Butler, a description of the basic function of labor's community services committees—not only on behalf of the older caller or his family, but for any working man or woman of any age, troubled by any problem or combination of problems.

Notes

1. Derek C. Bok and John T. Dunlop, *Labor and the American Community*, p. 363.
2. Howard N. Fullerton Jr. and James J. Byrne, "Length of Working Life for Men and Women, 1970," *Monthly Labor Review*, February 1976, p. 31.
3. Cornelius Justin and Mario E. Impellizeri, *The Mirage of Private Pensions*, pp. 13–14.
4. Paul P. Harbrecht, *Pension Funds and Economic Power*, p. 6.
5. Joseph E. Finley, *The Corrupt Kingdom*, p. 178.
6. Ibid., p. 184.
7. IUE programs and resolutions adopted at the Fourteenth Constitutional Convention, August 1970, pp. 15–16.
8. *The Aging and the Community*, AFL-CIO publication no. 128.
9. *Stress on the Job* (Ithaca, N.Y.: New York State School of Industrial and Labor Relations, Cornell University, 1975), pp. 21–22.
10. Boris Shishkin, "Organized Labor: Champion of Cooperative Housing," *Co-op Housing*, Winter 1964.
11. Lawrence N. Butler, *Why Survive? Being Old in America*, pp. 91–92.
12. Ibid., pp. 336–37. (N.B.: Cruikshank resigned as NCSC president in mid-1977 to accept the posts of Counsellor to the President on Aging and Chairman of the Federal Council on Aging.)
13. $24,000 annually; report of the AFL-CIO Executive Council, 1975, p. 31.
14. Letter to the author, 7 July 1976.
15. Butler, *Why Survive?*, pp. 435–36.
16. Ibid., p. 141.

7.
Community Service

Eighteen AFT locals and the AFT administrative staff local of the Newspaper Guild have made contributions to help rebuild Guatemala's schools damaged in an earthquake this year. The Guatemalan Relief Fund is being administered by the American Institute for Free Labor Development/Guatemala.

Over 60 percent of the schools in Guatemala were damaged, and AIFLD's work is to reroof these schools. Contributing to the fund were five locals from New York State . . . The Scranton and Philadelphia Federations in Pennsylvania sent money, as did the Toledo and Cleveland AFT locals in Ohio. In Minnesota, both the Minneapolis and the St. Paul Federations contributed. Other locals responding were Portland, Ore.; Hawaii; Jefferson Parish, La.; Lynn, Mass.; Brillion, Wis.; Providence, R.I.; and Putnam, Conn.

American Teacher, June, 1976

Leo Perlis is convinced the community service program of the AFL-CIO is "the most important happening in the labor movement since collective bargaining."

As national director of community service activities (CSA), Perlis may be forgiven his exuberance. His devotion to "areas not covered in the contract, but responsive to the need of the members," accounts for the tremendous range of services available. But he shrugs off all personal credit.

While the millennium is not at hand, there is a thirty-year success story in CSA. The people want it and George Meany backs it, and we are responsive to the needs of the members. CSA is developing a sense of greater responsibility of the union toward the member. After all, what is a trade union for? To serve the people! The original concept of the union was as a fellowship. I am my brother's keeper.

Perlis has a staff of four people working with him in the Community Services Department in the AFL-CIO headquarters on Sixteenth Street not far from the White House. But that staff is only a fragment of the vast network of community service representatives and counselors covering the United States and Canada.

The directory published annually by the Community Services Committee of the AFL-CIO (whose chairman is Peter Bommarito, president of the United Rubber, Cork, Linoleum and Plastic Workers of America) lists in thirty-one pages the names, addresses and telephone numbers of members of the national CSA committee and department, CSA staff of international unions, liaison representatives to national organizations, state and central body CSA staff and CSA liaison representatives with local chests, funds or councils of the United Way.

There are employees of unions on the national, state and central body levels who are on the payrolls of their respective organizations. In addition, representatives nominated by AFL-CIO bodies are on the payrolls of public and private social agencies. Two hundred liaison people are on the payrolls of United Way organizations alone, representing local AFL-CIO organizations.

The directory for 1977 indicated there were fifty-six liaison staff members with national and international unions and thirty-four with state AFL-CIO federations. A total of forty-nine were serving with six national voluntary agencies—United Way, Red Cross, the National Council on Crime and Delinquency, Boy Scouts of America, National Council on Alcoholism and the National Institute on Alcohol Abuse and Alcoholism—and with one state agency, the Pennsylvania Council on the Arts.

The figures do not include community service personnel of independent unions, such as the United Auto Workers, or the untold thousands of volunteer workers on community service committees of local unions, state and central bodies, international unions or labor agencies. Nor does it include the army of union counselors who spearhead the entire program, for it is the counselors who provide the information and referral services for rank and file members seeking help in the shop and union hall.

What does it cost to operate the federation's CSA program? Perlis was more concerned with the quality of the services performed than with the costs and brushed aside the question with the remark that the figures could be found in the financial report to the convention.

> I do know we have an economy drive once in a while, but usually we simply order supplies from central purchasing, submit vouchers that are approved and our payrolls are met. In a sense, we don't have any income because we don't accept funds from any other sources but the AFL-CIO. We join councils in applying for grants, but the grants go to agencies, such as the National Institute on Alcohol and Drug Abuse, for instance. We don't accept money, don't grant it, don't supervise it. Our funds come from one source—the members, who pay a per capita tax.

The AFL-CIO Executive Council report to the 1975 convention included a financial report indicating the Community Services Department's expenses totaled $211,691.25 in the fiscal year ended June 30, 1975.* That's a small part of the total cost of CSA, which cannot even be estimated, considering the number of unpaid man-hours clocked by an army of volunteers. But it averages out to less than 5 percent of the AFL-CIO budget that year—a remarkably low proportion, considering the extensive CSA program.

Obviously, overhead and administrative costs would be excessive if every volunteer—counselors, the mainstay of the program, are volunteers—were on the payroll. But their time and energies are freely given to help their fellow man—something extremely difficult for the public, and especially representatives of the press, to understand. This brings to mind the question of the *Newsday* reporter who was trying to comprehend the rationale for organizing the Long Island Education and Community Services Agency.

"But what's in it for you?" he asked Anthony J. Costaldo, executive director, finding it hard to accept that trade unionists would volunteer their services. One answer to that question came recently from Harry Fisdell, executive vice president of the New York Newspaper Guild: "A union is a family."

In that family, CSA trained approximately 80,000 counselors in its first thirty years, Leo Perlis estimated, although, he went on to concede, "Not all of them have really worked at it."

What were they trained to "work at?"

The Basic Training Manual for Union Counsellors, which was revised in 1974 after being in use for thirty years, is a fifty-six-page handbook designed to instruct central labor bodies how to recruit and train counselors, organize a community service program and follow up a recommended ten-session training course. It is a meticulously detailed guide which even the least sophisticated trade unionists should be able to adopt, since it includes specific instructions, planning checklists, outlines for each session's program, discussion guides, casework problems, sample referral forms and even suggested letters to instructors—usually representatives of agencies to which problems will be referred.

CSA also makes materials available at a nominal cost, including leaflets, pamphlets and a film, *Tell Me Where to Turn*, which may be rented from the Film Division, Department of Education, AFL-CIO. There's a wealth of information designed to aid the counselor in responding effectively to the problems that will confront him. They include:

---

* Two years later, the CSA budget amounted to $247,000.

Family Counselling for the Union Member, published in cooperation with the Family Service Association of America

How to Reduce Your Chances of Becoming a Victim of Crime, published in cooperation with the National Council on Crime and Delinquency

Toward a Safer America, also published in cooperation with the NCCD

Debt Counselling

Labor and Alcoholism, issued in cooperation with the National Council on Alcoholism

What Every Worker Should Know About Alcoholism, published in cooperation with the NCA

What Every Worker Should Know About Drug Abuse, issued with the American Social Health Association

Strike Assistance

Fluoridation for Your Community

Disaster Services

Crime, published jointly by CSA and the National Council on Crime and Delinquency

Who Cares? The Education to Action Project, issued with the NCCD

Services for the Unemployed

Labor-Red Cross: Partners in Community Service

Beyond the Picket Line: How to Organize a Strike Assistance Program

A Joint Union-Management Approach to Alcoholism Recovery Programs, an NCA publication

What is the intrinsic value of this literature distributed to counselors and community service committees by CSA? It provides the union counselor with pertinent information describing problems affecting workers and their families and instructions on how to secure help to resolve the problem. Consider the leaflet, *Who Cares? The Education to Action Project*, which is "specifically designed to divert children from a life of crime." The essence of the pamphlet may be found on two pages. "What Can You Do?" gives four answers:

1. Contact the National Council on Crime and Delinquency for further information on criminal and juvenile justice systems.

2. Obtain the NCCD's assistance in preparing an educational program on the juvenile justice system.

3. Invite to this program concerned citizens and representatives of interested organizations such as legal services, minority groups, neighborhood associations, civil liberties groups or associations of professionals in the criminal justice field.

4. Form an action committee to work on the problems that surface during the course; for example, evaluate the local home for juveniles, study the feasibility of halfway houses, or study the effectiveness of the probation department. Research the local jail.

Skeptics, obviously, will sneer, pointing out the gap between leaflets and effective action. But the Education to Action Project can point to effective steps taken in Akron, Kansas City, and Kokomo and Marion County, Indiana, among other places, as well as a follow-up program, the Community Citizen Mobilization Project, conducted in cooperation with the National Council on Crime and Delinquency under a grant from the Law Enforcement Assistance Administration. By mobilizing trade unionists and other community members in long-term programs to improve the criminal and juvenile justice systems, the project has come to the aid of ex-offenders in Des Moines and Cleveland, rehabilitated first offenders in Portland, rescued juvenile delinquents in Fort Worth and started an innovative foster care facility in Dallas.

Cleveland's United Labor Agency may be singled out for establishing the Leo Perlis Remotivation Center, which counsels ex-offenders, trains them in marketable skills and then helps them find jobs. In less than a year, more than 900 ex-offenders, probationers, furloughees, pretrial-diversion candidates and juvenile delinquents were served by the center, which is expanding its facilities to meet the extraordinary demand.

Given the direction and impetus, trade unionists become involved in community affairs, going far beyond assisting the individual with his personal problems. That is because community service implies an active interest in community affairs. In a scholarly study, Professor Alice H. Cook of Cornell University has described this interest:

> Labor's interest in community affairs . . . is twofold: To represent the economic and social interests of working people generally in community affairs and to put community resources at the service of union members.[1]

But the essential mission of CSA, according to Anne Nelson, a Cornell associate, is "providing an effective mechanism for bringing together the problems of workers and the resources available to aid in solution."

That should be the business of every trade union, and the Nelson study sums up the reasons why:

> There are good reasons cited by involved unions as to why community services should be the business of every local union. First, it is the union's business to protect the worker's job. A worker is absent, comes to work late, is nervous and absent-minded about what he is doing. Nobody tries to find the reason and that worker is fired. A union with a counseling program and a place where the workers will receive attention, can say to the employer, "This worker has a problem and before you fire him, we are going to try to do something about it."[2]

That would be the case in the International Ladies Garment Workers Union, which has at least one counselor in each shop under contract, equipped to cope with the problems of any of the union's 400,000 members. They have been trained in the information and referral techniques essential for counseling by professionals from the Columbia University Graduate School of Social Work. They know the agencies, private and public, which can resolve the members' personal problems. They know whom to talk to at the agencies and how effective it is to stress, "This is the ILGWU calling," rather than name the individual counselor.

In general, ILG locals conduct community service activities on their own, under guidance from the international, but some are referring their problems to the appropriate central labor council's community services representative. Assistant President Gus Tyler maintains the services are used extensively, because each new member learns of the services in an orientation program and there are frequent reminders in the local union's newspaper. Why does the ILG go to these pains?

"We're concerned with the social wage of our members," said Tyler. "It's not enough to get another dollar in the pay envelope if he can be ripped off for two dollars. We're concerned with the total life of the member."

That's an admirable attitude, but hardly representative. In lecturing to New York trade unionists, the author discovered few shop stewards were aware of community service functions. In a class of sixteen shop stewards of Local 16, National Association of Broadcast Employees and Technicians, the only person (aside from the instructor) who showed familiarity with CSA was the local's business manager. That was understandable, for where else can a union on strike turn to for help, if not to CSA? Strike assistance is a basic function of a community service committee. In a strike, members have pressing needs—for drugs, medical care, food, rent, utilities and clothing—and turn to community agencies through CSA for assistance. A business manager obviously would be well informed on CSA.

The rank and file, however, show less awareness of a service virtually each one could use at least once in a lifetime. But once informed, the member inevitably asked, "Please give us a name and phone number to call in an emergency."

This should not be considered representative, either, since some unions repeatedly bring to the attention of the rank and file the services available to them. The National Maritime Union publication, the *Pilot*, regularly carries (in English and Spanish) the following information:

To help NMU members, pensioners and dependents with information, social aids and assistance covering Social Security, Medicaid, Medicare, Food Stamps, Retirement, Home Economy, Nursing Homes, Financial Planning, Family Problems, and Personal Problems.

This is a free and confidential service offered by the NMU Pension and Welfare Plan with the help and cooperation of the Graduate School of Social Work of Hunter College.

GO TO: 346 West 17 Street
Lobby Floor, Rear
(Inquiries by mail will be answered in writing when possible.)
SEE: Mrs. Carmen M. Ortiz, Mr. Daniel Molloy, Personal Service Workers.
Al Zeidel, Director of Social Services.
HOURS: Mondays, Wednesdays, Thursdays, Fridays from 10 a.m. to 4 p.m.
TELEPHONE: 675-7300, Ext. 821, 839.

Do members take advantage of these services? In a one-month period, a statistical report prepared by a Hunter College student social worker showed that 104 members were served, of whom sixty were active seamen and forty-four pensioners. The office staff handled 138 interviews and correspondence with fifty-seven members.

That one month's case load was a full 35 percent more than the total a year earlier. The difference was attributed to the addition of a Hunter College student, a social worker, so that the office was open four days a week rather than three. The report, prepared by Dan Molloy of Hunter College, noted that financial needs "consistently represented about 50 percent of the seamen and their families who are seen" from 1974 through 1976, reflecting high unemployment and the steadily rising cost of living. Some seamen, indeed, were so acutely in need of help "that seamen had to accept the Men's Shelter or the Seamen's Church Institute, who were the only agencies willing to help." Aside from the NMU, that is!

While the image of Joseph Curran will undoubtedly remain in the public mind as that of a labor leader who retired on a pension with benefits aggregating a million dollars, he was a dedicated trade unionist who played a decisive role in establishing the Personal Services Department of the union in 1941, just four years after the NMU was chartered. The department, which continues to this day, was established by convention vote, Bertha Capen Reynolds recalled:

At the 1941 convention of the union it had been voted to establish a personal services department to take care of personal problems of the members, which were an increasing burden on the elected officers. An old seaman, equipped with a desk and a secretary, took charge of the new ser-

103

vice. There were urgent questions of claims for injuries and personal losses suffered at sea. War brought a multitude of problems, from small services needed . . . up to help for distressed families in locating seamen who were often stranded by injuries in parts of the world from which it was not easy to get return passage. As casualty lists lengthened, there was need for help to bereaved families for immediate living problems, and in filing claims for War Risk Insurance. The secretary, a young woman who had been a portrait painter and had turned to labor organization to express her love for people in a more significant way, was learning how to use the structure of social agencies in the community for services to seamen and families.[3]

Shirley Ross Backner, who worked in the department during the war years helping alien seamen secure visas and citizenship papers, recalled it was "a beautiful kind of organization which worked closely with the membership, benefiting each other." Curran, who was even then under attack from some of his members for remaining "topside," i.e., in his union office, rather than shipping out with the rest of the membership, will be considered thoroughly corrupt despite what he achieved for his members. That has been almost entirely forgotten.

The involvement with the members' problems is shared, not only by union officers, but the volunteer community services counselors as well. A striking example occurred in January, 1976, at the fifth class of a twelve-session training course conducted by the Long Island Education and Community Services Agency. A member of Long Island Merged Branch 6000, National Association of Letter Carriers, spoke up in class, troubled by a problem he'd encountered on his mail route. A retired worker who told him he hadn't received his Social Security check appeared to be starving. The class discussed the problem of what could be done, without questioning whether the retiree was a member of Branch 6000. (He was not.) Still groping its way, the class decided the letter carrier should call the agency's director, Anthony J. Costaldo, the next morning and leave the problem in his hands.

"Oh, no, you don't," came a voice from the class. "Now that we know whom to contact at Social Services, you handle it yourself!"

The letter carrier did and returned to class the following week to relate with glee how he had gone about expediting delivery of the Social Security check and how he had handed it to the old man. The reaction of the class was pure joy. There was something to this community services business, after all! It's a reaction that is endlessly repeated.

Two other students in the same course were elementary school teachers from Deer Park, Long Island. They were members of Local 2598, American Federation of Teachers, but only one of them could remember the local's number. Both completed the twelve-session course, held on the coldest, snowiest winter nights the area had known in many a year, but this was after the two women signed up "out of curiosity," just to find out "what it was all about." During the seminars, they said later at the graduation exercises, they became aware "much to our surprise" of the extent of the services available to them. They realized the need to organize a community service committee as much as they needed the services. Both assured the author Local 2598 will have such a committee—soon.

The personal reaction, however, as frequently as it is cited, may be adequate rationale for the individual, but not for the commitment unions have to serve the member. Nor is it sufficient to examine only the union point of view; the community, too, through its public and private social agencies, actively seeks the involvement of trade unions, not only in fund-raising, but in wide distribution of information on available services and even in the administration of agency affairs. Labor's cooperation was sought a score of years ago, John A. Fitch notes:

> Officers of Community Chests and Councils—the national coordinating agency for similarly named local bodies—succeeded in effecting a joint relationship with the [AFL and CIO] labor committees, making possible cooperation between the public and private social agencies and the unions.

> As a result unions and social agencies have been working together on both the national and local levels for social betterment. Both AFL and CIO had members serving on the boards of community chests and social agencies all over the country and on committees of such bodies. At the end of 1955 it was estimated that as many as 25 to 30,000 union members were serving in this manner. Both federations regularly assisted in raising of funds. Of the more than $300 million raised for community chests in 1955, about a third came from individuals, a third from employer organizations, and the remaining third from employee groups, including organized labor.[4]

One other factor may not be dismissed idly: reaction to management paternalism and the development of personnel management. The challenge to unions for the loyalty of workers who were seduced by welfare capitalism becomes apparent in these observations by Richard A. Lester:

> The second program was the development in the 1920's of personnel management and welfare capitalism. Containing overtones of management paternalism, it stressed a battery of techniques including employee representation, profit-sharing, stock ownership, suggestion systems, company magazines, and benefit programs such as group life insurance, pen-

sions, and sickness pay. In this approach, management concern for the individual welfare and loyalty of plant employees becomes evident. That concern is given additional emphasis in the "human relations" approach that began to capture management thinking in the 1930's . . . [T]he human relations movement is based in good part on applied psychology. Initially the therapeutic value of individual interviewing, employee counselling, and small group communication was emphasized. Later this "new image of the worker" as a personality whose inner feelings need expression and respectful treatment, led to a broader range of company activities designed to improve employee satisfaction on and off the job.[5]

What better way to win the loyalty of the union member than by showing an interest in his welfare, both on and off the job? Virtually all of the literature on union participation in community activities considers this reaction merely as a ploy to buy the votes of the rank and file and to gain respectability for the union as a vehicle of social change.

Even Lester, who may be considered one of the more objective critics of American trade unions, fails to observe (in the single page he devotes to community service) that unions serve their members, but stresses the value of community service to the union:

> AFL-CIO encouragement of such labor participation is understandable in view of the fact that union members contribute to and use both the volunteer and public welfare agencies. Such activities on the part of unions have the advantage that they get credit for them and have an influence in policy determination.
>
> In addition, participation with management at a high level in a non-conflict endeavor emphasizes common interests and increases the social recognition and respectability of unions and labor leaders. It reduces the feeling that organized labor is a group apart from the community, and increases the reliance of workers and the community upon unions. Undoubtedly integration of unions into community activities is a moderating influence on union leadership.[6]

The bias in these observations becomes apparent a few pages further on where Lester concedes there is a missionary spirit apparent in the trade unions:

> Zeal for the cause of unionism is likely to be particularly prominent during the early stages of a union's development. Personal loyalty and devotion supply much of the volunteer work, so essential to the life of a union, especially at the local level. It is the "actives," mostly unpaid for their services, who constitute the grass roots of trade unionism. They account for much of a union's vitality and moral tone.
>
> The ethical aspects of trade unionism help to explain its humanitarian aims and resistance to the corroding influence of material success . . . The

importance of a missionary spirit is evident in the history of such unions as the Amalgamated Clothing Workers, the International Ladies Garment Workers and the United Auto Workers. To a considerable extent these unions reflect the vision and crusading spirit of Sidney Hillman, David Dubinsky and Walter Reuther.[7]

Without detracting one iota from the vision and crusading spirit of Hillman, Dubinsky or Reuther, it might prove rewarding to reflect it was within the trade union movement—and not elsewhere—that these men were able to improve the lot of their fellow men.

Contrast the views of critics of organized labor with the attitude expressed by Perlis in considering the question of why CSA cooperates with adversaries in the community:

> We work with many types of people, many of whom we do not agree with on their views and policies. But we work with them for the common good. If we are to have a viable, open, flexible society, we must not extend hostilities, but must cooperate. It is important, too, to create a climate where unions agree in an established, fragmented society. We must awaken a sense of responsibility.

But on whatever premise cooperation with public and private social agencies is sought by unions, it is inevitable that labor's demands for a voice in the administration and allocation of funds lead to an adversary relationship with the corporate sector of the economy that is inclined to think of the agencies as dependent upon philanthropy, i.e., corporate gifts.

While there is an adversary relationship between labor and management in collective bargaining, Perlis has gone beyond the labor contract to conceive a "human contract" in which labor and management "cooperate in serving the company employee-union member (remembering at all times he is the one and the same person) beyond the plant gates and beyond the union contract."

The concept of the "human contract" includes a policy, program and process in which labor and management work together with the assistance of social agencies to bring about "what both the company and the union desire—a "happy" fellowship of working people . . . "the best insurance against instability, poor morale, absenteeism and turnover." The "human contract," Perlis maintains, is the "heart of the AFL-CIO Community Services program."

Working hand in hand with management "do-gooders" has not always been a practice of the labor movement. Indeed, there's a history of hostility between the two. Unions were cool to the first "do-gooders" who strove to bring education to the masses, care for the working women of the New England textile mills, feed the starving families of coal miners or ease the burdens of apprentices who were little more than indentured servants. Unions haven't always taken an unequivocal stand on social welfare for their own members, whether the product of legislation, collective bargaining or the philanthropy of "do-gooders."

As AFL president, Samuel Gompers was opposed to compulsory health and unemployment insurance and equally unenthusiastic about old-age pensions. "Social insurance cannot remove or prevent poverty," Gompers said. "It does not get at the causes of social injustice. The only agency that does get at the cause of poverty is the organized labor movement."

In 1916 at the AFL convention, he said, "The measures themselves and the people who represent them, represent that class of society that is very desirous of doing things for the workers and establishing institutions for them that will prevent their doing things for themselves and maintaining their own institutions."

Despite this, the federation did endorse old-age pensions in 1908 and Gompers said he favored a noncontributory old-age pension. While he opposed health insurance, the executive council of the AFL endorsed the concept in 1918, but with little enthusiasm. Today, however, trade union leaders sit on the boards of directors of the "do-gooders'" social welfare agencies, working for the common good, not only by invitation, but because of labor's insistence that it has a right to sit there.

The result has been that boards of directors are peppered with the names of prominent labor leaders, while their *Who's Who in America* listings grow tediously long. Consider this one paragraph excerpted from the profile of Albert Shanker, president of the American Federation of Teachers, and an AFL-CIO Executive Council member, as distributed by the AFL-CIO public relations staff:

Active in civil affairs, Mr. Shanker serves on the Board of Directors of the A. Philip Randolph Institute and League for Industrial Democracy. He is also a member of the boards of directors of the United Housing Foundation, the Building and Development Fund of the Wiltwyck School for Boys, and the United Fund of Greater New York. In addition, Mr. Shanker is a member of the Executive Committee of the Workers Defense League, Vice President of the Jewish Labor Committee, an Associate of the University Seminar on Labor at Columbia University, and serves on the Board of Directors of the New York City Council of Economic Education and on the Advisory Council of the Edward Corsi Labor-Management Relations Institute of Pace College. He is a member of the President's Council of the School of Education at New York University and is a member of the Advisory Committee of the National Center for the Study of Collective Bargaining in Higher Education of Baruch College of the City University of New York and a member of the Boy Scouts Labor Committee.

That may be taken as fairly typical of the involvement of the top echelon of union officers in civic affairs. (Murray H. Finley, president of the Amalgamated Clothing Workers, listed sixteen positions held in various organizations plus twelve he formerly held, usually on boards of directors, in his 1975 biography.) But what is true at the top is equally true of the lower echelon of unions involved in local civic affairs.

Throughout the nation, union officers and members serve on school boards, city councils, state legislatures and on the boards of directors of social welfare agencies ranging from the Red Cross to United Way. And when it comes time to erect a rehabilitation center for retarded children, corporate funds pay for the donated building materials, but it is the building and construction trades unions that donate free labor to put up the building! The highly publicized corporate philanthropy is rarely matched in print with recognition of labor's help, as in the following excerpt from a magazine article:

The opening of the Suffolk County Rehabilitation Center for the Physically Handicapped next month will give the crippled, the handicapped and the palsied children of Suffolk new life and hope. And it will also demonstrate that labor and management, working in harmony, have a heart that pours out its quality of mercy for the good of the community.

The million-dollar building on Indian Hill Road, Commack, which will open its doors in February [1961], was made possible at no cost to the taxpayer through the generosity and cooperation of labor and management.

Labor, represented by the Nassau-Suffolk Building and Construction Trades Council, provided the skills of more than twenty crafts free evenings, Saturdays and Sundays, while building contractors donated the materials—free concrete for the foundations to the lighting fixtures.

Each easily gave the equivalent of half a million dollars in labor and materials. Why? Community service is the flip answer, but it goes much deeper than that, obviously.

The guiding hand behind the project, John E. (Buddy) Long, president of the construction trades council, puts it this way, quoting from his favorite Biblical passage:

"I shall pass through the world but once.
"Any good thing, therefore, that I can do, or any kindness I can show to any human being,
"Let me do it now.
"Let me not defer it or neglect it. For I shall not pass this way again."[8]

Professor Cook, in her study, *Labor's Role in Community Affairs*, added up three considerations of why labor should participate in community affairs:

1. Union members want to find out about community services.
2. Many community organizations want closer working relationships with workers via the unions.
3. The unions, as important community organizations themselves, representing a high proportion of the working people, want increasingly to help make policy on public questions.[9]

That is a scholar's evaluation, but how does labor see its role in the community? The answer can be found in the resolution adopted by the first constitutional convention of the AFL-CIO setting up community service departments. The objectives "in the area of community organization for health, welfare and recreation" were declared to be:

1. Encourage equitable labor representation on agency boards and programs.
2. Stimulate labor participation in formulating agency policies and programs.
3. Develop techniques and methods to interpret for union members agency programs and practices.
4. Assist union members, their families and other citizens in time of need.
5. Plan for union participation in civil defense and disaster relief programs and operations.
6. Help in the development of health and welfare services, such as blood banks and multiple medical screening.
7. Coordinate fund-raising drives, through voluntary federation wherever possible, for voluntary health and welfare services.
8. Cooperate with other agencies in dealing with and in solving social and health problems.
9. Participate in all genuine efforts designed to improve social work standards and practices.

Those objectives, adopted in 1955, have yet to be changed.

They have provided an effective guide for labor involvement in the community in the intervening decades. The first objective—labor representation on agency boards and programs—may appear self-serving, but should be understood as requiring total involvement. Helping to make policy on public questions requires not only votes on boards of directors, but active participation of the rank and file on the local level. Where else would the votes come from to seriously influence legislation and regulation?

While there are unions which discourage members from registering to vote in elections for fear registration makes them liable to jury duty and hence loss of pay, far more unions plunge into community affairs in efforts to bring about reforms. One recent effort, running counter to the usual nonalignment with civic groups, received national notice in the *Progressive*:

In Pittsburgh, many members of Local 575 of the Service Employees International Union (SEIU) have joined a community campaign for utility reform. The local's leadership is giving strong support to the People's Power Project (PPP), a broad-based coalition fighting for a utility "lifeline" which would provide a minimum amount of electricity to consumers at a fixed lower rate. The PPP, with union support, is also pushing for a change in the utility rate structure to compel large industrial users to pay higher rates.

Paul Garver [business representative] of the SEIU local and an earlier organizer of PPP, says his union allows its locals great latitude in community political action. The decentralized structure of the union and its growing recognition that broader coalitions between workers and the community are essential—especially for public sector employees—has prompted participation of individual union members in a number of other causes in the Pittsburgh area. Some have given active support to the Action Coalition for the Elderly (ACE) in efforts to reform nursing homes and improve hospital patient care . . .[10]

But the account in the *Progressive* failed to indicate the extent of the involvement of SEIU Local 585 of Monroeville, Pennsylvania, and 668 of Harrisburg in community affairs in the Keystone State. Correspondence with Garver revealed:

SEIU Locals 585 and 668 have supported various measures for utility reform . . . including Lifeline . . . The People's Power Project is a smaller activist group which I personally work with and which has helped to put together the broader coalition of labor, consumer, environmental and senior citizen groups that include the SEIU locals.

Similarly, Local 585 is not directly related to the Action Coalition of Elders, but rather works through the Committee to Improve Kane Hospital, which is a coalition effort of some 50 community, senior citizens and church organizations assisting the Action Coalition in correcting the terrible conditions at that huge county institution.

Our particular contribution has been to work for full cooperation of the workers at Kane Hospital, represented by several unions, including Local 585, with the community struggle, to improve conditions for both patients and workers there. We have also found that our members working at several county nursing homes in adjoining counties have found the report, *Kane Hospital—A Place to Die*, useful in improving staff and supply situations in their own institutions.

The report, a 100-page book published in 1975 by ACE,[11] calls for a public investigation of inhuman conditions observed and reported by two nurses aides and a social worker at John J. Kane Hospital, a public, government-financed, extended-care facility for 2,200 elderly and chronically ill people of Allegheny County, Pennsylvania.

Lifeline, referred to in Garver's letter, is the "low-fixed, fair price for the amount of gas and electricity necessary to meet the energy needs of the average residential consumer." The PPP, in a legislative campaign, is seeking passage of House Bill 2060 in the state legislature to establish substantially lower utility rates for consumers. SEIU Locals 585 and 668 "have been active" in the coalitions which testified in favor of the bill in hearings held by the Consumer Protection Committee throughout the Commonwealth, the *Pennsylvania Service Employee* noted in its Spring, 1976, edition.

Do these coalitions have fruitful results? They do, on two fronts: Aligning trade unions with the public in a consumer protection campaign does far more to brighten labor's image than mountains of public relations releases possibly could, while the combined strength of all participants in a coalition raises enough clamor to be heard effectively in the legislature.

It can hardly be coincidence that Michael Johnson, executive vice president of the Pennsylvania AFL-CIO, and Helen O'Bannon, a Pittsburgh economist, were sworn in as commissioners on the Pennsylvania Public Utilities Commission late in 1975. Both are considered to be consumer advocates. And both are members of the community.

Notes

1. Alice H. Cook, *Labor's Role in Community Affairs*, p. 2.
2. Anne H. Nelson, *The Visible Union in Times of Stress*, p. 14.
3. Bertha Capen Reynolds, *Social Work and Social Living*, pp. 54–55.
4. John A. Fitch, *Social Responsibilities of Organized Labor*, p. 150.
5. Richard A. Lester, *As Unions Mature: An Analysis of the Evolution of American Unionism*, pp. 37–38.
6. Ibid., p. 45.
7. Ibid., p. 51–52.
8. Austin H. Perlow, "Suffolk County Rehabilitation Center to Open in February," *Industrial Bulletin*, January 1961, p. 6.
9. Cook, *Labor's Role in Community Affairs*, p. 3.
10. *Progressive*, July 1976, p. 9.
11. *Kane Hospital—A Place to Die.*

8.
Neighborhood
Service Councils

It's a principle of the union, not just to fight for wages and hours, but to take an interest in the community, in the life of the people, because we believe in what we are doing.

Jay Rubin, president of the Hotel and Motel Trades Council of New York, spoke slowly and clearly. After a moment's thought, he went on:

This is the only Hotel Trades Council in the country. We can't stand still and fight for our members only. We must fight for the entire community. We must bargain for fair conditions, especially in our industry, but we must also consider the entire community.

In general, the labor movement is fighting for more than the contract, like trying to obtain health insurance for everybody, a minimum wage, which affects not only the union member, but all workers. More and more the labor movement is coming to represent the interests of the community. No, we're not the only body doing so; many others are, too. We're concerned also with the cultural field, that involves the whole community.

Mrs. Shirley Kronberg, director of the council's Neighborhood Service Councils at 707 Eighth Avenue, New York City, picked up where Rubin left off, effusively expanding on his statements: *

"In 1961, the union felt that servicing the membership in terms of the contract alone was inadequate. We had been setting up committees from time to time for special services, like legislation, but they didn't fill the bill. So, we divided up our membership geographically and opened up headquarters for the Neighborhood Service Councils in each of the five boroughs.

"At the center in each borough, we have a staff and volunteer workers making up committees, but we also have a citywide committee. The purpose is to deal with everything in the life of the worker not

---

*Mrs. Kronberg's story is told in her own words as taped in an interview; it has been edited only to excise the remarks and questions of the author.

related to the contract or the job. And that's exactly what we do. For this service, our membership pays an additional fifty cents a month to pay the costs of operating the council.

"The Hotel Trades Council has 23,000 members affiliated with ten unions—Local 3 Electrical Workers; Local 6 Hotel, Restaurant Workers; Local 56 Maintenance; Local 94 Operating Engineers; Local 144 Front Service; Local 153 Office Workers; Local 1005 Telephone Operators; Local 1 Carpenters; Local 1422 Painters; Local 43 Upholsterers—all of whose members work in hotels and are covered by one contract negotiated by the Hotel Trades Council.

"We've been losing jobs in recent years. We had 30,000 members only seven years ago. Hotels are closing down.

"We handle problems outside the contract only. We have no authority to do anything else. What do we do? All right, this is what came in today. Here, we keep a sheet on everyone who calls. Here's a Social Security problem. When —— retired in March, he was told he would not be eligible for Social Security until October, because he was overpaid in 1971. He was sick in the hospital when he was sixty-five and they paid him and now they're taking back $1,700. We went through all his papers. There was nothing to indicate it was in 1971. So I spoke to Social Security about this letter. A result of interceding, we got the breakdown.

"We found out, actually, they paid him more. They were going to collect more than they paid him. Let me explain: When Social Security evaluates what they pay you, it's what you may earn for that year. For example, in 1971, you were able to earn $1,680. Everything you earned over that—this year it's $2,760—every two dollars you earn the government keeps one dollar and you get one dollar. They claim he owed them something like $1,900.

"Figuring out his Social Security, I found he only received less than $1,700, some of which was already returned. So I called and asked, 'Can you take more than you gave him?' Well, no, then you got to stop counting on what he overearned and start counting what you gave him. This was something he could never do himself. The bureaucracy is so vast, there is no one person who will know what the entitlements are in the areas of unemployment insurance, Social Security, medical and health, Medicare, Medicaid, compensation, etc. It's impossible. Nobody knows it all.

"The second case today? This lady came in; she also was overpaid in Social Security. But she is also sixty-five now and I instructed her on how to convert her Blue Cross to senior care. It was something she didn't know about. She had been paying Blue Cross premiums and I told her not to pay any more and to convert.

"They don't tell you when to convert. And if you wind up in the hospital, first of all you are overpaying.

"And the third case today: ——— went to Presbyterian Hospital for some clinic visits and he got this bill for $229. But he has four kids and can't pay the bill. It's important to reach the hospital before they turn it over to the collection agency and lawyers and garnishees. I called the accounts department in the hospital and tried to find someone who knew about it. I asked for the name of the administrator because I wanted to send a letter. And I found this very lovely lady, Miss Jones, yesterday. And she said he has a clinic card and on the back of the card he has a rating, according to what rate he should pay. So he came back with it today and I read it to her. He has a special rate and they will review the bill. So I helped him.

"Then there was this lady who received something she did not understand. She got a big fat thing with a lot of carbons all made up. She called me up and said I got something from the Board of Health and I don't know what it is. Can I bring it up? But of course. It was a medical order form for special shoes from Medicaid. The doctor filed for it. But they never know if it is going to be granted. I had to tell her what it was and to take it back to the doctor for his signature.

"He'll tell her what shoe store to go to for the shoes. Then there was another one, a Mr. ———; what did we do for him? This is an interesting one. This is a Catch-22. This man was in the hospital. See, this is his bill. Okay? He was covered for twenty-one full days and he had four discount days which under our contract means four days at 50 percent. Okay? That's what he got the bill for.

"He came in on April 1. He was discharged from the hospital January 31. We found that he was still eligible for Medicaid because Medicaid covers you for ninety days retroactively. But for an in-hospital bill, it has to be filed in the hospital. The hospitals are refusing to file once you are out of the hospital. You can't file on the outside. Okay?

"Since they have an obligation to check with somebody if he has Blue Cross and is going to pay the bill, their social services department should do the checking. But they let him out and then said they are not allowed to file. So I called Medicaid and called around until I got somebody who said the hospital has got to file or tell us why not. So I got the head of their accounting department. This was way back in April and I spoke to him and I told him if you don't file for Medicaid, we'll send him to a lawyer to sue you for denying him the rights he is entitled to. So they said send him down.

"Did I intimidate them? Yes, that's right, I did. So he went down and he filed for Medicaid. Now he's got another bill from them, which he brought in to me today, and which he is not supposed to have, since once they've filed, they're supposed to submit his bill to Medicaid. But it might be the computer didn't know it, right? So I called the hospital and told them he filed for Medicaid through them.

"Do I keep a record on all of them? Sure, otherwise, I don't know what we did last. We keep these records and have files and files full of them. Here's a record on the number of cases we handled in a 10-week period recently, a total of 342 cases.

"What's housing relocation involve? That's about people who are burned out or living in subhuman conditions. I had a ninety-year-old man who was living in a boarded-up house. No one knew he was there, so I got Relocation to send a building inspector to condemn the building. So they condemned it and then he got a bill from the city for $1,700 for all the time he was living there at $100 a month. They want the money. But some plaster fell on his head recently, so they're liable. So, he's suing the city. That should cancel out the $100 a month. Yes, I agree with you; it's insane. You're right, but you don't know what's going on until you see it.

"And here's another one—a mother with three children, two boys and a girl. You have to tell Housing how many so they'll know the number of rooms they'll need. The boys are seventeen and fourteen; the girl, eighteen. She's on unemployment insurance now; the mother, I mean. She's applying for a job soon. So I told her not to apply for housing until she gets the job.

"Does the fifty cents a month cover it all? No. But we just had a dance and raised $4,000. We try to raise money. We went to Albany Monday a week ago; no, it was Tuesday, as part of the tenants' lobby and the workers raised the money in the shops. They collected $732, so we sent two busloads.

"We try to handle all the problems of the members on a personal level. They come here because it tells them to in our union paper. They're told to come here for help. Every once in a while we list the addresses of the borough councils and tell them what's going on and at what time. We also have ballet lessons for the kids, music lessons, one day a week at each council and a luncheon for the pensioners. We do income taxes for all our members. We also did election registrations. And camp registration for away-from-home camps for the Central Labor Council. Now we're planning to hold a dance, a raffle, a concert. In July, we'll have a picnic.

"Why? Because we have, we found in all our years of experience as the increased wages are raising the standard of living of the people, that the other problems are so overwhelming that it's not adequate.

"A union has to do more than provide an increase in salary, another holiday, and whatever else you can get for them. It's just not enough just to change the standard of living if all these other problems are killing the people.

"You're still not satisfied [with the answers]? First of all, the union is the membership. It's not some abstract thing that's made up of officers. It's true that workers elect the leadership, but whatever is in the interest of the membership is the function of the union. It's mandated by the membership, so it may be [President] Jay Rubin's idea, but if it didn't sit well with the membership it would never be approved.

"I'm involved in this. First of all, everybody employed by us is a hotel worker. We all come from the industry. I was a waitress. I think we're unique in this that all of us come from the industry. You know, they go in a lot for hiring the college people. We don't have any professionals. I don't think professionals have the kind of understanding that's necessary, or the empathy with our people.

"Everybody here has worked in a hotel or is the spouse of a hotel worker. This job Vicky does; she's the wife of Juan, who was a waiter from the [Waldorf] Astoria, and he worked on trips and social and recreational activities and he died three years ago and we brought Vicky in because she was most familiar with the kind of thing he did.

"Right, you have to have empathy with your members. But it isn't just hotel problems. It's that by having a cross section of your own members you know, here, you know, they don't have to lie to us. Somebody comes in here and is doing a fake story, you know, I tell them, to me you don't lie. If you have to lie, I'll tell you what. I'll tell you when to lie. If I say what are you making as a bellman in the Plaza, you know, and he says $80 a week, don't tell me that, tell it to somebody else. So that first of all they're making straight talk and secondly, we're on their side. What we are all trying to do is to beat the system.

"I think that what all of us have is a strong sense of anger over what is being done to people, the people that deserve it the least. You should see what is being done to the elderly who have worked all their lives.

"Life is so ugly for them it is monstrous. It's not easy growing old. We have a lot of people who were immigrants. There was a time, for instance, when Irishmen came here in droves and many of them were not married. A lot of single women, no families."

And then, after a telephone call which broke her train of thought:

"You know, the day you stop getting indignant is the day you're dead. You might as well kiss it all goodbye. However, you know, I used to say to my husband, who does the same thing at the bakers union, we each come in with our little two spoons every morning and we empty the ocean and by tomorrow morning it's all filled up again. So that any thinking person has to know this is not adequate for the need. There have to be greater changes.

"What do I get out of it? Well, first of all, absolutely, absolutely, I identify with them and we're on their side. Like the other day, Belle and I had a young man in who's picked up, he's not charged with homicide, but he's involved in what turned out to be a murder. We strongly suspect he was a pusher.

"Right now, he's out on bail and he has no job. We told him, you know, how to go for unemployment insurance. We are not the judges, neither moral or legal. By the time they get to us they are so down they don't need us to kick them, too."

Then, reminded of the alcoholic waiter she had referred to the Central Labor Rehabilitation Council:

"Yes, he lost his job, so he went to Local 144 [SEIU]. He was a doorman, but he was in no shape to work. They sent him up here for a job. He hadn't eaten in two days. He had slept on the subway after his wife threw him out of the house. We sent him to June [Crawford] because he needed hospitalization for alcoholism. He was hospitalized and de-toxed and placed in a health unit, I don't know, Alcoholics Anonymous, or whatever, and when he got out, dried out, he got a job and it all worked out. I've no idea what happened to him eventually, but he was straightened out and got a job, but that's not unusual; no, not unusual. And I'll tell you something else. I make it a practice: I'm here if someone needs me, but I'm not their mother and I don't have to follow them beyond. If he'll need us again, he'll come back. I meet people in the elevator all the time years after they have been here. . .

"I had a woman come here who had been threatened with arrest by her daughter. Her daughter had a child out of wedlock and was living with mama and the baby. The baby was ill. The daughter wanted to move and take the baby because that was the only way she could get welfare. The mother refused to give the daughter the baby. The daughter went to Legal Aid Society and the Legal Aid Society called up the mother and said if you don't give the kid back her baby we're going to have you arrested.

"The mother came here. Okay? I called the Legal Aid attorney. I'm on the Legal Aid board and we talked it over and persuaded the mother to give the kid the baby. Now the daughter, the grandchild and the mother are all together. But you see, I had met this woman many times. I make it a practice, never ask her anything personal. If she'll want to tell me, she'll tell me. So, there are many people who come with many kinds of problems, but I never refer to them, I never ask.

"Do they ever say thanks? Yes, very often and in many ways. People drop in here and try to *shtup* us money. Yes, like a five-dollar bill. Right! We get very indignant. If they ask Belle in advance, she warns them, you don't want to get thrown out, don't do it.

"If somebody gave me a box of candy, I'd take it, no, not for the candy, I'm on a diet and won't eat it, but if I refused it would kill them.

"I've been here now since 1961. I was a hotel worker when the councils were organized. I was elected first chairman of the Bronx council. When the coordinator of the council left to become professor at Wayne University in Michigan, I put in for the job and was coordinator for three years and when the girl whose job I got died of lung cancer I took her job. So I'm here about eleven years. I have two wonderful sons. They're union people, of course.

"Jay Rubin is president. The idea of the councils was his. Jay has for years been looking for organization forms through which the membership can express itself—in legislation, in politics, every way. Without that kind of support the council couldn't do much."

9.
Labor Rehab

Jerry stared off into space, as though he could see through the wall of his office on the sixth floor of 386 Park Avenue South.

"There are all kinds of services out there," said the administrator of Central Labor Rehabilitation Council, with a wave of his arm. "But in a crisis, panic seems to set in and they don't know where to turn, where to go for help.

"We're a kind of catalyst because in that panic the thought comes up, 'Maybe the union can help me,' or 'Maybe Labor Rehab knows the answer.' Well, we do know the answer, because we damn well know where to turn for help. We know how to meet the needs of the people."

And then, obviously proud of the job Labor Rehab does, Jerry Waters glanced at the shelf of ledgers behind him, adding, "My records show that 68 percent of all our referrals are closed satisfactory to the client."

The term *unique* applies only to the financing of the Central Labor Rehabilitation Council of New York, not its operations, since the council, familiarly known as "Labor Rehab," serves working men and women and their families—regardless of union affiliation—throughout New York City as a community service activities committee organized as a labor agency. That's a pattern repeated widely elsewhere.

It is funded by voluntary contributions of unions, companies and agencies and government grants, because Labor Rehab has grown so large in the scope of its activities that support by the United Fund of Greater New York alone would no longer be adequate. The scope of problems referred to Labor Rehab is endless because workers' problems are endless, and more than 1,200 persons come to the council annually seeking help. According to Virginia Viglietta, statistician, the council "closes" an increasingly larger case load each year. A decade ago, less than 700 appeals were closed annually, but the figure was well in excess of 1,000 by 1979. That doesn't mean each case was immediately resolved to Waters' satisfaction; a large number of cases remains open at year-end, but may be closed a day, a week or month later. That figure, too, mounts rapidly, reflecting the heavy case load and could number in excess of 700 on any December 31.

The statistics are deceptive, since they fail to reveal the results achieved. But Waters knows at first hand what the results are:

> It's gratifying to know we are bringing help to people, to see the results in a man put back on the job, a broken family pulled together, a kid's life saved with heart surgery, a drunk dried out and sobered up for the rest of his life. There was a little girl who sat on that chair the other day and she smiled when I handed her one of those "I Paid My Dues" buttons. I'll never forget that smile.
>
> Why do I do it? No, it's not just a job and to hell with the money. I get gratification out of it. What's it all about? What is a union for? A union is to help people and give them direction and the leadership they need.

Labor Rehab trains 300 to 350 counselors annually so they'll know how to refer callers to the appropriate social agencies for assistance. That, after all, was the original concept of the Community Services Committee of the New York Central Labor Council: to provide referral and information services for union members. For how many business agents or shop stewards can cope with a family bankruptcy, the loss of a limb in an industrial accident, a paranoid spouse, a critically ill child, drug addiction, alcoholism or a broken family? Who has the time or skill to devote to resolving such problems?

More pertinent, what worker, shop steward or business agent knows where to appeal for help, even if he can overcome the member's reluctance to "beg" an agency for assistance? Labor Rehab realized this when it undertook its first major project, as the final report on Project Rehab shows:

> Agencies as a group are associated in their minds almost exclusively with memories or experiences with "home relief." With this attitude labor people are not likely to take the initiative nor are they apt to take readily to a suggestion that they apply for service with their problems.[1]

The final report points out that the services are available, but not being used by those who need them:

> Members of the affiliates were not taking advantage of available services despite obvious need. In some instances this was due to the lack of knowledge, but more frequently it seemed to result from the frustration experienced in trying to understand how the agencies operated and conditions to establish eligibility. The professional agency world and the trade union would not speak the same language.

Another obstacle was the reluctance of union officers to get involved in what they considered members' personal problems. "They had considerable uncertainty even about the wisdom of union representatives getting involved with the purely personal affairs of individual members."

But they were convinced, once the Community Services Committee organized Project Rehab in 1961 under the impetus of Harry Van Arsdale, president of Central Labor Council. (There had been a committee since 1946, but it was chiefly a fund-raiser for the United Fund; that is, until 1951, when the late Michael Quill, Transport Workers Union president, assigned Louis L. Levine to be community services director for CIO affiliates in New York. With a mandate from Quill, Levine created his own operation of "helping the rank and file with their problems," since there was no program to follow. Levine laid down his own rules, formulated from day to day.)

Waters recalled how project Rehab started:

> Van Arsdale started it. It was crazy. There was this conference at the Hotel New Yorker by the insurance companies and the news said they thought the state ought to be doing something about rehabilitating injured workers. Of course, it was their job, the insurance companies, that is, but they were passing the buck to the state.
>
> Van Arsdale heard about it and he said to Lou Levine, who was labor "rep" with the United Fund, "Why haven't we done something about this? It would help the injured worker get some help." Van Arsdale asked Lou and me to get to work on it.

To understand what a suggestion such as that meant, one must understand Harry Van Arsdale—no simple matter. The man who has led the Central Labor Council since 1957 and will continue to do so as long as he wishes, had already involved his own union, Local 3, International Brotherhood of Electrical Workers, in an extensive community services program long before he thought of Project Rehab. Some facts about Van Arsdale are on record, but he is an elusive man, never granting interviews, remaining cloaked in an impenetrable, authoritarian garb which repels personal contact. But over the years it has become clear he is fanatically devoted to trade unionism, which he calls "my hobby." It is his entire life. Associates reveal he is convinced he has a mission in life: "to help the working people."

This conviction is borne out by the zealous devotion Van Arsdale has shown to his cause, working a long, hard day all year around and compelling everyone in his entourage to work equally hard. His wife said recently, "He leaves the house at 7 A.M., and doesn't get back before midnight."

Because Van Arsdale has been a public figure for so long, it is not difficult to track down biographical data. The son of an electrician who was a charter member of IBEW Local 3, he was born in 1905 in the section of New York City known then as Hell's Kitchen. After attending Townsend Harris High School two years, he went to work for Western Electric and other firms, until he was initiated into Local 3 in 1925. By 1934, he was business manager of the union. By 1957 he was president of the Central Labor Council. That's not a rapid rise to power, but reflects a broad acceptance of his views as he acquired prestige and power. Any disinterested observer must concede he used his position in the interest of union members and not for personal gain.

One cannot fault Van Arsdale for being aware of the power he wields, since he has been the inspiration and driving force behind Central Labor Council and Labor Rehab, reflecting his concept of a union with a social conscience. "A union is not just wages and hours," he said years ago. "It's brotherhood. It's the worker who visits you when you are sick. It's the vehicle for a better life. It's a classroom."

He amplified this theme recently in a rare burst of candor that was illuminating: "The union which negotiates a contract only is not a union. It must go further and try to improve the life and welfare of its members in many other ways, too. Of course, the contract helps in that direction, but it's not enough."

Was that why Van Arsdale worked so hard at a score of union jobs (but accepted only one salary)? To give the union member a better life? If so, he was working on a rigorous schedule that appeared self-destructive; but Van Arsdale was unconcerned: "I only do what I like."

Does he ever take a vacation, or does he always stick to a routine that could easily wear out a man considerably younger than his seventy-four years? "Of course, I take vacations. I went to Hawaii one year and you can't get more vacation than that!" (But it turned out Hawaii was the site of an IBEW training school session that year.)

In his usual paternal manner, he remarked, "When you get to know people, you have a tendency to like them," but an hour later in addressing IBEW Local 3 members who were being awarded high school diplomas, he revealed what he meant. Putting the program down on the table, he suggested taking note of the ages of the graduates.

The names of the graduates who had passed the union's examination for high school diplomas were followed by their ages. One was sixty; another, sixty-six. It wasn't quite clear what point Van Arsdale was making until he added, "And you ask me what I get out of this!" His face beamed with pride.

In his remarks to the graduates urging them to go further with their educations, Van Arsdale summed it up: "People who work with their hands or their brains produce the wealth of this country. Their aims and aspirations are to make a better life for themselves and their children. That's what it's all about."

And what better way, than through a trade union?

Van Arsdale transformed the Community Services Committee into Project Rehab in 1962, when under his urging the committee, whose chairman then was Michael Sampson, applied for a grant from the Department of Health, Education and Welfare. (Sampson's recollection was that Van Arsdale "kept the application in his pocket for a year before he acted on it.")

When the project got under way, Levine, because of his training and education (City College and New York University studies in sociology and industrial relations and a certified social worker), was named director, and Sid Lew succeeded him at the United Fund as labor "rep."

Project Rehab was created as a community service referral program to assist workers who required rehabilitation. The final report on the project could serve as a classroom guide for other unions. For that reason the conclusions deserve wide dissemination:

> It was important to locate Rehab in the same building where Central Labor Council met and where representatives of the affiliated unions regularly came to confer. . . . Union representatives were constantly made aware that the project was an important activity of the council.

The point was critical. The service to the member is not an activity by a professional social worker, an agency or an employer. It is a service provided by the union, and that makes the service acceptable to the member! What follows flows from this concept and was designed to create identification with Project Rehab for the union official and the rank and file.

Wide publicity in the labor press was designed to make union officers as well as members familiar with the project. Staff members took part in counseling classes so they could become familiar to the counselors. Professional titles were "not unduly stressed."

Staff members became Miss Y and Miss X, not professional rehabilitation counselors or nurses. And one rule was followed: "Don't talk down or give the impression of being patronizing." The staff was taught to "clear procedures with elected officers," learning, "so far as possible, to use the union approach, emphasizing always that the project was organized to help because of the union's genuine concern for the member's welfare." That meant the social workers on the staff had to learn about union procedures to overcome the distrust union members have for professionals:

> [Members] are accustomed to grievance procedures and they tended to equate the personal problem of the union member with a grievance, ex-

pecting prompt solution. When a member believes that something is wrong on the job . . . his union representative is expected to solve the problem as quickly as possible. Direct confrontation between supposedly injured parties is far more usual than a subtle, indirect approach. "This is a problem. What are you going to do about it?"

That meant the staff occasionally had to see clients after working hours and listen to them unburden themselves without the need to make out "forms" in order to win their confidence.

But to get clients to come to the social workers, union members had to be trained as counselors and informed how to obtain the required help. A manual was prepared and courses given under the guidance of the Community Services Committee. These courses still continue and annually as many as 250 union representatives are trained as counselors. The manual, written in 1965, was revised in 1973.

In brief, the handbook[2] describes the job a counselor performs, instructs him (or her) how to elicit the information on the problem from the member and direct the member to the proper social agency for solution of his problem. Essentially, the role of the counselor is to refer problems to the proper agency for resolution and then to follow up the case to make certain it is resolved. But with the proliferation of public and private agencies in recent years, that is no simple matter. What is needed, to begin with, is a directory of services available, but it must go beyond a name, address and telephone number.

The counselor must know the eligibility requirements. A further need is a personal contact in the agency; dealing on a first-name basis expedites the service.

It is doubtful many New Yorkers have the knowledge to reach out and tap the resources of the one agency which will best serve in a particular area. Nor is it simple to reach for a telephone and ask for help. The manual devotes an entire page to "How to Telephone an Agency." In part, it directs:

Collect your wits first. Know exactly what it is you want to find out. Make your call before 4:30. Most agencies close at 5 p.m. However, Labor Rehab is usually open after 5 p.m.

Tell them you are a Community Service Counselor for your union. Many switchboards, specially large ones, may have a person on the switchboard who does not know who you should talk to. Consequently, you are likely to be routed around from one person to another until finally they locate someone who can answer your question. WRITE DOWN THE EXTENSION AND NAME OF THE DIVISION YOU GET ROUTED TO. Then, if you have to call back, you won't have to go through the same rigamarole.

But telephone etiquette is a small part of contacting agencies. Which agency to call? The handbook lists agencies in New York City, plus those in nearby Nassau and Suffolk counties, giving addresses and telephone numbers of branch offices and services available.

There is nothing esoteric about such categories as "aged and retirees," "alcoholism," "armed forces," "children," or "consumer protection," but they are collected, classified and compiled in a handy, readily available form. Some of the notes appended to the data are unlikely to be found elsewhere. Under "Small Claims Court," for instance, there is this note: "If you want more information, call one of the Small Claims Courts. The Manhattan number is very hard to reach. To get information quickly, you may call the Staten Island Court even though you may present your case in another borough."

The organization which was set up for Project Rehab continues to operate as Labor Rehab. When the demonstration project funds ran out, the need the project had filled in rehabilitation indicated it could do equally well in related fields.

During the term of Project Rehab—April, 1963, to August, 1968—a total of 2,361 cases was handled by the staff, with only a small proportion (302 out of 2,361 referrals) coming to the attention of the staff from the union member affected. More than twice as many, 791, came from union officers, but the majority, 1,430, or 43.9 percent, came from counselors.

Other referrals came from newspapers (191), other union sources (302), nonunion referrals (174) and the staff itself (71).

Only union members were served by Project Rehab. The record indicates 54.6 percent of the cases involved union members; 13.5 percent were wives of members; 16.5 percent, their children; and 15.4 percent, close relatives. But what does not appear in the record is that the first referral concerned a nonunion family. When this came to the attention of HEW, the project was notified this endangered the demonstration grant. But freed of the restrictions of a grant, Labor Rehab today serves working men and women and their families without regard to union affiliation.

What sort of problems did workers bring to Project Rehab (presumably because no other institution of society offered help on the same terms)? A rundown of referrals shows an overwhelming majority of cases involved vocational or education problems, but hundreds more concerned employment, while significant numbers of cases had need of training or guidance or schooling.

Many clients presented more than one problem. Unemployment, for example, was linked with physical impairment or mental or emotional disturbances; indeed the mental illnesses outnumbered the physical disorders. What did Project Rehab do for these troubled people? The staff contacted 3,261 agencies to handle their problems with medical and psychiatric evaluations, medical inpatient or outpatient treatments, psychiatric inpatient or outpatient treatments or (in 151 instances) physical rehabilitations.

But the tremendous range of cases handled is revealed in the other "treatments" recommended, including nursing, custodial nursing home, "other" nursing home care, physical aids, medicine, blood treatments, dental care and "sixty other cases."

And the results? Did Project Rehab accomplish anything? Indeed it did; the number of working people helped back to rewarding lives was so encouraging that Labor Rehab continues to this day.

Waters, who became director when Levine was named to the New York State Labor Department, runs a tight ship at Labor Rehab, keeping meticulous records on referrals, cases open and the percentage of cases closed. He's obviously proud of the job CSA does and rattles off figures from his ledgers to prove his case:

> To date this year, 652 unions have made referrals to us, and that includes a great many unaffiliated unions, like the Teamsters and the court clerks and independents you've probably never heard of. As of June 30, 1976, a total of 14,501 referrals were made to us in the seventeen years of our existence.

Project Rehab's results were so encouraging a second project was undertaken in 1967, a year before the work of the first ended. True, there is an innate tendency for any organization to perpetuate itself, but another consideration was the need to continue the service. Fortunately, there was a will to go on. Said Guy F. Robbins, M.D., consultant, in the preface to the final report on the Job Development Project, "My experience with labor has been a most satisfying one. They care, they can see the problems and they face them."

Job Development ran from January 1, 1967, through May 31, 1970, although the final report[3] considered cases handled only through December 31, 1969. Funded by HEW, the demonstration project undertook to conduct an intensive educational program with the unions, not only Central Labor Council affiliates, but independents as well. The union-based placement program asked unions to "share the headaches" in finding jobs for the disabled. Thus it grew out of Project Rehab, providing "an expanded rehabilitation service for the union member, the retired worker who wants to return to the labor market and any members of the unionists' families," as Harry Van Arsdale said in his foreword to the report.

The project called upon the skills and techniques of retired trade unionists, aged sixty-five and over, to work with the staff in

September, 1968, but a difficulty soon appeared. The retired members had been selected because they had "experience gained through years of labor"—a point worth stressing because it reflects an attitude frequently encountered in unions. The retired member is not only an asset, but a source of pride to the union. Because he is still wanted, he retains his *dignity*, feeling he is still wanted. But he did find it difficult to explain how any one could function on a job despite a disability. And so special classes were arranged to clarify this point.

The retired members ranged from sixty-five through seventy-six in age. Eleven men and one woman were in the group. They were paid three dollars an hour plus travel expenses. Each was given an ID card, "which they proudly carried."

But the grant funds soon ran out. However, the aides showed an aptitude for their work and a willingness to continue as volunteers, as much as they needed the money. The final report notes:

> Without exception, all volunteered to help the project whenever they could . . . despite the fact that the moneys being received were in most instances important to the aide to supplement his Social Security or pension. Thus, the role of the Job Development Aide filled two needs: The project's need for additional union contacts and the self-need for additional income.

The principal responsibility of the aides was to find work for union members by enlisting the cooperation of union affiliates and informing them how they could assist in providing employment for the disabled. Visits to unions achieved not only this end, but made it easier for the professional staff to appear at union meetings. The approach worked, since "union officers invited us to attend," and care need not be taken to pressure them in accepting Job Development as part of Labor Rehabilitation Council. "To exercise pressure might have resulted in quick job placement, but not lasting employment."

Three common objections were overcome at the 103 union meetings attended by project staff members: Handicapped workers were not trying to displace men on the job; workers were not being asked to cover up for a returning worker because he would not produce as well as before; and established work routines would not be adjusted because a handicapped worker was on the line.

To overcome the "show me" attitude of workers, Labor Rehab arranged for promotion of "Labor's Health Week," during which labor leaders were taken on tours of community agency facilities. The week ended, by design, in the annual community services institute, a daylong program at which counselors were graduated and panel discussions held on timely, pertinent community services topics allied with the project. The institute is customarily attended by 500 to 1,000 trade unionists, agency representatives and concerned employers.

Another avenue opened by Job Development was with management, whose cooperation was essential if jobs were to be found for disabled workers.

> The selected method recognized the line of protocol existing between labor and management. Additionally, the fact of the matter was labor had a better relationship with management than the JD staff could possibly hope to develop within the time limit of the project.

Union counseling classes were also requested by union officials who could not readily understand "how one can vocationally function within the limits of a disability." One problem was specifically raised: "How can a man with his voice box removed or half his jaw gone, or a nose removed, possibly work? Never mind his problem. I have men who just would not accept the looks of him."

The answer was given by a prominent head and neck specialist from a center for cancer and allied diseases, who spoke to the group. He was accompanied by a dental surgeon and three former patients. One had had a laryngectomy, one had had his nose removed (the class never knew this until they were told), and one had had part of his palate removed. And they all held jobs.

At other classes demonstrations were given by amputees and stroke victims who, following rehabilitation, returned to their former jobs or found other suitable employment. Other classes dealt with drug addiction—a major problem in 1969, especially among younger workers enrolled in apprenticeship programs. When that problem became acute, unions were assured they could refer the cases directly to Labor Rehab. The unions' concern was not only with the drug addicts, but the investment the unions had in them in time, money and effort expended on apprenticeship.

Based on the experience gained from Project Rehab, Job Development was far more successful, since there was an increased number of referrals, attributable to the growing familiarity of the staff and union personnel. Of the 465 cases considered in the final report, by far the greatest proportion came from counselors.

There was a high proportion (84.3 percent) of union members among the clients, who ranged in age from seventeen to seventy, with more than half of them (54 percent) between the ages of thirty-five and fifty-four. Of the 465 persons assisted, almost four-fifths were unemployed when they appeared at Job Development. Of those holding jobs, the report said, "Most of them required help in order to remain in their regular employment, but some needed help in securing a job that was more appropriate from a medical standpoint and felt they could not afford to quit their present jobs in order to look for new work.[4]

All 465 cases presented some type of problem related to jobs or education, but all the clients had disabilities, over 95 percent of them either physical or pyschosocial—or both. About 72 percent had physical disabilities or impairments, the great majority due to muscular skeletal problems, while clients with heart disease ranked next in frequency. Alcoholism and drug usage affected 37 percent of the group with psychosocial problems. The drug users were mostly under twenty-five years of age, while the alcoholics fell in the mid-age group of thirty-five through fifty-four.

The figures are deceptive, giving little indication of the complexity of the problems encountered by the worker, his family and the Job Development staff. But the final report does give a hint:

> For instance, a member needed help in getting a prosthesis so that she could eventually return to work. While this specific request was turned over to a select agency, other problems faced this member and her family: Social Security benefits were applied for; the husband required assistance in securing his sick benefits during a brief spell of illness, alternate arrangements had to be made for financing the prosthesis after one agency ran into difficulties with the supplier, and so on.

Despite the difficulties of the 465 cases handled, 397 were closed as having arrived at "a solution or decision." Specifically, 222 clients (47.7 percent) returned to work and twenty-nine (6.2 percent) were far enough along in training or treatment to suggest probable success in job placement. Allowing for thirty-eight cases open and being worked on, twenty-four incomplete cases which dropped out and could not be located, six others who died and eleven who accepted pensions or went on Social Security, a third of the closed cases remained "unsatisfactory" in results.

The report's conclusion, however, makes it apparent that the rate of success was not to be sneered at:

> The success rate of 66 per cent is high as compared with other attempts at vocational rehabilitation. It is the opinion of the staff that these results could not have been attained without the combined efforts of the Project, union, employer, co-workers and the client's own unusual motivation. The cooperation, consideration and understanding of those unionists and agencies who supported and augmented the efforts of the limited project staff should not be underestimated.

With the final report in and the last of the federal grants expended, the project came to a formal end, but Labor Rehab goes on as a counseling and agency referral service incorporated as the Central Labor Rehabilitation Council of New York Inc., under the aegis of the Central Labor Council, whose community service chairman is James Joy Jr., business manager of Local 1-2, Utility Workers of America. Waters has been named administrator of services, and Frank Vivert succeeded him as director.

Operating on an annual budget of about $420,000, Labor Rehab has a staff of twenty-four persons, including four full-time social workers. The staff is housed in offices adjacent to the Central Labor Council, which pays the rent, electricity and postage.

As an affiliate of the United Fund of Greater New York, Labor Rehab receives an allocation from the fund annually, but the $17,500 allocated in 1979 came to only 11.9 percent of its budget. The major part of its funds is raised through contributions of unions, agencies and individuals, as well as a number of foundation and federal grants.

Sponsors in 1979 included Group Health Inc., the Health Insurance Plan, South Oaks Hospital, United Fund of Greater New York, Dr. Guy F. Robbins, director of educational planning at Memorial Sloan-Kettering Hospital, and the Educational and Cultural Fund of the Electrical Industry (in New York City). Each has signed an agreement with Labor Rehab, in which the sponsor and Labor Rehab (referred to as "the corporation") mutually agree:

1. The Corporation shall provide to all workers, covered employees, pensioners or other persons referred to by the above referred to organization and to the dependents and members of the families of such persons, all of its services, including but not limited to vocational, social and other counselling, so as to enable such persons to maintain or regain their status as useful members of the community. The Corporation agrees to provide all of its services to all individuals referred to it by said organization without charge to the individual.

2. The above referred to organization believes that the purposes and aims of the Corporation are in furtherance of and beneficial to the welfare of the entire community and it subscribes fully thereto. As evidence of its concurrence in the aims and goals of the Corporation, it hereby applies for sponsor membership in the Corporation and in connection therewith it voluntarily agrees to contribute the sum of $——— to the Corporation.

3. Upon the execution of this Agreement, and the making of the voluntary contribution, referred to above, the above referred to organization shall be accepted by the Corporation as a sponsor member and it shall be entitled to all the rights and privileges of such membership therein persuant to the Bylaws of the Corporation.

Waters mentioned a large union which annually donates $5,000 to

Labor Rehab. Asked what they "get in return," he said, "When they had a strike in 1968, they got that much back and more in a single week of services when members appealed for help in filing for unemployment insurance benefits and hospitalization."

Strike or no strike, there's more than enough work for three full-time social workers and an army of volunteers. And that is rather strange, for despite the record of Labor Rehab, community service is not too familiar to the rank and file trade unionists in New York.

"It's appalling to me," said social worker Bess Kaye at Labor Rehab, "how few members know about community services. I don't believe they read much. But word gets around. One tells another, 'If you've got a problem, Mrs. Kaye will help you.'"

Mrs. Kaye finds most of her cases are referred to her by the union, either through an officer or shop steward who has heard of a member who is "in trouble." But can she help the member?

Of course, we are helping people. We don't turn anyone away. There is no one answer to what kind of problems we handle, unless I say there are only universal human problems. There was the Brooklyn Union Gas worker who had tuberculosis, for instance. Because he owned an auto, he couldn't get welfare aid. But he needed the car for his work. The problem was not only tuberculosis and getting medical treatment; it was financial as well. Financial problems and illness go together.

But I get lots of satisfaction out of helping people. I don't do it for the money. Of course, I put a lot into it, more than I have to. The satisfaction of helping people. Yesterday, for instance, a woman phoned me after I did what I felt was nothing—there's so little in the community to help people. But she was surprised at what I had squeezed out of the community for her. I'm useful, creative and productive here. Of course, there are frustrations, too. I can't follow up each case as I'd like to. There's not enough time in a day. If we had twenty counselors, we'd still be busy.

Mrs. Kaye is a professional social worker with experience in nursing, social work, psychiatry, nursing homes, hospitals and elsewhere. She has no trade union background. But Halo Hartwell, senior social worker on the staff, is a trade unionist. Despite their differences, the two women agreed on virtually all points. Said Mrs. Hartwell:

Most cases are referred to us by union officers. But we get a few from counselors, even after they have taken courses here. Why do we help them? Because members expect their unions to help them. "What are you doing with our dues?" they ask. "Why the large salaries for officers?" No other fraternity they belong to do they feel as close to. The worker depends on the union and the union should help them. After all, if [the union] can't solve their problems, they can't earn a living. But business agents can't handle the problems; they become exasperated . . . Why do union members expect so much? Unions should have their own staffs. But many which contribute liberally to Labor Rehab don't use us at all. In fact, unions don't use us enough.

Mrs. Hartwell, who has been involved in trade union causes since the 1920s, was administrator of the International Association of Machinists' Welfare and Pension Fund, Division 15, before she came to Labor Rehab in 1972. Why did she take the job?

Well, I do need the money, but I don't like to stay at home. I like the structured life of working and like being in contact with people. I have a trade unioh background and I want to play more of the advocate role. I was always a fighter for causes. This is a place where I can make a contribution. I feel we are helping people, even if only in a small way. They don't have the tools to help themselves, what with disability benefits, workmen's compensation, unemployment benefits and all the rest. There's no doubt about it; we are helping people.

The third full-time staff member, social worker June Crawford, devotes half of her time to drug and alcoholism problems, finding them a challenge, since it is "very rewarding to get them dried out, sober and back to their families and job." Why is it a challenge? Questioning revealed she had been involved with an alcoholic.

She agreed that too few of the rank and file even know about community services. "It's too expensive to get our story around. Then, too, you talk to a union officer and he's too busy and he doesn't spread the story. I remember when Local 153 Office Workers invited Labor Rehab to address a meeting on alcoholism, and only 200 members showed up."

There may be disappointments, shortcomings, even a feeling that so much more could be done if more unions were involved, not only as supporters of Labor Rehab but beneficiaries of its services. Overall, however, if a judgment can be made of Labor Rehab's effectiveness, that of Dr. Robbins, listed as a "corporate sponsor," is undoubtedly the least biased, the most objective. Dr. Robbins, who is not a trade unionist, annually contributes a substantial sum of money on his own behalf, and not of Sloan-Kettering's, because as a consultant to the staff, he knows, "They care about people and are trying to help them."

Notes

1. *Project Rehab Final Report.*
2. *The Basic Training Manual for Union Counselors.*
3. *Job Development Project Final Report.*
4. Ibid.

10.
The Community-minded Union

VICE PRESIDENT BOMMARITO: Joe Beirne was neither the first chairman nor the last chairman of organized labor's Community Services Committee—but he was a good chairman. He was an active, dynamic and perceptive chairman.

Joe was a true believer. He believed, first of all, in the labor movement. "Let me put it this way," he wrote in 1969. "There is only one substantial private institution in the United States whose primary dedication is to the best interests of all the American people. That institution is the American labor movement represented by the AFL-CIO."

He believed, second of all, that the future of the labor movement lies in its complete identification with the health and welfare of the total community. When it came to choose a slogan for his own international union, the Communications Workers of America, he proclaimed that it was "the community-minded union," not by virtue of its slogan—but because its officers and members, under the leadership of their founding president, have blazed new trails in community participation and involvement. Joe himself became the first labor leader in history to serve as president of the United Community Funds and Council of America, and he had served actively for many years on the boards and committees of many national health and welfare agencies.

That excerpt from the speech delivered by Peter Bommarito, chairman of the AFL-CIO Community Services Committee, in presenting the AFL-CIO's 1975 Murray-Green Award posthumously to Joseph Beirne, president of the Communications Workers of America, gives an indication of the rationale for the CWA's community services program.

The reasoning behind the commitment to the image of the "community-minded union" is worth reflecting on. It is, however, more than an "image." CWA *is* involved—in helping teen-agers help themselves in Houston; in setting up blood banks in Miami and Atlanta; assisting handicapped children in Des Moines; remembering orphans with gifts at Easter in Trenton, New Jersey; sponsoring a Little League team in Winston-Salem, North Carolina; and, odd as it sounds, "providing a sound system for the elephant trainer at the Oakland, California, zoo."

Why? Here we have no rhetoric, no self-serving, sanctimonious pleading; merely an outspoken explanation in the CWA's *ABC's of Community Service*:

Community Service is one of the three integral parts of the CWA Growth Program. The others are organizing the unorganized and public relations. The three parts are closely knit and interlocking . . .

The reason for community service is to help people. And in the process build a stronger, more prestigious union. Service to the community by CWA officers and members dates back to the earliest days of the union. CWA President Joseph A. Beirne, for example, has been active in volunteer fund-raising projects almost as long as he has been in the labor movement.

"There has always been a need to help other people. There are those in this great country who suffer. Some need a toy or other small item, some need money to buy food and clothing, and others need companionship and guidance. The needs of the people transcend the imagination," Beirne explained . . .

CWA members have been active for years in contributing voluntary hours, work and dollars (to United Chest and United Fund drives). Often, in the past [the] work was performed in the name of the telephone company or other business—and CWA received no enhancement of its image as "the community-minded union." Part of the purpose of the Growth Program was to change this . . . to gain a fair share of the credit for CWA. Why? Some argue it makes no difference who gets the credit, so long as the work is done.

CWA leaders knew that many services were being performed by locals and where it was public knowledge the union's image was more powerful. CWA was able to sit at the bargaining table with strength from community support backing them up.

"One thing that makes the company react to our collective bargaining demands is any hint of criticism of the company," Beirne said. "And where there is an active CWA local in a community, and where that CWA local has a good image, we found collective bargaining was successful. We got better contracts.

"The reason was simple. People in the community, including mayors and councilmen, and other centers of power, were embarrassing management by asking them why they couldn't negotiate a contract with a reasonable 'community-minded' union" Community service, then, is an additional tool in the CWA collective bargaining arsenal.

The motivation for a community service program is a compelling one, as the CWA sees it: to give the union a better public image so that it may prosper in its basic bread-and-butter functions. In that, the union is not unlike the corporate executive who gives his time and efforts to United Way, United Cerebral Palsy Association or the YMCA.

But it would not be farfetched to extend the comparison to the zealous churchgoer who bestows charity on earth to the underprivileged so that he, himself, may reap the reward in the hereafter. Consider that the community-minded trade unionist, the corporate executive and the theist are enriched spiritually and psychologically by the act of helping one's fellow man.

One area in which organized labor has been extremely generous is in support of youth movements. It is difficult to ascribe any insidious motive to the unions which sponsor Boy Scout troops. Is it a diabolical scheme of the American labor movement to pervert Boy Scouts into becoming trade unionists? While that sounds implausible, it is difficult to fault unions for the "crime" of teaching boys that unions are an integral part of the economic structure, especially since Scouts are not union members and do not pay dues to the unions chartering their troops. Indeed, unions underwrite the costs of sponsorship, just as churches, synagogues, service clubs and fraternities do.

Do many unions sponsor troops? The question shouldn't arise, but unions ordinarily do not publicize this service. It is so routine that unions have chartered over 200 Scout units and are providing leadership ship for more than 122,000 Scout units across the country.

In the leaflet *AFL-CIO and Scouting* appears the statement, "Twenty-five percent of all Scoutmasters are union members," a surprisingly high proportion that stirred disbelief in at least one reader, since it was an undocumented claim. The statement has been given wide currency in *Labor in the American Community*, which attributes the estimate to George C. Freeman, director, Local Council Finance, Boy Scouts of America, in 1968. But now it has been confirmed by the BSA as based upon "a survey conducted by the BSA in the 1960s."

Involvement with scouting is not a local union option, but an AFL-CIO program which annually calls forth a message from George Meany to all affiliates. In 1976, Meany said:

> A positive approach is necessary to capture the attention and interest of all youth. I am pleased that the Boy Scouts of America has launched BOYPOWER '76. Of course, BOYPOWER '76 is not the only solution to the turmoil which confronts America, but it is one which offers a program of proven ability to develop better citizens. Reaching one boy in three is a monumental task, but it can be achieved.

> I urge, therefore, all AFL-CIO affiliates, in line with our Community Services Program, to continue their support for Scouting and to respond particularly to BOYPOWER '76 goals.

(Boypower '76 aimed to involve a third of all American boys in scouting, with the focus upon the poor in low-rent and public-housing projects. Recall that many trade unionists have such backgrounds; bear in mind also that men of the trade union movement were once boys.)

International unions do develop scouting programs in cooperation with the AFL-CIO. In appeals to affiliates to sponsor troops, the internationals not only tell their local unions to sponsor troops, but tell them why. Two excerpts should suffice.

Francis S. Filbey, general president, American Postal Workers Union, wrote in the leaflet *The American Postal Worker and Scouting*:

> Our effectiveness as an organization is not determined solely by what we think of ourselves, but rather how others see us. And others may never see us—unless there is some kind of postal crisis—until we make ourselves visible through action in the community. There are many ways, of course, to achieve useful visibility. Not the least of them is through a working partnership at the local level with the Boy Scouts of America.

Another comes from Martin J. Ward, general president of the United Association of Journeymen and Apprentices of the Plumbing and Pipe Fitting Industry, in the leaflet *UA and Scouting*:

> The Boy Scouts of America are involved in an attempt to bring the benefits of Scouting to a representative one-third of all American boys—regardless of race, creed, or even physical handicap.
>
> They have asked the assistance of the labor movement to help them meet this ambitious goal. I wholeheartedly endorse their program and urge UA local unions to support Scouting activities in their communities.
>
> The sponsorship of a Cub Scout or Boy Scout troop is a worthwhile extension of any local union community involvement program. Scout units are virtually self-sustaining. Their modest requirements are things that our local unions are rich in: leadership and a place to meet.
>
> Many union members are already making outstanding contributions to the youth of their communities through Scouting programs. Increasing and systematizing our involvement is desirable for many reasons. In addition to performing a valuable community service, the sponsorship of a troop provides a vehicle to interpret the labor movement's objectives to the youth of our nation.

The Boy Scouts of America, as well as the AFL-CIO, is happy with the relationship. George Atkinson, AFL-CIO-CSA liaison with the BSA in North Brunswick, New Jersey, who represents the BSA as much as he represents the AFL-CIO, wrote:

> Organized labor provides substantial financial support for Scouting, prin-

cipally through United Fund contributions. The Scout councils across the country receive close to 50 per cent of their support from local United Ways, and, as you know, organized labor contributes substantially to these funds. In addition, there are many unions that provide direct financial support to Scouting. There are also many local unions that provide in-kind contributions through manpower to build camps and other Scouting facilities.[1]

In recognition of labor's contributions to the youth of our nation, the AFL-CIO established the George Meany Award, presented annually to "any adult male or female union member who has made a significant contribution to Scouting." One award is permitted by each city central labor council, plus another for each state central labor body to "recognize the recipient's outstanding service to youth through the programs of the Boy Scouts of America."

If unions are involved with the Boy Scouts of America to such an extent, have they neglected the Girl Scouts of America? It wouldn't be surprising, considering the lack of recognition women receive in the labor movement. But the truth is, the relationship between unions and Girl Scouts is good. The public relations director of the GSA knew offhand that "we have 350 councils and 156,000 troops," but did not know how many were sponsored by unions, citing differences in organization between the BSA and GSA.

While no data were available on the number of troops with union ties, the relationship was termed "pretty good," and a brochure, published by the AFL-CIO in 1976 was cited as evidence of this relationship. The brochure is being distributed to AFL-CIO affiliates, asking them to support the Girl Scout movement.

If scouting is indebted to unions for financial support through United Way, then countless health and welfare agencies across the country that survive only with United Way's support are equally in debt to labor, drawing major financial support from the donations and payroll deduction plans in which labor and management play co-determinate rolls.

Giving through United Way is well-established labor policy which dates back to the concept of supporting community institutions through industrial plant and office collections. But the close relationship between United Way of America and the AFL-CIO can be seen in the memorandum of understanding signed November 22, 1971. It provides, *inter alia*:

All AFL-CIO representatives being considered for membership on the UWA Board of Governors and other committees will be nominated by the AFL-CIO.

The AFL-CIO will be represented on the Executive Committee of UWA by two members.

AFL-CIO will be represented in officer positions of UWA.

The Director of the UWA Labor Participation Department will be nominated by AFL-CIO subject to the approval of UWA . . . There will be at least six full-time AFL-CIO Community Services representatives in a professional capacity on the staff of the UWA in addition to the director.

The entire nineteen-point memorandum reads more like a labor contract than an understanding; e.g., the item on salaries provides: "This provision is subject to any subsequent recognized bargaining agreement between the employer and his employees." That is understandable, however, and does not detract from the commitment made by labor and United Way. It is an understanding based on "these and other good and sufficient reasons as well as for the purpose of defining the mutually advantageous relationship of many years standing."

What has the outcome been? To an effective extent, employees of unionized shops have been enrolled in payroll deduction plans which are a significant source of funds for United Way. While there is no doubt of the often-attested-to contributions made to United Way by AFL-CIO-CSA representatives, there's a dearth of data on how much union members contribute to annual fund-raising campaigns. But labor's contributions to the United Fund were summed up on request by Richard E. Booth, executive director of the United Fund of Greater New York:*

After 20 years in New York, I am more convinced than ever of the importance of labor participation and support in the United Way movement. Over the years I've seen labor play an increasingly bigger part, not only in dollar contributions, but in its membership's involvement in community activities. This continued involvement is due, in part, to local United Way labor staffs and their involvement with Central Labor Council community services programs. Through these labor staffs, union memberships have gained a better understanding of the United Way concept and have consequently become more generous.

But there seems to be some question of just how much union members contribute to United Way fund drives. That's because UWA claims it cannot separate union and non-union employee contributions. Mounting skepticism over the years has finally drawn from UWA an estimate that labor's share amounts to about 48 percent, but the AFL-CIO considers "on the order of one-half or more" of the $1.2 billion in donations to UWA to be more reasonable. And the contribu-

*Subsequently executive director of Tri-State United Way; retired in 1978.

tions of union members would undoubtedly be increased considerably if labor received even a fraction of the recognition given corporations.

It would be shortsighted to assume fund raising is the sole assistance of unions to United Way. Equally important is the role played by CSA "reps" across the country. Full-time, salaried employees of UWA, the "reps" encourage and promote labor participation, but they also work with community service committees of independent unions, as well as with AFL-CIO affiliates.

They develop programs, such as summer camping for under-privileged children, and community service seminars, and, most importantly, act as referral agents for unions and individuals with problems requiring the services of public or private social welfare and health agencies. While their role is now accepted as indispensable, both by labor and United Way, only some twenty-odd years ago it was a moot point whether there was any justification for paid labor "reps" on United Way staffs.

Indeed, Louis L. Levine, as a community services "rep," wrote a lengthy tract, *Why Labor Staff*, in 1955 to justify the role of the paid labor representative:

> The union is of great importance to the individual member. The loyalties developed in the union group are particularly strong—much stronger, in fact, than the loyalties of members of other groups. The union member looks to his organization for improvement of his economic status, for consideration of his grievances, and, in a very real sense, for the protection of the health and welfare of his family. In addition, union organizations are a fact of life in industrial communities. Community organizations for health and welfare cannot ignore the opportunity to use these channels. There is no other effective way in which to reach union members.[2]

There's no need now to try to justify the use of salaried labor representatives on United Way staffs. Quite the contrary. Despite having its own staff, Labor Rehab in New York has not put an end to the practice of having two "reps"—Sid Lew and Frank Livolsi—serve full-time with the United Fund of Greater New York.

In a sense, Labor Rehab is the prototype, indeed, the forerunner, of the Labor Agencies which the AFL-CIO Community Services Department is now actively organizing across the country. Labor Rehab was organized in 1961, but the first mention of a Labor Agency was in 1971, when the AFL-CIO Executive Council adopted a resolution calling on central labor bodies to develop labor community services agencies "to perform, extend and expand their community service functions." The reasons for setting up agencies were outlined in the resolution:

> More people must be reached. Better service must be given. Experimental

programs must be developed to meet unmet needs. Successful programs must be extended. Additional methods of financing must be discovered. New relationships with governmental and private agencies must be developed. Organizational and administrative relationships must be clarified and made more effective.

Three years later, CSA director Perlis, who was responsible for carrying out the new concept, was able to report the first agency had completed an experimental, eighteen-month trial and had been funded as a permanent member of United Way in Denver. That was Labor's Community Agency, a member of Mile High United Way of Denver. Perlis has tirelessly traveled the air lanes, addressing community service committees on the ways and means of organizing agencies.

Incorporation as a nonprofit, membership corporation is a complex matter best handled by an attorney, but there was and is decided opposition from United Way, which has been understandably loathe to allocate funds to special interest groups of unproven value. Rolland E. Hoffman, executive director of Mile High UW, was candid in explaining his reluctance to accept the concept. In a report to his board of trustees, Hoffman said:

> I was very honestly opposed to this concept. I felt it would create a schism between Labor and United Way. To safeguard the UW, I proposed a pilot program to give the Agency time to produce and give us time to evaluate. What has happened over that period of time has been a very pleasant surprise. The staff of this Labor Agency has bent over backward to work cooperatively with the United Way staff. There has been much greater support by Labor leaders and rank and file members to the UW campaign than before.

> I have come to the conclusion that even though this is funding of a program that at first looks like a special interest group, it would be advantageous for the United Way Board of Trustees to accept Labor's Community Agency as a member Agency.

The board did accept Labor's Community Agency as a member of UWA under an agreement signed November 20, 1972. The concept has spread, but it has not been easy to achieve. The Long Island Labor Education and Community Services Agency, for example, was incorporated in 1973, two years after it was first proposed, but it did not win developmental funding from the Nassau-Suffolk United Way until 1976 and full acceptance as a member agency until 1977. From first-hand involvement, the author can describe the dispute.

The Community Services Committee of the Long Island Federation of Labor first broached the idea at the prodding of Perlis, eager to broaden its services to members. Lacking funds and staff, the committee of volunteers and a single labor "rep" at United Way were able to do little more than act as a referral agency. Any intensive follow-up on any case was impractical.

Incorporation made it possible, in accordance with AFL-CIO recommendation, "to receive financial support from local united funds and to enter into contractual arrangements with appropriate governmental and voluntary agencies for contributions and grants for special programs and projects." These capabilities substantially extended the functions of CSA "reps." Equally important, it was the agency that became the service organization, thus involving not only independent unions, but the entire community.

This became apparent when one of the first appeals for help came from an employee of the unorganized Grumman Aerospace Corporation, seeking a summer camp for a handicapped child. The arrangements were made, following adoption of a resolution that the Labor Agency had been created to provide "those services deemed necessary to meet the social, health and educational needs of Long Island's working people," regardless of union affiliation.

That excerpt from the minutes indicates part of the purposes for which labor agencies are organized. Other purposes outlined in the incorporation papers included:

To provide professional, vocational, social, educational and other counselling for workers and members of their families whose medical or related problems result in impairment of their ability to obtain or continue in their jobs.

To develop, sponsor, promote and conduct comprehensive programs to provide services deemed necessary to meet the social, health and educational needs of working men and women . . .

To establish a referral service whereby members of the community with . . . problems . . . would be assisted in obtaining the necessary help from other community organizations . . .

To provide continuing education programs for training union specialists in community services, consumer education, educational resources, mental health programs and occupational health programs . . .

To provide an organization through which trade unions will become involved in the development of labor studies, liberal arts programs and other union leadership training programs.

To recruit and train trade union representatives to serve on boards, committees and advisory groups of other planning, health and welfare, community services and educational institutions; and to develop training for those trade union members . . . to become consumer representatives with the agencies that provide such services . . .

To raise, collect, procure and assemble funds, credits and gifts as well as grants from governmental and private philanthropic organizations for the purpose of financing the programs of the corporation.

It was undoubtedly only the last of these purposes that drew any fire, since there is an understandably reasonable reluctance to spread United Way allocations any thinner by admitting any untested organization that appears to be a special interest group. And one more agency applying for funds leaves that much less for the competing agencies. The reluctance to welcome the Labor Agency appeared to foreclose any thought that a Labor Agency affiliated with United Way would stimulate union members to give more to fund drives.

More union support proved to be a convincing selling point, especially when the labor participation chairman of the fund raising drive was an officer of the Labor Agency. Part of the money, after all, would be going to labor's community services arm. Amicable relations prevailed between labor and United Way on Long Island, with two trade unionists serving as vice presidents of UW and six others on the UW executive committee. Labor representatives also took part in the allocation of funds and the Labor Agency has been assured of an allocation of funds annually, even if not up to labor's expectations.

Across the country, by the middle of 1976, despite all opposition and stumbling blocks, nineteen labor agencies had been incorporated and twelve of them were in operation, or "somewhat better," Perlis said, than he had expected two years earlier. His goal had been five agencies in full-time operation, another operating but as yet not incorporated and six more incorporated, but not operating. Two others were being formed.

Incorporated and in full-time operation at the end of 1977 were:

Labor's Community Service Agency, Phoenix, Arizona
Labor's Community Agency, Denver, Colorado
United Labor Agency of Greater Washington, D.C.
United Labor Agency, Jacksonville, Florida
Labor Agency for Community Service, Baltimore, Maryland
Union Organization for Social Service, Camden, New Jersey
Labor Education and Community Services Agency, Melville, New York
Central Labor Rehabilitation Council of New York, New York
United Labor Agency, Cleveland, Ohio
Lorain County Labor Agency, Lorain, Ohio
Labor's Community Service Agency, Portland, Oregon
Bucks County Labor's Community Service Agency, Bristol, Pennsylvania
Whatcom Community Services Labor Agency, Bellingham, Washington
Labor Agency, King County Labor Council of Washington, AFL-CIO
    Community Services Division, Seattle, Washington
Marathon County Community Services Agency AFL-CIO, Wausau, Wisconsin

Not incorporated but operating was the Labor Agency of Mentor, Ohio. The six agencies which had been incorporated, but were not yet in full-time operation, were the Community Service Agency of North Carolina, Raleigh; Organized Labor's Agency for Community Services, Greater Kansas City Area; Community Services Activities, Omaha; Labor Community Services of Merrimack Valley, Lowell/Lawrence/Haverhill, Massachusetts; and United Labor Agency, Atlanta.

In a closely related field, unions have a symbiotic relationship with the American National Red Cross in areas which go beyond fund raising, since union members frequently require the services offered by the Red Cross in floods, storms and fires, in case of injury, illness or surgery requiring first aid or other assistance, especially blood donations.

It is a close relationship because so many problems faced by working people can be resolved only by the Red Cross. An added factor is the widespread use of union volunteers and union halls during disasters, while the official AFL-CIO attitude on the sacredness of human blood tends to make close allies of labor and the Red Cross:

> The American Blood Commission is an organization brought about largely as the result of AFL-CIO action. Since the Executive Council called in 1971 for "a nationally controlled blood program . . . which would insure adequate quantities of volunteer blood," the American National Red Cross, the White House and others have responded in favor of a national blood policy designed to eliminate "commercialism."
>
> It is possible, of course, that the commission may achieve one voluntary, non-commercial, high-quality blood system, but its history of compromise leads one to suspect that this new effort may once again result in failure to meet a major health need of the American people.
>
> The AFL-CIO position is based on three major concerns—moral, medical and economic.
>
> It is morally unacceptable for a humane society to permit the sale of human tissue, such as blood.
>
> It is medically inexcusable for an advanced society to permit the sale of high-risk, commercially bought blood which causes sickness and death among thousands of its citizens.
>
> It is economically unsound in any society to sustain competing blood banks with complicated bookkeeping and credit systems as well as high prices for the blood itself.[3]

The AFL-CIO position on blood banks is that "low-risk blood should be made available, free of charge, to all who need it," a position which dates back, at least, to the Statement of Understanding signed

October 18, 1960, by Perlis, as CSA director, and Dr. Sam T. Gibson, Red Cross blood program director. It provided for "strengthening and development of a coordinated blood program" based upon the principles of the two organizations.

Labor's insistence on high standards appears to be paying off. In June, 1977, the *New York Times* reported that the "nation appears to be moving slowly toward almost total reliance on volunteer non-paid donors" in the use of 10 million pints of blood a year collected for transfusion.

New York City, a union town if ever there was one, requires from 800 to 900 thousand units of blood annually for its hospitals, Bill Jones, labor liaison to the Metropolitan New York Division of Red Cross, estimated. Among the unions which have "good blood bank programs," Jones named the following: Local 3, International Brotherhood of Electrical Workers; District Council 9, Brotherhood of Painters; Metallic Lathers Local 46; United Store Workers; Transport Workers Union Local 100; Local 1-2, Utility Workers of America; International Ladies Garment Workers Union; Local 1-S, Retail, Wholesale and Department Store Union; and Local 3036, New York City Taxi Drivers Union.

And yet Jones had to concede, "If 5 percent of the trade unionists participated in the blood bank program, we'd have no problem getting enough blood for New York's daily hospital needs. As it is, we have critical shortages every year in July and August and from Christmas to New Year's Day."

The appraisal was revealing because it came from a trade unionist, not in rancor, but sadness. (Jones was formerly president of Hospital Workers Local 420 AFSCME.) His data on blood donated by union members went back to 1969, recording that as many as 150 New York City unions had made blood donations in a single year, accounting for as much as 46,000 units of blood donated.

Considering there has been better than a 413 percent gain in blood donations since 1969, and Jones' anticipation that "we will do even better during the next five years in working toward a total blood collection service for the division areas," his disparagement of labor's contribution indicates he'll be satisfied with nothing less than perfection.

But Jones was more sanguine in reflecting on labor's other contributions to Red Cross programs. Not only are unions a source of money through the United Fund, but in donations made directly to Red Cross. (These latter gifts to the Metropolitan New York Division are turned over to the United Fund.) He described the reaction of ILGWU members to a first aid training program: "Two of the graduates told me they were able to revive a woman who fainted in the shop. They were elated over the quick way their training paid off."

Jones recalled a union family which lost its home on Christmas Day in a fire. Red Cross had helped resettle the family, and the help was appreciated.

"Some time later," he recalled, "the head of the family came up here to see me and volunteered to work for the Red Cross in any way we wanted. We put him to work."

But overall, Jones was not satisfied with the response he was getting from New York's unions after spending years on the job plugging away for more union participation.

> I get calls from community service people asking for help. Union members come here asking for blood, but few of them want to take first aid training. I get calls from unions to come to their meetings to explain our programs, but I don't get many such calls. We need volunteers to man vehicles, to relocate families in emergencies, to be on call, to help out as instructors, to act as clerical workers. But we don't get enough union members as volunteers.

That seems to reflect an inbred American personality trait: *never volunteer*—a trait which has given rise to many a tale, especially in the armed forces. But it is equally true that in an emergency—a flood, hurricane, catastrophic fire or tornado—volunteers need not be called; they appear as though by magic.

The roll call of union ties with community agencies could be continued indefinitely, with only the certainty that the farther one looked, the more would be found, indicating labor not only has a stake in the community, but has accepted the responsibility and become deeply involved in its survival. Not enough, to be sure, not nearly enough; that is a point which may not be attained, but will remain a goal.

But involvement in community life is no more incongruous for organized labor than Nelson Rockefeller's lifelong devotion to government. What is extraordinary is that the concern workers show for community institutions should necessitate comment. After all, workers and their families constitute a preponderant proportion of the population. What would be extraordinary would be a total lack of interest in the community by either workers or their unions.

As workers, consumers, taxpayers, voters, members of fraternal orders, churchgoers (or agnostics), environmentalists or hard hats, sick or well, labor is as much part of the community as the clergy, the medical profession, the bankers, the Confraternity of the Blessed Virgin or the mom-and-pop delicatessen owners.

Labor has had as distinguished a representative on the highest court of the land as any other facet of the community: Supreme Court Justice Arthur J. Goldberg, the author of the merger agreement between the AFL and the CIO.

147

It was a former international secretary-treasurer of the United Mine Workers of America, Representative William Wilson, who introduced the bill in Congress creating the U.S. Labor Department. And another Wilson, President Woodrow Wilson, appointed him the first secretary of that cabinet post.

Labor today has a handful of representatives in Congress—not, to be sure, representing organized labor, but their constituents, who include trade unionists. The Congressional Directory of the Ninety-fifth Congress listed twelve members whose biographical sketches included union affiliations.

There were others, presumably, who were serving in Congress during 1977 who did not reveal past or present labor affiliations. For example, Representative Bruce Frank Vento, D-F-L, fourth district of Minnesota, stated he was a former teacher, but the American Federation of Teachers hailed his election by claiming him as a member of the Minneapolis Federation of Teachers, Local 59.

Two labor representatives did not come back to Congress in the November, 1976, election. They were Representative Joseph E. Karth of St. Paul, Minnesota, who had been an international representative of the Oil, Chemical and Atomic Workers for ten years, and Representative Ken Kechler of Huntington, West Virginia, who proclaimed in the directory of the Ninety-fourth Congress that he had "actively campaigned for the late Jock Yablonski and for reform of the United Mineworkers of America through election of Arnold Miller."

Unions are composed of workers and workers are people, people who not only sit in Congress, but on state, national and international deliberative bodies as well. They are so much a part of the establishment that at least three labor leaders were members of the prestigious Tripartite Commission assembled by David Rockefeller in 1973 to consider, *inter alia*, the "excess of democracy" that afflicts the industrial economies of the United States, Europe and Japan.[4] Labor's representatives were I.W. Abel, Leonard Woodcock and Lane Kirkland. But seventy-five years ago Samuel Gompers hobnobbed with Andrew Carnegie, Mark Hanna and William Howard Taft in the National Civic Federation, which was equally concerned over the economy. Very little changes over the decades; American labor remains part of the community.

The community is no longer provincial, but worldwide, and so is American labor's participation. The AFL (and subsequently the AFL-CIO) has been part of the International Labor Organization since its formation in 1919. Gompers played a key role in shaping ILO as a supporter of President Wilson's program to channel international labor into a conservative direction calculated to avert revival of the Socialist International after World War I.

The ILO has long been effective in promoting labor and social justice through the adoption of "conventions" on international work standards. In 1976 alone the ILO was responsible for changing ninety-five pieces of legislation in fifty-five countries, while in 1977 the ILO was gratified to see Spain adopt its conventions on freedom of association and the right of workers to organize. Annually the ILO spends about $40 million to provide technical assistance to underdeveloped countries, including management training for some 25,000 persons in ILO projects.

The unique agency, composed of tripartite delegations from labor, employers and governments of 135 nations, had the warm support of the AFL-CIO until the Soviet Union resumed its membership in 1954 after a fourteen-year absence. Resentment crystallized in 1974 when the Red-Arab Axis pushed through a resolution condemning Israel as racist, leading the AFL-CIO and the U.S. Chamber of Commerce to insist on U.S. withdrawal from the ILO.

"The ILO has been operating on a double standard for some 21 years," said Kirkland. "The double standard is characterized by a contradiction: the uncritical acceptance of the nondemocratic, repressive system of government represented by the Soviet Union."

The U.S. filed notice of intent to leave the ILO on November 5, 1975, and did withdraw on Novermber 1, 1977, with an announcement by Secretary of Labor Ray Marshall that touched off bitter criticism in the United Nations. But labor was not united on the issue. Ernest Lee, director of the AFL-CIO International Department, echoing George Meany's unswerving anti-Communist stand, said, "We won't play if the game is crooked—even if it is the only game in town."

But UAW President Douglas Fraser felt that pulling out of the "one international agency which has played such a central role in promoting human rights for workers, our hope of improving the lives of many will greatly diminish."

George Meany's hope was that somewhere "down the road" the U.S. would rejoin the ILO. Labor must remain active in the world community, even if only to lessen the inroads that Communism is making on the existing corporate economy.[5]

Notes

1. Correspondence with George Atkinson, AFL-CIO-BSA liaison, Boy Scouts of America, 6 May 1976.
2. "Why Labor Staff?" p. 5.

149

3. Report of the AFL-CIO Executive Council, 1975, p. 203.
4. Vide Michel Crozier, Samuel P. Huntington and Joji Watanuki, *The Crisis of Democracy* (New York: New York University Press, 1975).
5. Vide Ronald Radosh, *American Labor and United States Foreign Policy* (New York: Random House, 1969).

11.
Labor and
the Nation's Health

Petrified with fear on hearing his physician declare, "I'm afraid we're going to have to take out most of your stomach," he trembled for the longest time in his hospital bed, unwilling to accept the verdict of a doctor he no longer trusted.

"What do I do now?" he asked himself again and again. "Where do I turn for advice? After all, Dr. G. is probably wrong." (He was, subsequent events proved.) A thought occurred to him, the same thought, he recalled with surprise, that had come to him a decade earlier when his father was dying of cancer in Los Angeles. In pain, he reached gingerly for the black book on the bedside table. Looking up the number of the Community Services Committee, he dialed.

"Tony," he cried out, breaking into tears, "I need help."

Unions are more concerned over the cost of health care than the state of the nation's health, but for obvious reasons. There is a pervasive illusion that the U.S. health record, like everything else in the best of all possible countries, is the finest in the world; the cold, hard fact is that the cost of health care has escalated beyond endurance and the health record testifies to the hazards of living in a highly industrialized society.

The ten leading causes of death in the U.S. are not led by homicide or suicide, as you might think, but by major cardiovascular diseases, including heart disease. While it's true that accidents, as a cause of death, do rank up near the top, influenza, pneumonia, diabetes, diseases of early infancy, cirrhosis of the liver, bronchitis, emphysema and asthma are also leading contenders.

Indeed, the U.S. has little to boast about in preserving life. The number of infant deaths is a shameful record, since the U.S. ranks fifteenth among the industrial nations of the world. And in life expectancy, the U.S. has ranked as low as nineteenth (for males) and seventh (for females).

The future may hold further fears, since questions arise daily as industry pours pollutants of undetermined toxicity into the air. The Environmental Protection Agency conceded it did not know whether "significant concentrations" of carcinogenic chemicals in the air around industrial plants to Staten Island, New York, and New Jersey's Newark, Hoboken, Clifton, Kearney and Passaic, were injurious. But it made the same "assessment" earlier of carcinogens which turned up "repeatedly" in tests conducted near plants in Baltimore, Houston and Los Angeles.

What may be responsible in large measure for two of the major causes of death—cancer and pneumonia—probably is not as obvious as the credulous would believe. Eighty percent of the incidence of cancer in the U.S. may be attributed to industrial pollution.

Unions cannot be said to be overly concerned with either environmental pollution or diseases. Indeed, far more attention has gone into coping with alcoholism and mental illness, undoubtedly because of the high proportion of grievances based on alcoholism and the danger inherent in working alongside an emotionally disturbed worker.

But there's no question of the intensity of effort unions have poured into attacking the high costs of the nation's health bill. If the American labor movement unswervingly believes in one concept, it is that a national health security program is vital to the future of the country. What has focused labor's attention on health security is the cost of medical care. Over $163 billion was poured into the health sector in 1978 to provide supplies, construction and research to an industry employing over 4 million persons, encompassing a billion physician visits and 250 million hospital inpatient days a year. But with 9 percent of the gross national product poured into health care, the results were far from satisfactory, Professor Rashi Fein of the Harvard Medical School is convinced. He pointed out: "It is inefficient. It wastes resources. It fails to deliver care to large numbers of people who cannot afford to pay for services or who do not find services available when and where they need them."[1]

The failure to deliver adequate health care at reasonable cost may be attributed in part to inflation, but also to fraud, estimated at as much as half of the $15 billion a year spent on Medicaid; unused or misused hospital beds; and 2.4 million unnecessary operations a year.

Organized labor has marshaled its lobbies in a campaign to seek enactment of a national health security program, impelled by the widespread loss of health insurance coverage for millions of unemployed during the 1974–76 recession as much as by the example Western European nations and neighboring Canada have set. (The United Kingdom's National Health Service has been severely criticized, but the critics neglect to mention the sad state of health care in England before NHS was enacted in 1946.) The U.S. remains the only industrialized nation in the world that does not have a national system of health care for its people.

Labor has been pressing for enactment of the Kennedy-Waxman bill establishing the Health Care for All Americans Act, but the legislation made little headway in four years despite a Democratic Congress. Any act which would call for a Social Security operation funded by payroll withholding was bound to meet with strong opposition. (Administrative costs plus profits of health insurance companies come to a combined $33.3 billion a year, the Department of Health, Education and Welfare estimated.)

The position of the AFL-CIO was expressed in 1975 by the Executive Council:

> America needs the Health Security program, the only national health insurance proposal which is based on social insurance principles and provides comprehensive care for all Americans. An improved bill . . . was introduced in the present Congress with Rep. James Corman (D–Calif.) and Sen. Edward Kennedy (D–Mass.) as principal sponsors. It is the best national health insurance proposal before the Congress.[2]

Labor's concern over national health is not a recent development, but reflects a deep-seated involvement in the health and welfare of the worker. It is a concern which made itself apparent in a variety of ways, dating back to the ten shillings a week paid some 200-odd years ago by New York carpenters to members "who fall sick, or through age or accidents are rendered incapable to getting his livelihood." It has resulted in union-sponsored educational programs on the early detection of cancer; collective bargaining agreements providing for health and welfare benefits, including medical, hospital, dental and prescription drug plans; group health, accident and life insurance policies; medical centers built by unions; drug abuse programs; and rehabilitation of alcoholics.

The Sidney Hillman Health Center, for example, was opened April 16, 1951, by the Amalgamated Clothing Workers and the Clothing Manufacturers Association as a "life extension institute that will not only cure illness, but prevent illness and prolong the lives of our members." In 1976 the center's physicians saw an average of 1,500 patients weekly, while hundreds of other patients came for a number of outpatient diagnostic, therapeutic and preventive services. The International Ladies Garment Workers Union Health Center provides diagnostic and therapeutic care for 150,000 members and their families. Its doctors make about 1,000 visits daily and the center provides 1,000 ancillary services through a staff of 200 employees.

But not all unions can afford medical centers or can bargain with employers to subsidize them. Most, however, are confronting the ever-present problem of alcoholism and, in recent years, drug addiction, too. Alcoholism is a major problem for the nation, which runs up an annual bill in excess of $25 billion to treat 10 million alcoholics, according to the National Institute on Alcohol Abuse and Alcoholism. Work-time lost, medical expenses and motor vehicle accidents underlie the high cost. And one of the major causes of grievances preoccupying unions is discharges for drinking.

While unions do not attempt to treat alcoholism, they do much to educate workers in understanding the nature of the illness, referring members to appropriate agencies for treatment; i.e., Alcoholics Anonymous, the Salvation Army, voluntary citizens' councils affiliated with the National Council on Alcoholism and state and local health departments.

Unions are encouraged by the AFL-CIO to develop community alcoholism action programs with the assistance of the AFL-CIO-CSA liaison representatives of the National Council on Alcoholism or the AFL-CIO Department of Community Services.

The United Steelworkers of America, through its education department, has developed an "action guide," outlining for its local affiliates methods of establishing labor-management rehabilitation programs for alcoholics. This approach is based on contracts between the USWA and a number of firms, which read, in part: " . . . the union and the company agree to cooperate at the plant level in encouraging employees afflicted with alcoholism to undergo a coordinated program directed to the objective of their rehabilitation."[3]

A veritable flood of literature is being circulated throughout the labor movement, not only by international unions, but by community service committees, labor agencies and the CSA Department, seeking to convince workers with alcoholism problems that the illness can be treated, that the alcoholic can be rehabilitated. Two examples are the leaflets, *What Every Worker Should Know About Alcoholism* and *Labor and Alcoholism*. The former, published by the AFL-CIO-CSA in cooperation with the National Council on Alcoholism, suggests what practical steps can be taken to develop programs to aid alcoholics, while the latter, issued by the National Council on Alcoholism in cooperation with AFL-CIO-CSA, outlines the labor-management joint approach in coping with the problem. And discussion, as well as the printed word, is used to convey the story, so that local unions will take action.

Alcoholism, however, is only one of several critical problems under attack by unions. Drug abuse and mental or emotional disturbances are also being confronted.

The AFL-CIO-CSA leaflet on drug abuse directs community service committees on providing treatment facilities for drug abuse victims, training counselors to handle the problem, obtaining materials explaining drug abuse and initiating community and labor-management programs. It is not a leaflet filled with sanctimonious platitudes but hard-hitting, practical recommendations on where to look for help, complete with names and addresses of the American Social Health Association and the AFL-CIO-CSA.

New York's Central Labor Rehabilitation Council has issued its own *Drug and Alcohol Rehabilitation Handbook for Local Unions and Union Counselors,* instructing them on how to refer drug users to Labor Rehab for treatment. Labor Rehab was instrumental in establishing a drug abuse referral service for union members and their families with the cooperation of the New York State Drug Abuse Control Commission, the National Institute on Drug Abuse and the American Social Health Association.

The United Auto Workers, General Motors, Chrysler, and Ford Motor are jointly conducting programs to help auto workers with their alcohol and drug problems. A comprehensive pilot drug abuse program covering five GM plants in Detroit with 30,000 workers was inaugurated in August, 1974, under a $260,000 grant, assuring workers they could seek help on a confidential basis without fear of disciplinary action. GM already had 100 labor-management committees in the U.S. and Canada dealing with alcohol addiction with marked success.

The announcement of the new drug abuse program also reported that 60 percent of the 3,000 alcoholics treated since 1972 showed substantial job improvement. Chrysler began its alcohol treatment program in 1968 and added the hard drug program in 1970, while Ford, also with the cooperation of the UAW, has a drug and alcohol abuse program coordinator at each work location, offering aid in contacting community agencies for referrals.

The UAW alcoholism program has been widely praised, not only for its effectiveness, but the initiative the union has shown in persuading auto companies to adopt its proposals. But the program goes far beyond treatment and rehabilitation.

In Missouri, for example, the UAW alcoholism program went outside the shop to help formulate policy in the community. The UAW took the initiative in forming the United Confederation of Labor to mount an effective lobby in opposing the liquor industry's campaign to resist tax increases on alcoholic beverages. Professor David J. Pittman, director of the Social Science Institute at Washington University, St. Louis, has cited the UAW in Missouri as "an effective model of collective responsibility."[4]

The same sense of responsibility has been shown by the maritime unions, which recognize that even though drinking is prohibited on

American merchant vessels, alcoholism is a critical problem on the high seas. The Seafarers International Union established an alcoholism rehabilitation center at Piney Point, Maryland, in January, 1976, and within a year could report it had treated more than 100 sailors. The National Maritime Union got its program under way in March, 1977, when it hired a guidance counselor and turned to the International Longshoremen's Association for assistance in setting up the program.

Alcoholism is as much a problem on the nation's docks as it is on the high seas. The ILA's alcoholism program should prove to be an exacting model for the NMU to follow. Underway for several years, the program covers some 25,000 employees of ninety-six companies under contract to the ILA as well as the employees' 60,000 dependents.

Initially funded by a federal grant, the program operates under a memorandum of agreement which is part of the basic agreement between the New York Shipping Association and the ILA of the Port of Greater New York, comprising some forty local unions. But make no mistake about it, the alcoholism rehabilitation program was undertaken by union initiative; indeed, it may be traced to the initiative of a shop steward who readily admits he is a recovered alcoholic:

> The grant itself is the outgrowth of the experience of one such shop steward who is himself a recovered alcoholic, John J. Hennessy. Having recovered from his illness, Jack sought help in making the same sort of recovery possible for others in the ILA. He first contacted Gerald R. Waters, Sr., administrator of the AFL-CIO Central Rehabilitation Council of New York Inc., and through him was put in touch with John R. Butler, associate commissioner of the New York State Division of Alcoholism.[5]

Hennessy today is program director and his staff consists of two full-time and two part-time employees. Vincent J. Dowling, a recovered alcoholic, works full time as the alcoholism counselor at the New York clinic of the NYSA-ILA Medical Center together with the program's secretary-receptionist, Margaret M. Brady. The program also employs two part-time field advisors.

Initially the program was publicized in a front-page article in the Local 824 Bulletin, and subsequently by a letter sent to every ILA member's home. This was followed up by articles in other ILA journals and on posters displayed in clinics, hiring halls, union offices, piers and terminals. The reaction was impressive: In its first year the program handled 1,128 referrals, an overwhelming proportion of whom were found to be alcoholics. The great majority of the alcoholics came to the program with little desire to do anything about their drinking problems. But some 714 agreed to enter the program. Despite the lack of motivation, 70 percent of them were rehabilitated. (Dropouts and drinkers were considered "failures," even though some of the latter may recover in the future.)

Each referral has his medical history checked, is given a physical examination and assigned to treatment meeting his needs, either in a hospital or other facility for detoxification, if needed, to a rest and rehabilitation center, if indicated, or directly to Alcoholics Anonymous. Where additional help is required, the alcoholic is sent to a treatment facility for a minimum of two weeks.

Treatment is paid for by the NYSA-ILA Welfare Fund, a trustee-governed body with a self-insured program. Eleven treatment centers are under contract to the alcoholism program, providing the best treatment available at significant cost savings.

Once the longshoreman has completed treatment, a follow-up phase of the program ensures he will not retrogress, since frequent attendance at unit meetings is mandatory.

What has made the program acceptable is the certainty that each case is kept confidential. Indeed, this assurance is embodied in the joint policy statement establishing the alcoholism program: "All medical records will be maintained in strict confidence."

Equally important in establishing the credibility of the program is the knowledge that Hennessy had been a shop steward and an alcoholic.

ILA President Teddy Gleason would like to see the program extended to the entire Atlantic and Gulf Coast District of the ILA in cooperation with the North Atlantic Shipping Association. His views on the alcoholism program, as might be expected, are enthusiastic:

> In my view, the development of a good alcoholism program in the industry is one of the most promising and exciting goals in our battle against the disease of alcoholism.
>
> Alcoholism not only affects profits, but ruins lives, and has a devastating effect on families. Through this new service, we expect to be able to offer aid to the ILA member or his dependent having a problem with alcohol, and thereby assist him in maintaining his job, his home, and his place in the community.

Counseling and referral are important aspects of rehabilitation in mental health as well as alcoholism. The scope of the mental health problem is staggering. More than 7 percent of all hospitals in the U.S. are psychiatric institutions, but the latter account for over 27 percent of all hospital beds.

Labor's community services counselors have long known what sociologists in recent years have begun to confirm: that prolonged unemployment during recessions and mental illness have a strong correlation. Family discord, child abuse, alcoholism and deaths from heart disease are other factors showing a strong correlation to unemployment rates.

The most common means of obtaining help for the disturbed worker is through the intervention of a counselor alerted to the problem by fellow workers or direct appeal of the troubled worker to the counselor, a CSA "rep" or a Labor Agency.

The plight of the mentally ill worker has long been recognized by the National Maritime Union, the United Mine Workers, the Amalgamated Clothing Workers and the Retail Clerks International Union. Admittedly, not enough has been done, but that's hardly strange, considering the popular reaction to "nuts," and the suspicions unions have about social workers engaged in psychiatry. In a study surveying labor's approach to mental health, Hyman J. Weiner observed:

> Unfortunately, however, the mental health field finds itself isolated and estranged from the world of work. For too long these two social networks have passed each other like ships in the night, each losing out by lack of real contact with the other. As a result of this situation the mental patient is usually left to his own resources in overcoming the barriers to finding and holding a job.[6]

Treatment for mental illness has at long last become part of the package of benefits covered by group health insurance programs—a field in which unions are active, and far beyond the scope of acting as agents for insurance carriers.

There are more than 762,000 persons enrolled in the Health Insurance Plan of Greater New York (HIP), the largest group health care program on the East Coast. As should be expected, unions have played a major role in the medical plan since it started operations in 1947.

At least 50 percent of the subscribers are New York City municipal employees, the remainder being residents of New York City and Nassau and Suffolk counties covered by labor or management health and welfare programs. The high proportion of municipal workers may be traced to HIP's origins. Mayor Fiorello H. LaGuardia urged his personal physician, Dr. George Baehr, to draw up a prepayment plan providing comprehensive medical care for city employees who, he noted, were frequently in financial distress due to indebtedness incurred during illness.

Since the city's municipal workers are union members, it was inevitable unions would play a major role in the administration of HIP. Its board of directors in 1976 included seven trade unionists out of a total membership of twenty-three directors. While that is hardly a controlling voice in board decisions, it should be pointed out that the chairman of the board was Barry Feinstein, president of Teamsters Local 237, and William Michelson, president of the United Storeworkers, served ten years as a member of the board and was chairman of the executive committee. It is also pertinent to note that the "users" or consumers of medical services have yet to attain any control over health costs. But their influence is not be be underestimated.

Union involvement is inevitable on two levels: through negotiation of health and welfare plans; and concern over the high cost of medical care, a factor which is impelling an increasing number of unions to undertake self-insured health and welfare plans.

Just how many labor unions have members enrolled in HIP? An annual report detailed 12.7 percent of the total enrollment to trade unions, but an additional 55.9 percent were employees of New York City and related agencies. This block of 411,319 persons was preponderantly made up of trade unionists and their dependents. Another 8.6 percent were covered by state and federal agencies, which, in New York City, means a high level of union members.

The prepaid health care which HIP provides through twenty-eight medical groups and eighteen other health centers covers everything from treatment of a cold to brain surgery, in the doctor's office, the medical centers or in hospital, but, when possible, at home. It does not, however, cover hospital expenses, only the doctor's services. HIP is more than an insurance carrier. Its facilities provide preventive medicine, all-inclusive, paid-for care, night and weekend emergency service and the use of so-called super-specialists when appropriate. More impressive is the constant auditing of all doctor visits, intensive research and feedback provided by thirty consumer councils.

If unions play an active but not controlling role in HIP, they do so, too, in other health insurance plans. Blue Cross and Blue Shield of Greater New York has been functioning for forty years and in all that time, Frank Donovan has been the labor representative on the staff. A trade unionist whose father was an organizer for Teamsters Joint Council 16, Donovan is a member of Local 153, Office and Professional Employees International Union. (Ben J. Cohan, manager of community services for Blue Cross, was formerly business manager of the local.) "This is a union-oriented organization," Donovan said. "Fully 70 percent of our business here is the result of union contracts."

That's a significant proportion of the 9 million subscribers in a metropolitan area of seventeen counties whose hospital and medical expenses are covered by Blue Cross-Blue Shield plans.

Donovan's not the only labor link to Blue Cross. The forty-one-member board of directors in 1976 included five trade unionists from as many unions—enough to give consumers a voice in policy matters, but far from adequate.

Donovan's dual role as promoter of Blue Cross "products" (he's one of seven on the staff serving labor accounts) and as developer of union pension and welfare trust funds—"so I can serve the members"—makes his job crucial to the union subscriber. Of all the Blue Cross plans in the U.S., the New York plan is, by far, the largest in enrollment. And Donovan estimates he has handled Blue Cross enrollments for 406 unions in close to forty years with Blue Cross.

Despite the constantly escalating costs of health care (1,000 percent from 1950 to 1977, President Carter estimated), Blue Cross does enable millions of Americans to meet their hospital bills, but no longer at a reasonable premium. Whether Blue Cross serves the community as a nonprofit organization devoted to promoting the social welfare, or whether it is a collection agency serving the American Hospital Association, are questions that must be answered before a national health insurance plan is enacted. The Health Law Project of the University of Pennsylvania contends Blue Cross is the financing arm of American hospitals.[7] What would the Blue Cross role be in a national health program?

While labor representation on Blue Cross boards of directors is inadequate to keep costs down, it is characteristic of the labor point of view that Donovan sees himself as "helping the union member" in an assessment of his work with Blue Cross. "I have a certain consciousness about the community," he said. "I want to do something for the community. And in Blue Cross I do this by relieving the strain on people who cannot afford good medical care...."

Meanwhile, Blue Cross broadened its operations, entering the field of health maintenance organizations (HMO), an area of great concern to unions. In New York, Blue Cross established its first community health program, offering prepaid group practice to subscribers in 1973. Four years later the New York State Health Department gave its approval to Blue Cross to expand the pilot operation in the metropolitan area.

While the HMO offers prepaid preventive medicine and hospital care under one roof as a means of containing spiraling hospital costs—subscribers do make less use of hospitals, pilot projects showed—the premiums are so high that in its first three years the Blue Cross Community Health Program of Queens-Nassau Inc., attracted only 14,000 subscribers and lost a total of $4.5 million.

Among the subscribers were the New York District Council of Carpenters, Operating Engineers Local 14 and 14B, Bakery Workers Local 3, Brewery Workers Locals 3 and 46, Local 802 Musicians, Provision Salesmen's Local 627, Joint Board of the Fur, Leather and Machine Workers Union, Metal Trades Local 638, Theatrical Stage Employees Local 4 and Plasterers Local 65.

Outside of New York, scores of labor groups are offering prepaid group practice to their members, with the heaviest concentration of union participants in Colorado and California. Other unions in Maryland, Pennsylvania and Rhode Island participate in prepaid group practice.

New York has but one of the 107 HMOs linked to Blue Cross. Another thirty are in the development stage and there is little doubt that prepaid group practice offering a full range of hospital and medical services will be the preferred health care delivery system of the future.*

Aside from Blue Cross, a union has pioneered in establishing its own network of HMOs. The Amalgamated Clothing Workers established the network in 1974 in an agreement with the Clothing Manufacturers Association and the assistance of HEW. The reason for the innovation, the ACWA Executive Board said, was that "costs for both health care and insurance premiums have risen steadily in the past few years, while there has been a simultaneous deterioration in quality, with the emphasis placed on treatment rather than preventive medicine."

The ILGWU has its own form of health maintenance: The union encourages its members to visit an ILG health center once a year for a physical checkup. "We pay our members to come in for a checkup," said Assistant President Gus Tyler. "It's cheaper for them than paying the bills when they are sick."

The ILG has at least eight health centers in the U.S., where members can go for examinations. In the wake of a survey the union undertook to determine the extent of tuberculosis (then an industrial hazard in the garment trades), the ILG opened the nation's first health center in 1913—a pioneering effort in third-party medicine.

The ILG efforts antedated the establishment of any prepaid group practice in the area it served. The oldest health care program in the northeastern United States is Group Health Inc., established in 1938 to offer health coverage to union members.

Unions were the first subscribers and union officers made up the first board of directors. The bulk of GHI's business is still in union coverage. Of the 1,034,928 contracts (employees plus dependents) in force as of December 31, 1975, covering 2,869,934 persons, 984,443 were government employees and their dependents.

The figures indicate a high degree of union involvement with GHI and this is borne out by GHI programs and personnel. For example, in 1976, GHI established an occupational health division to provide

---

*By 1979, HMOs were serving 8 million members in 200 groups.

periodic health examinations as an early warning system of known hazards; to provide detection and elimination of other hazards; to educate (in cooperation with Empire State College and Cornell's State School of Industrial and Labor Relations) employees and physicians in occupational health and to provide consultation services to unions and industry on specific risk problems.

This development is exemplary of GHI innovation. While it is providing health insurance coverage, GHI also operates a hospital and a group of vision service centers and has a homemaker service that provides home health care. But it was also first to offer benefits for in-hospital medical care, medical care in the patient's home and the doctor's office, out-of-hospital psychiatric care, out-of hospital diagnostic X-ray and laboratory tests and dental care.

If GHI goes beyond its role as a nonprofit health insurance carrier, it would not be hyperbole to attribute its innovations to the input of the trade unionists who help determine policy.

Stephen C. Vladeck, who served as chairman of the board of directors of GHI, was a celebrated labor relations attorney who was counsel to many unions. His deputy was Louis L. Levine, who started out his career as director of the New York Central Labor Council's Community Services Committee. The board of directors has included seven trade unionists, representing as many unions, a minority on a board of thirty-seven members, eleven of whom were medical doctors or dentists.

On the West Coast, the Kaiser Foundation Health Plans represent the largest group practice plan, if not the oldest in the nation. They owe their start to the medical services industrialist Henry J. Kaiser made available to his workers, first in construction projects, such as the Grand Coulee Dam, and then, during World War II, in a shipyard in Richmond, California.

Wage deductions paid the costs of the group practice plan for Kaiser employees. After the war, Kaiser's initiative and financial assistance made possible a community-wide prepaid group practice which grew over the years to serve 3.5 million persons in California, Colorado, Ohio, Oregon, Washington and Hawaii. Under six regional plans, Kaiser-Permanente owns and operates twenty-six general hospitals with more than 5,700 beds and sixty-eight outpatient centers. They use the services of 3,100 full-time physicians and 27,000 other employees. Late in 1977, the health plan was certified as a health maintenance organization (HMO).

Labor-management welfare funds are enthusiastic supporters of the Kaiser-Permanente Health Plan, but union willingness to take advantage of such group health plans is not to be equated with union initiative in establishing its own programs. But unions have been instrumental in this area, too. The Labor Health Institute was started in St. Louis in 1945 by a CIO warehousemen's union. The United Mine Workers' welfare and retirement fund started its own medical program in 1949 and, despite all the scandal and controversy attached to the fund's operations, the medical program was effective.

In a critical review of the program, Richard Carter has observed that of the 97,000 disabled workers rehabilitated in the first six years, 6,500 went back to work in the mines, 15,500 found work in other industries and 5,800 became self-employed. Not only were the lives of disabled men rebuilt, but in large part they became self-supporting, earning over $6 million a year, compared with the drain they had been on the economy before the fund was organized.[8]

The fund made good medical care and hospitalization available at reasonable cost, much to the dismay of the American Medical Association, which blustered that "free choice of physician should be preserved." The point of mentioning AMA opposition is not irrelevant. The lack of adequate hospital facilities in Kentucky led the fund to establish a chain of hospitals in the Appalachian coal fields, seven of them in Kentucky. This led to the blacklisting of the physicians in the miners' hospitals by the AMA. It was not an isolated instance. Over the years the AMA has been consistent in staving off "socialized medicine" by opposing every new concept in health care delivery.

It has opposed public health vaccinations against diphtheria, venereal disease clinics, health insurance of any kind, group practice, salaries for doctors, Blue Cross, Social Security, fee schedules, federal grants for mother-and-child welfare programs, the elimination of means tests for crippled children, the extension of Social Security benefits to the disabled and more, Roul Tunley asserts in *The American Health Scandal*.[9]

It has not been easy for labor to take care of its own. The American Medical Association and the American Hospital Association have seen to that. And as long as providers, rather than consumers, of health care services continue to dominate the boards of directors of health insurance carriers, the task will be no easier. An Associated Press survey of the boards of Blue Cross and Blue Shield health insurance plans in 1975 found that even the few "public" members named to boards in recent years in answer to widespread criticism were elected by incumbent board members and not by Blue Cross subscribers.

Blue Cross claimed there were 1,775 board members for all its state and local plans. Of these, 1,138, or 69 percent, were "consumer representatives."

But the AP survey reported 161 of the "consumer representatives," or 14 percent, were also hospital trustees, and most of the rest were corporate executives, bankers and lawyers. Connecticut Blue Shield, cited as typical, has a twenty-man board that is self-perpetuating, electing its own new members. Of the twenty on the board in 1975, eight were practicing, one a retired physician; the others were the president of Connecticut Blue Shield, five corporation executives, a lawyer, a vice president of Southern New England Telephone, a union official, a bank president and a woman affiliated with the Connecticut Housing Authority.[10]

Increasingly, unions are being compelled by high costs to establish self-insured hospitalization plans. One example is the National Maritime Union, whose 37,000 members and families are covered by a self-insured plan, even though seamen can make use of U.S. Public Health Service facilities. The NMU's benefits, after a $100-deductable step, cover 80 percent of hospital costs up to $2,500, then 100 percent of the bill after that.

If there's any avenue of hope for holding down hospital costs, it may lie in the 200 Health Systems Agencies (HSA) created in 1976 by HEW under the National Health Planning and Resources Development Act to coordinate the development of health facilities.

The law mandates that between 51 and 60 percent of HSA board members must be consumers (rather than providers) of health care, thus giving unions representation, which they are pursuing intensely. But the danger is that overzealous consumers will seek to equip each crossroads hospital, nursing home and clinic with costly facilities that could be used cooperatively at far less cost. HSA may add to the cost of the health delivery system, rather than reduce it.

Notes

1. Rashi Fein, "Health Care Cost: A Distorted Issue," *American Federationist*, June 1975, p. 13.
2. Report of the AFL-CIO Executive Council, 1975, p. 168–69.
3. *The World of Work and Alcoholism* (United Steelworkers of America Education Department, n.d.).
4. "A *Center* Report: Alcoholism," *Center Magazine*, July-August 1976, p. 44.
5. "A Union-Based Alcoholism Program," *NCA Labor-Management Alcoholism Journal*, January-February 1976.
6. Hyman J. Weiner, "A Group Approach to Link Community Mental Health with Labor," *Social Work Practice*, 1967, p. 178.
7. Sylvia A. Law, *Blue Cross: What Went Wrong?*, p. 2.
8. Richard Carter, *The Doctor Business*, p. 182.
9. Roul Tunley, *The American Health Scandal*, p. 99.
10. *New York Times*, 6 August 1975, p. 69.

12.
Education: Labor Goes Back to School

This is a simple expression of my appreciation for your foresight in making the labor studies courses available to union members. I have just completed the two-year Cornell program and was granted a certificate. Although the course work was not likely to lead to advancement on my job (I am a meat wrapper at Waldbaum's), I am profoundly gratified by having had the opportunity to pursue such a well-structured program. In fact, my studies have so whet my appetite that I want to pursue further education.

But more immediately, the course work gave me a greater admiration for unionism. Tracing the development of the labor movement was somewhat of a revelation, learning about the long and arduous struggles made by the thousands of valiant soldier-workers of preceding generations. The discovery of their "overcoming" has given me much more appreciation of the working conditions and fringe benefits [I enjoy] today.

Moreover, I am happy to see that unions are not simply satisfied with the gains won in the workplace; they also want to make the worker feel good about himself outside the work arena; they now encourage workers to get involved with his community and society at large. And in this respect I have already begun looking at my neighborhood and my neighbors, with the feeling that I have some value and can be useful in making where we live a better place. The labor studies program did this for me and more—one who in the past wasn't sure of her next door neighbor's name. Again, I thank you for making the program available.

Thelma Keyes, Queens Village

Unions are sending their members back to school in increasing numbers (yet to be estimated) to complete or, at least, to add to their interrupted formal education. The response has been more than appreciative. Trade union students demonstate just how well their collective bargaining skills enable them to take advantage of the opportunities offered. This was clearly illustrated in the battle students mounted to win college credits for their studies in a two-year labor-liberal arts program. The fact finder, Dr. Julius J. Manson of Baruch

College, City College of New York, stated the issue: "The students claim full Cornell [University] credits retroactively, for courses taken under the Labor Studies Program conducted under Cornell auspices at Farmingdale, Long Island, starting with the Fall, 1974, semester."

The students, who were, with few exceptions, trade unionists, claimed they had been promised college credits for completing courses with a passing grade, but this was disputed by the State School of Industrial and Labor Relations (ILR) at Cornell. By going to fact finding, the Student Committee of the Labor Studies Program at Farmingdale not only made use of their negotiating skills, but demonstrated the high value they placed on education, gainsaying the popular notion that "unions have no use for college longhairs."

Professor Manson's report and recommendations underline the eagerness with which union members react to college-level studies. He not only ruled "the students . . . should receive full Cornell credit, retroactive to September, 1974, for courses which they have successfully taken," but complimented the students upon the thoroughness with which they collected documentary evidence supporting their contentions. (The Student Committee submitted more than fifty documents, letters, brochures and memos to the fact finder.)

The committee (composed of William J. Dietz, manager in charge of maintenance of equipment manpower on the Long Island Railroad; James Sottile, general chairman of the LIRR Brotherhood of Railroad Signalmen, and William G. Benson, recording secretary of Local 100, Service Employees International Union) won the plaudits of fellow students, faculty and guests at graduation exercises on June 30, 1976.

While the union members taking ILR courses at Farmingdale had had some formal education in their youth and thus were easily able to adapt to the demands made on them, few had completed four years of high school. But they were highly motivated, as the following excerpts, taken from homework papers, illustrate:

> Labor History gives the origin and struggle of union's [*sic*] to survive the early years. This course enables students to become leaders in their unions in the future.

> All this knowledge reflects back to the local. The local reaps the rewards of a member that is interested in his job. Hopefully, he will pass this interest on to other members. This can only serve to unify a union.

Like most Americans, these trade union students, with few exceptions, could not cope with the English language, although they were superior to youthful SUNY-Farmingdale students. The need for continued education was obvious.

Fortunately, opportunities exist and colleges all over the country are offering courses that are well attended—to such an extent, Workers Education Local 189 is composed solely of labor educators. (An intra-union dispute in 1976 ended its ties with the American Federation of Teachers.) The University and College Labor Education Association listed forty colleges and universities in twenty-six states, the District of Columbia, Puerto Rico and Canada in its 1975 *Directory of Member Institutions and Professional Staff* as offering regular and continuing programs providing education for workers and their organizations. Two years later the total had grown to forty-seven, but in mid-1978 an additional thirty institutions were offering or preparing to offer labor study programs.

There are other labor study centers open to workers, including the Meany Center for Labor Studies in Silver Springs, Maryland, as well as courses offered by the education departments of sixty-three international unions, which are listed in the Local 189 *Directory of Labor Education*. No directory, however, can possibly be all-inclusive, for unions are extensively involved in continuing education, which has suddenly been discovered as the "wave of the future" by university regulars who long viewed it with disdain.

The most obvious reason, at least in the United States, is declining college enrollment, which is moving university authorities to look to adults for tomorrow's student body. The demand is certainly there, since the qualifications required to succeed in the highly technological labor market demand higher education. And, as Fred M. Hechinger pointed out, "Highly educated older professionals are in danger of becoming obsolete, their success and earning power threatened by younger professionals."[1]

Trade unions are aware of the need to educate their members to meet the needs of changing technologies. The Utility Workers of America, confronted with the first commercial nuclear reactors, had to learn the lesson overnight. Engineers and technical workers in the International Union of Electrical Workers did not in the 1960s, when "second generation" electronics systems were developed, and overnight they found their skills and training were obsolete. The building and construction trades unions, which appeared to be impervious to technological changes over the years, have at last shown growing concern over environmental pollution and nuclear radiation.

Education is overcoming the prejudice which fostered the display of this kind of sign in offices of the building trades unions:

IF YOU ARE OUT OF WORK
AND HUNGRY
EAT AN ENVIRONMENTALIST

There's a growing awareness that saving the environment will not only create jobs, but also save the lives of construction workers.

The back-to-school movement has the wide support of unions in the United States. The Oregon AFL-CIO in 1975 unanimously adopted a resolution introduced by H. Landon Ladd, international vice president, director of research, education and collective bargaining coordination for the International Woodworkers of America:

> Resolved, that the Oregon AFL-CIO hereby establishes as a matter of the highest priority the passage of a bill creating an Oregon Labor College meeting the following criteria:
>
> 1. That the labor college shall be established as a separate specialized institution within the Oregon State System of Higher Education.
>
> 2. That the primary purposes of the labor college shall be to provide research, education and other services for officials and members of unions and employee associations, as well as appropriate public services.
>
> 3. That there shall be an Oregon Labor College Advisory Commission composed of representatives of unions and employee associations to work with the Oregon State System of Higher Education to ensure worker reality and confidence in the institution by means of policy recommendations concerning the labor college . . .

The resolution was based upon a series of "whereas" clauses, including the absence of any "worker-oriented, state-supported institution for labor research and workers education in any of the states of the Pacific Northwest," despite the increasing demands on union officials and members "because of economic complexity and conditions and laws and regulations concerning labor relations."

Will there be an Oregon Labor College such as labor wants? Perhaps, but Roy A. Ockert, coordinator, Department of Research, Education and Collective Bargaining for the International Woodworkers of America, was dubious after his union's five-year campaign met with innumerable obstacles, including the "anti-labor attitudes of the higher education administration."

The campaign for the Oregon Labor College produced approval in 1976 from the chancellor of the Oregon State System of Higher Education for an Oregon Labor Research and Education Center, not a School for Labor or a Labor College. And a year later, the state legislature and governor authorized establishment of the Labor Education and Research Center at the University of Oregon in Eugene, under a two-year budget of $247,000, calling for a director, three full-time faculty members and a classified staff person to develop a statewide program. The labor advisory committee, which wanted a labor college in Portland, the state's population center, was not consulted on the site, but had a voice in selecting the director.

The Oregon State AFL-CIO waged a stiff battle for the school. Keith W. Johnson, international president of the International Woodworkers of America, exemplified the spirit of the five-year campaign in addressing the 1976 convention of the Oregon State Industrial Union Council:

> We in the union movement cut our eye teeth on fighting against injustice to workers. Our greatest strength—our finest times—are when we are fighting for the rights of working people. And millions of dollars of taxpayers' money for business and not one cent for labor, is most certainly not justice. They are nonsense because no self-respecting union will knuckle under at the first sign of opposition to a necessary demand.
>
> We did not get where we are by throwing in the sponge every time the boss said "no." And make no mistake about it, the statement that we have to accept whatever the Chancellor is willing to give us, or get nothing, is a challenge to labor.

In the face of such determination it is likely there will be an Oregon Labor College located in Portland, where labor wants it. After all, there is a Labor College in the Empire State College, a division of the State University of New York, because trade union graduates of a two-year labor-liberal arts program fought for and obtained it with the help of Harry Van Arsdale.

More than 400 students were enrolled in the autumn term of 1976 at the Labor College, taking a variety of courses at four campuses in Albany, Hicksville, the World Trade Center and 326 West 42nd Street, Manhattan, under the guidance of Labor College and Cornell's State School of Industrial and Labor Relations (ILR) faculties. The curriculum included courses in labor law, work and contemporary social issues, economics, collective bargaining in the public sector, comparative industrial systems, literature of social protest, theories of personnel management, industrial psychology and communications.

It was Van Arsdale, as a delegate to the 1975 AFL-CIO convention, who introduced a resolution calling for establishing labor colleges in all the fifty states:

> Resolved: That the AFL-CIO call upon state AFL-CIO bodies to petition their state legislatures to establish labor colleges in the state universities, and be it further
>
> Resolved: That President George Meany and AFL-CIO be commended for establishing the college degree program in the AFL-CIO Labor Studies Center.

169

The resolution was adopted by the convention with the amendment, "where feasible," inserted after the words, "state universities."

If American trade unions have openly embraced the concept of labor education, it was not always thus. The history of labor education has been marked by a wide range of attitudes, objectives and cooperating institutions, reflecting the changing nature of trade unions over the years. One of the earliest mentions of education as a goal of American trade unionists came in 1827 with the formation of the Mechanics' Union of Trade Associations in Philadelphia—the first effective city central organization of wage earners in the world, formed for two principal reasons: to secure a ten-hour day, in order to have enough leisure for political activity, and to secure free public education, so that political activity would be feasible.

The Colonial mechanic, disenfranchised if he did not own fifty acres of property or its equivalent, did not win suffrage until the 1830s. And it took almost another 100 years for women to gain the right to vote.

Suffrage had to precede public education, since it was highly unlikely the landed gentry would tax themselves to support public schools for the benefit of the children of mechanics, nor were they eager to take children out of the mills or fields, cutting off a source of cheap labor.

A particularly touching description of the plight of child labor and women, too, appears in *History of Labour in the United States*:

> The condition of females and children in factories attracted particular attention and the New England Association of Farmers, Mechanics and other Working Men declared that this subject "ought to receive the sedulous care of the respective departments of government."

> "If children must be doomed to these deadly prisons," said the New Haven delegate to the 1833 convention, "let the law at least protect them against excessive toil, and shed a few rays of light upon their darkened intellects."

> "Workingmen! Bitter must be that bread which your little children earn in pain and tears, toiling by day, sleeping at night, sunken under oppression, consumption and decrepitude, into an early grave, knowing no life but this, and knowing of this only misery."[2]

It was the mechanic, the workingman, who through the New England Association, the New York Workingmen's Party and the Mechanics' Union of Trade Associations in Philadelphia, fought for universal suffrage (yes, for women, too, and as early as 1831 in Delaware!), public education and public libraries. What was the motivation which impelled the early trade unions to champion these causes? We have an explanation in the preamble to the constitution of the Mechanics' Union of Trade Associations:

The real object of this association is to avert, if possible, the desolating evils which must invariably arise from a depreciation of the intrinsic value of human labour; to raise the mechanical and productive classes to that condition of true independence and inequality[*sic*] which their practical skill and ingenuity, their immense utility to the nation and their growing intelligence are beginning imperiously to demand; to promote, equally the happiness, prosperity and welfare of the whole community—to aid in conferring a due and full proportion of that invaluable promoter of happiness, leisure, upon all its useful members; and to assist, in conjunction with such other institutions of this nature as shall hereafter be formed throughout the nation, in establishing a just balance of power, both mental, moral, political and scientific, between all the various classes and individuals which constitute society at large.[3]

But it was not until the middle of the nineteenth century that the fundamental pattern of public education was established in the U.S. Labor education did not follow until the 1900s. The term, "labor education," requires rigid definition, since it is neither training in specific job skills nor "a means to the liberation of the working class." Dr. Lois Gray has clarified the term:

In the American context, labor education is a specialized branch of adult education; it is a non-credit service for mature persons, but it is not vocational education, i.e., training in specific job skills. Labor education is distinguished from adult education generally by the occupational status of its clientele, by its organizational ties, and, to a lesser extent, by its content. Its students are workers (non-supervisory level, including blue-collar and white-collar, employed and unemployed); it is typically attached in some way to the organized labor movement; and its subject matter relates, directly or indirectly, to the worker's interest in his economic position, his employment relationship, and his union membership. Within this framework, labor education encompasses a wide range of programs which may be grouped together in terms of their objectives. These include (1) ideological (based on a commitment to social change), (2) institutional (designed to build organizational loyalty and participation), (3) professional (preparation for leadership), (4) remedial (raising the level of the educationally disadvantaged), and (5) cultural (for life enjoyment).[4]

Within those limits, labor education in the United States has undergone extensive change over the years—in the curricula and the sponsorship of programs as well, at times when social reformers' kind intentions were met with antipathy, if not downright hostility, by "business" trade unionists. There was a basis for that hostility in the post–Civil War days of the Knights of Labor, as well as later, even until contemporary times. According to Norman Eiger:

After the Civil War the growth of national unionism largely paid lip service to educational opportunity for workers. The Knights of Labor were suspicious of higher education, stating in one publication: "Our boys and girls do not need a higher education but should be trained to become useful citizens." They found ample justification in those days for their views that the universities were strongholds of privilege and anti-unionism.[5]

While the belief that the "wealthy classes" were opposed to public education a century ago undoubtedly had some merit, the social reformers of the early 1900s, including some who were wealthy, could hardly be held to share the same views. Yet few unions received the offer of labor education courses with open arms. As Dr. Lois Gray indicates, "Labor education in the early 1900s was largely the work of 'friends of labor' and received little direct support from the labor unions, which were weak, organizationally and financially, and engaged in a desperate struggle for survival."[6]

Certainly, Dr. Gray's assessment is accurate. Yet there is another factor which holds true now, as it did then: the barrier of language. Academe and labor do not speak the same language—any more than labor and social agencies do. The barrier tends to lead unions to sponsor educational programs of their own, rather than cooperate with and accept what "friends of labor" offer with the best of intentions. There is an argument implied that labor needs education to break the language barrier, but equally true, academe should learn to communicate with trade unionists in their own terms.

Gus Tyler, a labor writer who communicates with both camps, is aware of the language barrier:

> Where will the future trade union leadership learn the needed insights into economy and society? Ordinarily, the broader view should be gathered from exposure to the intellectual friends of labor—economists, sociologists, industrial relations experts, political scientists, educators. Yet, unfortunately, there is a kind of built-in hostility between the intellectual and the practitioner . . . the gap is widened by the simple fact that the two sides don't talk the same language . . . Out of this nondialogue arise mutual suspicion and contempt . . . The gap between intellectual and practitioner is as unfortunate as it is common.[7]

But social reformers and universities did make notable contributions to the education of trade unionists—especially women, who were shamefully neglected by unions—for many years. The groups ranged from the Workingman's Institute founded in 1874 by Johns Hopkins University through the Women's Trade Union League school for women workers in 1903 to the first Bryn Mawr summer school for women workers in 1921. (Bryn Mawr President M. Carey Thomas, convinced that workers required educational opportunities, conceived the summer school experiment after witnessing workers' schools in England while on a trip to Europe.)

The motivation for these educational programs was self-evident: Humanitarians were eager to make education available to workers so they might be better equipped to function effectively in the community. That, at least, was the attitude of the YWCA, whose industrial department educated industrial women workers. As for the educators involved, Dr. Gray has observed they were "motivated by visions of a new social order and viewed education as a major tool for changing society."

That was undoubtedly the attitude of the Rand School of Social Science, founded in 1906 by the Socialist Party. But it was so blanketed by an ideology of social reform that few unions, aside from the International Ladies Garment Workers and the Amalgamated Clothing Workers, could tolerate the school. Another was Brookwood Labor College, founded by A. J. Muste in 1921 in Katonah, New York, as a two-year resident college for workers. Despite the distrust of radicals shown by the labor movement, each endured for at least a decade and made notable contributions to the development of labor leadership. Thomas R. Brooks noted:

> Over the years Brookwood trained an impressive number of people who played a leading role in the founding of the Congress of Industrial Organizations and have since filled many positions of leadership in the unions. Among them were the two Reuther brothers, Victor and Roy; Julius Hochman, a vice president of the ILGWU; Rose Pesotta, an ILGWU organizer active in the Akron sit-downs, and Clinton S. Golden, who with other Brookwood graduates was active in the founding of the Steelworkers.[8]

In a closely allied area, the Works Progress Administration launched an educational program in 1933, directed by Hilda Smith, who had been director of the Bryn Mawr summer school. The WPA Workers Education Program enrolled a million workers, two-thirds of whom were men, and employed two thousand or more unemployed teachers. Brendon Sexton concluded that labor education in the 1930s was "in fact, largely a WPA activity."

> The effects of the WPA program were lasting and deep. The vitality of present-day labor education largely derives from people who were associated with it. Rich in resources far beyond the dream of people now engaged in this work, it had certain advantages that cannot be replicated.
>
> Qualified academics and intellectuals were available and eager to accept

173

teaching assignments, and WPA had the money to pay them to organize and teach classes for as few as three or four students.[9]

If there were doubts voiced by trade unionists over the educational programs created in the past on behalf of the worker, the educational programs the unions are conducting in our own time have brought forth a harsher reaction. As soon as the validity of these programs is questioned—and radical intellectuals invariably raise the point, much to the detriment of the unions involved—the courses are described as "trade union schooling," devoid of any social consciousness, self-serving to prop up leaders in office, lacking in ideology, "bread-and-butter oriented" and totally lacking in the elements of what B. J. Widick calls a liberal education.

Widick decried the disappearance of the traditional worker's education of the 1930s, attributing it to the lack of idealism and the indifference of today's trade unionists. That view does not match the experience of this writer and teacher, who can testify to the eagerness, the spirit and idealism of his students in the ILR-Cornell labor liberal arts program. Nor does Widick's view consider the insistence of trade unionists on credit and degree programs in labor studies. Can it be that it was Widick and not the trade unionists who changed since the 1930s?

The truth is, Messrs. Widick, Harold Wilensky, Jack Barbash, Joseph Mire, et al: Labor education not only retains its "traditional" values, but is alive and well in colleges, universities, labor schools, in-service union programs and weekend retreats because there is a demand for labor education and the means (even if starved for adequate funding) to satisfy it. And there is as little point in questioning the motives of the sponsoring unions as there would be in questioning the value of the curricula.

Going far beyond the "almost exclusively trade school" education offering courses in collective bargaining, parliamentary procedure, labor union administration, labor relations law and writing grievances, the centers for labor studies are now offering courses in labor history; social behavior and work; science, technology and labor; critical urban problems; conflict resolution; society, industry and the individual; international affairs; and even "Labor Surveys the Arts," which should please the radical hungering for a "liberal arts education."

The motivation for sending officers, staff members and the rank and file to such courses is self-evident. Sexton says:

> If a union—especially a mass union—is to be democratic, if it seeks membership participation, it will sponsor classes in which members may quickly acquire democratic skills. Elected shop stewards and business agents rarely come armed with the ability to write and negotiate

grievances. They can, and most do, develop skills slowly and laboriously on the job—at considerable expense to themselves and the people they represent—or they can acquire rudimentary negotiating skills more quickly in practice sessions under the guidance of experienced unionists and informed academicians. Similarly, they can learn to interpret agreements, make a speech, run a meeting, lead a discussion, or get a committee going. They can gain understanding of the provisions of workmen's and unemployment compensation laws and of laws governing industrial relations. They can be shown how to see through the "black arts" of the time-study man, whose use of stop-watch and clipboard may affect pace of work and pay received.[10]

Such a union, it should be observed, is hardly likely to be corrupt. Yet the lack of any labor education for its members should not be presumed to indicate the converse. Apathy is not unknown in any area of American life.

But beyond the fundamental motivation of building a successful union (successful in organizing and negotiating), there is the desire to give the member a broader and richer life by awakening his intellect to an awareness of his own potential and his relationship to society.

Is that a conceit? Or merely an appraisal of a union's function? And hasn't the thought been expressed times without number by trade union leaders? Murray H. Finley, president of the Amalgamated Clothing and Textile Workers Union, said on the day before the clothing and textile unions were merged:

I believe in building a better world—not just a better house or more material things for myself—but to better people's lives. And I believe trade unions are necessary to preserve the American way of life. I don't think we can have a free democratic society without a free democratic labor movement.

Both the ACTWU and UAW have education departments—and they are not recent developments, either!

The Walter and May Reuther UAW Family Education Center on the shores of Black Lake, Michigan, houses an unusual, "perhaps unique kind of adult education program," according to Al Nash. The students are members of the union and their families attend the center as recipients of scholarships from the union covering the payment of lodging, food and program costs for two weeks:

The center describes its method as "learning by doing," the phrase commonly used in adult education to describe role-playing, simulated exercises and other techniques which lead to "doing." In the center "learning by doing" is essentially carried out by establishing several mock local unions to each of which 25 to 30 members and their spouses are assigned and in which they discuss, make decisions and act upon administrative problems and economic and social programs similar to those encountered in actual locals.

In addition there are a number of workshops in which, for example, negotiations, communications, political action, time study and shop steward roles are informally discussed during the two weeks.[11]

What is the value of the UAW educational program? Nash, an associate professor at ILR-Cornell, assessed the contributions of the center: "[It] has created, in effect, a total environment which increases the ability of the union member and his or her family to engage in meaningful democratic learning, to acquire insight in union administrative roles and activities, and to develop personal capabilities."[12]

The Amalgamated Clothing Workers has had a continuous educational program since its formation in 1914. Indeed, it would be no exaggeration to say education in the Amalgamated preceded its founding by many years, having its roots in the Education Alliance (founded in 1883), the Henry Street Settlement (equally old), the United Hebrew Trades (1883) and the *Vorwarts* (the *Jewish Daily Forward*), each of which made valiant efforts to educate and Americanize the Jewish immigrants who toiled in the sweatshops of the Lower East Side of New York long before the Amalgamated was organized.[13]

In its early days, the Amalgamated sponsored everything "from socialistic propaganda and workers' universities to pure recreation and social guidance as workers' education, [but] it has never advocated learning for its own sake. Education has always been conceived of as an integral part of the union and therefore to be utilized for union purposes." This assessment by Lottie Haid Tartell[14] might possibly be quarreled with by the Amalgamated today, but Tartell also noted that the purpose of education in the union's first decade was "to broaden the cultural background of their workers and activities to meet the trade union needs as a trade union organization."

Education, in the view of the early Amalgamated leaders, was not to be restricted to the classrooms. On the contrary, newspapers came first—a lesson trade unions, for the most part, seem to have forgotten. "One of the most effective means of education is undoubtedly the press . . . . Our press must not be a mere official record of the work of the organization, but a weekly educator for the members, informing and enlightening them on matters pertaining to our organization as well as the labor movement in general," the General Executive Board reported in March, 1916.

The purpose of using newspapers for education, wrote Joseph Schlossberg, first editor of the union paper, the *Advance*, in 1919, was "to give them that which will make of living wealth producers, of human machines, a higher species of human beings, which will enable them to understand society and themselves."

The Amalgamated adopted a number of programs which evolved over the years as the clothing industry, the members and officers changed with the times. These programs included support of the Rand School, lectures and courses sponsored by joint boards, social get-togethers, courses offered by the United Labor Education Committee, cultural activities offered by the United Education League, mass meetings during strikes and/or lockouts, an active workers' school, an officers' school, numerous pamphlets, establishment of the National Education Department in 1936, recreational programs, correspondence school courses, a readers' packet service and a Department of Cultural Activities. But always the commitment to education and social reform remained firm; only as circumstances altered, so did the tools.

An exception to usual practice? Hardly! There are many instances of unions with educational programs of long standing. The ILGWU appointed Theresa Wolfson its first education director in 1916—a year before the ACW and the United Cloth Hat and Cap Makers held their first classes for members. Indeed, after World War I, there were so many education departments flourishing that the National Workers Education Bureau was formed in 1921 to "collect and disseminate information relative to the efforts of education on any part of organized labor." (The bureau coordinated educational programs conducted by unions until 1954, when it was absorbed into the AFL as its education department.)

Lawrence Rogin and Marjorie Rachlin estimated that by 1968 about forty of more than 180 national unions were sponsoring some form of educational activity, but these unions included some of the largest in membership, so that the forty involved over half the trade unionists in the country.[15] A 1977 directory of AFL-CIO affiliates reveals fifty-two international unions with officials listed as education directors. Another eleven listed research directors, but the line between education and research appears to be vague, since nineteen unions listed education and research posts held by the same official.

The AFL-CIO itself has not only a standing committee on education, whose chairman is Hunton P. Wharton, president of the Operating Engineers, but a Department of Education, whose director is Walter G. Davis, and a standing committee on research, whose chairman is Rudy Oswald, AFL-CIO research director. There is also the George Meany Center for Labor Studies, whose executive director is Fred K. Hoehler.

The Education Department, with a staff of seven and an annual budget of $1.5 million, carries out an extensive program of preparing and distributing legislative and leadership training manuals for affiliates, sponsoring educational conferences, co-sponsoring short-term institutes with state or regional AFL-CIO bodies, planning or developing symposia, researching data for testimony before legislative committees on education in Congress, distributing films to unions, public schools and other institutions and acting as a clearinghouse on education materials for education directors of affiliates.

How many trade unionists are involved in labor education? Associate Professor John R. MacKenzie, director of the Labor Studies Center at Federal City College, Washington, and president of the University and College Labor Education Association, stated that there is no satisfactory estimate. He added, "This is one of the needs of our field, but as of the present, there is no statistical base anywhere in the U.S. that ties union and university programs together either from the number of offerings or students taking part in the programs."[16]

Dr. Gray, chairman of the association's Committee on Academic Standards and Degree Programs, confirmed Dr. MacKenzie's opinion, but was able to shed some light on trade union involvement in education: "There are 6,000 trade unionists currently enrolled in credit programs," she wrote, "but this is only a small part of the total enrolled in non-credit programs."[17]

The number of trade unionists enrolled in labor studies programs appears to be growing constantly, undoubtedly in response to technological and economic pressures. The newest and most ambitious program of all, the Meany Center for Labor Studies, is opening up new opportunities for many more would-be students. When the campus was dedicated in 1974, George Meany, as chairman of the board, noted the "very significant occasion" was the culmination of years of hard work and planning to provide the staff training and leadership preparation for trade unionists, so they could better carry out the goals of the labor movement.

Union leadership today, Meany pointed out, has to know as much about an employer's business as the employer himself knows if collective bargaining is to work effectively on behalf of workers. Said Meany:

> We realize the need for education not just for the citizenry as a whole, but special education for our own people . . . This is why we are here today, dedicating an institution to build up the educational standards—to make our people better, more intelligent trade unionists so that they can do their job better, so that they can make a better contribution, not only to the people we represent, but to this nation.

The center was established five years earlier and was attended in that period by more than 3,000 men and women who went to class in the basement of a building on Massachusetts Avenue in Washington, D.C. In 1973, however, the AFL-CIO acquired the college campus for $3,051,024 and spent an additional $3,039,861 to improve and expand the property so that college credit programs could be offered to union staff employees and full-time elected officers.[18]

Complete residential facilities, conference rooms, food service and limited recreation facilities are available on the campus. The original residence hall with forty-four rooms to accomodate fifty-six persons was inadequate, so a second hall with 100 rooms, housing about 120 persons, was added.

In a two-year period, the campus was the scene of ninety programs attended by 2,000 full-time union staff and elected officers. Additional programs have been presented for various unions pursuing their own special studies. What are the courses offered at the center? The catalogue offers a wide range of institutes of one or two weeks' duration, covering such subjects as union administration, improvement of skills in public speaking, dealing with the media, conducting meetings and reading efficiently and writing effectively; effective leadership, economic directions, international affairs, the economic power of multinational corporations, trade union women, arbitration, education techniques, civil rights, collective bargaining, labor law, negotiated health plans, organizing, safety and health, and a variety of special programs for particular groups, such as the building trades or labor editors.

The labor studies center should be regarded as one of the brightest developments on the labor front in many a year, offering solid hope that labor will make progress in solving one of its major problems: poor communications.

The center's program, however, is only one facet of the AFL-CIO's interest in education. Trade unionists may use their Labor Studies Center experience to go on to earn a Bachelor of Arts degree in Labor Studies from Antioch College by working independently on selected courses of study, completing assignments and conferring with their instructors by telephone and mail. The AFL-CIO has also been conducting an internship program since 1970, providing full-time jobs at AFL-CIO headquarters at $240 a week in the fields of civil rights, legislation, public relations, social security or political education.

Two interns are selected from each AFL-CIO region annually, the selection being made on the basis of academic study, background experience appropriate for training and an interest in organized labor. The interns work at the AFL-CIO for six or seven months and then are placed in jobs with unions or labor-related programs.

What is the outlook for labor's pursuit of education? In training a new generation of leaders, broadening the lives of its members and improving the public image of unions, labor is taking a measured risk of transforming the entire trade union movement.

Fears have been expressed that the educated young rank-and-file member may be a union-buster or a radical reformer. But Ed Sadlowski, United Steelworkers insurgent, who began working in the mills at nineteen after a stint in the Army, and who has kept his ear open to the rank and file ever since, thinks otherwise:

> I don't think the young kid has sold labor off. I don't hear any of these kids asking, "What the hell do we need a union for?" They'll bitch and moan because they don't get the service they're looking for. They're telling you what the labor movement should be. They're not trying to destroy it. That's a plus . . . The question is, can the labor movement pick up that ball and run with it? I think we have a whole new situation here. With the influx of young people into the labor market and the economic situation being the way it is, labor can be on the march again as it was in the 1930's.[19]

At the other extreme, in view of the increasing number of white collar, professional and government employee unions, Gus Tyler sees a revival of the mix between intellectuals and workers which characterized turn-of-the-century interplay in the early needle-trades unions. An additional factor to consider, in his opinion, is that, "In still other unions, the contact of union leadership with labor intellectuals will be formalized through employment of college graduates for specialized work: Research, writing, editing, industrial engineering, education, legal work . . . "[20]

Going a step further, the technology of the age must produce educated workers who can fill the needs of the knowledge sector. And educated workers can be the most militant of trade unionists. Two examples may be seen in the programs of District 65, Distributive Workers Union, which sponsors labor studies degree programs for its members at Hofstra University, and District Council 37, AFSCME, which has its own Education Fund, taking in a broad range of services, including a high school equivalency certificate, educational advice or counseling, remedial writing in a learning lab, preparation for college and college classes for credit at the College of New Rochelle. "The key concept in the union's Education Fund is 'transition,'" according to Irving Rosenstein, administrator. "The program is designed to help individual members or groups of members to take the next step to get from where they are to where they want to go."

The American labor movement, which has had but three leaders in ninety years (Gompers, William Green and Meany*), will be shaken up by what Tyler called the "new class" of workers, "made up of men and women with higher education who wield decisive economic and political power:

> They are managers, professionals and technicians who are the real power in corporate America. They are the ideologic spokesmen for that huge class of employees in our service economy—now about two-thirds of the labor force—and therefore can swing national elections. Because this class is well-educated, it is liberal—with a sensitive social conscience. It can, therefore, be counted on to use its strategic economic posts to give corporations a sense of social responsibility and to use its political clout to move America along progressive paths.[21]

Tyler may be too sanguine; he is ever optimistic about labor's potential, but it is inevitable that given the changing nature of the "working class," unions, too, will change in direction, ideology and leadership, under the impetus of the educated, dissatisfied member. But it will be no revolution; evolutionary change is already under way in the scholarships virtually every union, from international to local, provides for its members and/or children of members, and in leadership training courses conducted by innumerable unions. The practice of awarding scholarships is so widespread, it warrants no further mention. But leadership training programs must be touched upon, if only to cite one choice example—that of the Communications Workers of America. "We spend more on education," said CWA Vice President Morton Bahr, "than we do on organizing."

While offhand he could cite no figures, Bahr did know that the CWA's 1977 budget called for $300,000 to be spent on administrative costs alone for educational programs, which start with the shop steward. Each new steward is required to attend a two-day training class taught by staff members, who instruct him in union structure, his responsibilities, the grievance procedure and the necessity of assisting members through community services. His CWA *Steward's Manual* is a handy, pocket-sized guide to duties as well as a reference work covering many of the crises he may encounter.

CWA educational programs also include classes for newly elected officers and a staff training program. CWA has close ties with several

---

*On January 10, 1980, George Meany died after a long illness which had forced his retirement as AFL-CIO president on November 19, 1979. Meany had served as president for twenty-seven years, but he left an unchallenged field to his protege, Lane Kirkland. Kirkland had never held an elective office in a union before Meany picked him ten years earlier to be second in command.

universities, including Cornell, Michigan, Rutgers and the University of Connecticut, where educational programs are conducted under CWA auspices.

The results of these courses are seen, not only in the sophisticated bargaining CWA does with an equally sophisticated management at AT&T, but in the widespread presence of CWA officers on the boards of directors of social welfare agencies across the country.

An equally significant by-product of schooling turns up in the leadership schools conducted by the Education Department of the International Association of Machinists. Leaders-in-training are instructed in how to explain trade unionism to junior high and high school students when they are asked to deliver talks about the labor movement. A few excerpts from the leaflet, *Explaining the Union to Students in the Public Schools,* point up aspects of a neglected area—educating the public:

> Generally, students have big, broad questions about unions on their minds. Often they are the usual questions: Why strikes, why corruption, why are we in politics, why do we need unions anyway, and so forth. Students' thinking will usually reflect what is in the newspapers in your area—for example, why do unions want to repeal Section 14(b); isn't the union shop undemocratic. These may be general, but they are important. A good way to bring them down to earth is to talk about your own experience—the way your lodge operates or the reasons your members went on strike, for example.

> Possible topics for a talk to students: Explain to the students who you are and give them a little background about unions. Why we have unions and how our union operates. What does the union stand for?

That last question, of course, is the crucial one, and the answers remain a mystery in many parts of the country. The IAM's answers help to clear it up.

"Better wages and working conditions for members" is the first response suggested, and that could be improved by pointing out that better wages for members invariably lead to better wages for all workers. But the IAM also lists these reasons:

> Community interest and responsibility for building a better town. Union work in the community is a good example—blood banks, cooperation with the community fund, Little Leagues, anti-poverty programs, such as the various Community Action programs, voting rights, etc., etc.

> Better legislation, which benefits everyone. Point out that we work for higher minimum wages, better unemployment compensation, education legislation, improved social security, expanded medicare, equal employ-

182

ment opportunity, etc. This is one of the main reasons we have gotten into politics. In the past, labor worked for child labor laws, free public schools, etc.

The IAM Education Department offers to help its members prepare their talks by making available copies of pamphlets and leaflets covering background material.

Members of the American Federation of Teachers have far better opportunities to speak to junior and high school students about trade unionism. In view of the anti-labor attitude displayed in some social study texts and the tendency of others to minimize the role of unions, teachers have a task merely to educate their students in the basics of trade unionism. AFT Local 2 has published *Organized Labor*, a compilation of source materials for the study of labor, to enable its members to teach the subject in secondary schools. In the preface, AFT President Albert Shanker explains why the book was published:

> The commercial press has, on the whole, misrepresented organized labor. Usually portrayed as reactionary and jingoistic, its policies are misunderstood and its programs largely ignored. The lack of systematic curricula on the secondary school level has seriously handicapped teachers wishing to present an authentic study of organized labor.

> New York City teachers, through their own organization, the United Federation of Teachers, have undertaken the publication of this resource kit. The author has selected documents which enable students to gain a deeper knowledge and a clearer understanding of labor's goals and achievements, the world of work, and the lives of the men and women, who, through their personal efforts and visions, have improved the lives of all Americans.[22]

Teachers may buy this book in the Teachers Book Store, just as they may buy *Puerto Rican History and Culture, Topics in Jewish-American Heritage* and *The History of Black Americans*—three other study guides published by the UFT so that teachers may relate their teaching materials to the needs of their students. But the guides are only one aspect of a nationwide AFT program to improve education in the public schools. The AFT Task Force on Educational Issues was established in 1975 to deal with a host of problems, including early childhood education, handicapped children, school funding and standardized testing.

There is one further type of labor education which is far more likely to offer immediate and substantial rewards, and that is the training and upgrading of workers holding menial jobs. "Trade school education" is the term used by radical intellectuals to describe this type of schooling. Yet there's undoubted merit in raising a worker's standard of living.

In the days of the majestic passenger liner, the National Maritime Union was accustomed to graduating about 2,000 members a year from upgrading and retraining courses housed in the union's Joseph Curran Annex in New York City. While the school still operates in the ship-shaped building, its scope has been sharply reduced, reflecting the reduced demand for seamen. The instructors, however, are still veteran NMU members whose service at sea qualifies them to teach courses for able seamen, deck-engine mechanics, electricians, refrigeration engineers, chief cooks, stewards and specialty chefs. Courses leading to the licensed officer rank of third mate and third assistant engineer have also been taught for many years.

The National Union of Hospital and Health Care Employees also has a training and upgrading program, jointly administered by the union and hospital management and funded by a 1 percent payroll deduction. And the American Radio Association sponsors training courses so that radio officers may qualify for certificates through the ARA Technology Institute for Maritime Electronics.

These few examples indicate it is still possible to move upward in the work force through the initiative of the union, thus fulfilling the American dream.

Notes

1. Fred M. Hechinger, "Education's New Majority," *Saturday Review*, 20 September 1975, p. 15.
2. John R. Commons, ed., *History of Labour in the United States*, vol. 1, pp. 320–21.
3. Ibid., p. 190.
4. Lois Gray, "The American Way in Labor Education," *Industrial Relations*, February 1966, pp. 53–54.
5. Norman Eiger, "Labor Education—A Past and Future View," *New Jersey Adult Educator*, Winter 1975, p. 14.
6. Gray, "Labor Education," p. 54.
7. Gus Tyler, *The Labor Revolution*, p. 237.
8. Thomas R. Brooks, *Toil and Trouble*, p. 154.
9. Brendan Sexton, "Staff and Officer Training to Build Successful Unions," *Readings on Labor Education* (New Brunswick, N.J.: Institute of Management and Labor Relations, Rutgers University, n.d.), p. 19.
10. Ibid., p. 18.
11. Al Nash, "The Walter and May Reuther U.A.W. Center," *Free Labour World*, May 1973, p. 14.

12. Ibid., p. 16.

13. Vide Hutchins Hapgood, *The Spirit of the Ghetto: Studies in the Jewish Quarter of New York.*

14. Lottie Haid Tartell, "Education in the Amalgamated Clothing Workers of America."

15. Lawrence Rogin and Marjorie Rachlin, *Labor Education in the United States.*

16. Letter to the author, 18 August 1976.

17. For a survey of institutions offering college credits and degrees in labor studies, vide Lois Gray, "Labor Studies Credit and Degree Programs: A Growth Sector of Higher Education," *Labor Studies Journal*, May 1976, p. 34.

18. Secretary-Treasurer's report to the AFL-CIO convention, 1975.

19. George Bogdonich, "Labor Maverick on the March," *Progressive*, August 1976, p. 18.

20. Tyler, *Labor Revolution*, pp. 238–39.

21. Gus Tyler, "A Labor View of the New Class," *American Federationist*, October 1973, p. 1.

22. *Organized Labor: Source Materials for the Study of Labor in America* (United Federation of Teachers, 1976).

13.
Labor's Assets
at Work

A bronze plaque, the gift of the international, was unveiled at the dedication of the new union headquarters. The building was magnificent; this was recognized within a year when the chamber of commerce awarded a trophy for outstanding architecture to the union.

"This building is a monument to the union," a visitor at the ceremonies remarked.

"Nonsense!" Irving retorted sharply. "The members are the monument. This is only a building."

When Manufacturers Hanover was boasting its auto loan rates were the lowest of "any major bank in the city," the Amalgamated Bank's rate was 2.5 percent lower. The annual rate on an auto loan at Manufacturers Hanover was 12.74 percent. But the Amalgamated Bank was charging 10.88 at the same time for a three-year loan.

Obviously Amalgamated Bank wasn't considered a "major" bank. Its total assets at that time were $735,210,000—hardly in the same class with Manufacturers Hanover's $31.4 billion in assets. But the Amalgamated is "major" in another sense: It is the only union-owned bank in the U.S. Not the first, but the only one to survive. Established in 1923 by the Amalgamated Clothing Workers, it still makes "a very handsome profit," according to Maxwell Brandwen, president.*

"I've been president so long," Brandwen said, "I don't remember. There were other presidents, but I got the charter for the bank in 1923. I was counsel then for the union and [Sidney] Hillman's closest friend."

The Amalgamated Bank got back at Manufacturers Hanover with its own advertising:

A major bank is claiming in its advertising that it offers the lowest auto loan rate of any "major" bank in the city. What is there about borrowing from a "major" bank to justify paying 2.5 per cent more for the same dollars?

---

* Retired in 1978.

When you buy a car, you shop around for the best value. Obviously, you should also shop the best value when you borrow.

The lowest financing cost of any bank, not just any major bank, is available at the Amalgamated Bank.

How does the Amalgamated Bank do it? Brandwen's answer reflected the acumen of a banker and lawyer and the philosophy of a trade unionist.

We do what no other bank does. Just because we are owned by a union, we are not immune to the ills of the industry. But this bank endures because of the quality of its management and supervision. We have the most liquidity of any United States bank. The first to make personal loans, we still charge the lowest rate [on these loans]. We were the first to eliminate all charges on checking accounts. And since most of our checking accounts have less than $100 balance, this costs us money.

The explanation of this approach to banking can be found in the quotations emblazoned on a wall inside the bank:

Righteousness Exalteth a Nation — Proverbs
To Secure to Each Laborer the Whole Product of His Labor as Early as Possible is a Worthy Object of Any Good Government—Abraham Lincoln
The Only Thing We Have to Fear Is Fear Itself — F.D. Roosevelt

The Amalgamated Clothing Workers controls and owns much of the stock of the bank, but Brandwen insisted the union "does not interfere" with the decisions of the board of directors. The board has seventeen members and all but two, Brandwen and Edward M. Katz, executive vice president, are ACW officers. The bank was organized by the union "to give the worker a break," and does so to this day. Brandwen pointed out unions use the bank "substantially," as do their members. Members not only maintain checking and savings accounts, but use the bank for personal loans. Despite some $27,113,919 in total loans made by the bank in 1975, Brandwen said, "Our modest losses amounted to $12,000 for the year." (That's equivalent to .04 percent!) The unions make use of the bank as trustee and custodian of pension and welfare funds.

"Our advice," Brandwen said, "is to avoid speculation and trading. We invest in United States and U.S. agency obligations only. We are very conservative, but our accounts show no losses and the yields are higher."

By "very conservative," Brandwen explained, he meant, "My philosophy is 'don't fill ratholes.'"

Union accounts also secure preference from the bank. During strikes, for example, Amalgamated can be "helpful," advancing large sums of money "in a way we wouldn't for a merchant."

Instead of suffering losses ("we don't operate that way"), the bank has been very profitable, "paying cash dividends and retaining earnings." In 1975, for example, total capital funds and reserves totaled over $44 million, of which capital stock consisted of only $5 million.

The main office is on Union Square in New York City, adjacent to ACW headquarters. There are only two branches: in Co-op City in the Bronx and at Fifty-fourth Street and Broadway, Manhattan. The bank also had a branch in Chicago, but it was sold in the 1960s, said Bert Beck, editor of the *Advance*, "because it was a headache to run, although it was doing quite well." While the name was retained, the bank was controlled by a group "with a philosophy like our own," and continued to be profitable.

While there was no other union-controlled bank operating in the United States in recent years, there is now. The Bank für Gemeinwietshaft, controlled by the German Federation of Labor, has opened a New York branch to handle investments and financial transactions on a large scale, while Israel's Histadrut has two branches of its Workers Bank, Bank Hapoalim, in metropolitan New York. There have been other labor-controlled banks in the U.S. in the past, although not on the scale of either of these institutions.

During the 1920s, when American trade unions were emulating big business, there was a rash of ventures into banking, starting with the International Association of Machinists, which opened the first labor bank in Washington, D.C., on May 15, 1920. Others quickly followed, launched by the Brotherhood of Locomotive Engineers, the New York State Federation of Labor, the Brotherhood of Railway Clerks, the International Printing Pressmen's and Assistants' Union, the Order of Railroad Telegraphers, the American Flint Glass Workers Union, the International Ladies Garment Workers Union and the Amalgamated Clothing Workers. But, with one exception, they did not last long.

"The decline of labor banking . . . was just as precipitous as its rise," Thomas R. Brooks noted. "The stock market crash of 1929 unhinged the labor banks just as badly as it did the regular banks. Only four labor banks reopened their doors after the crash. Two have since folded, leaving the Amalgamated Clothing Workers' banks in New York and Chicago as the sole survivors of the labor bank era."[1]

A more recent venture, by the United Mine Workers, reflected no credit on the union. John L. Lewis found a repository for the union's welfare and retirement fund when the UMW acquired a controlling interest in the National Bank of Washington in 1949. By depositing millions in funds in no-interest checking accounts, the UMW prospered in its banking, acquiring other banks and wheeling and dealing in loans and investments in utilities, coal shipping and mining, with little regard for the members or their interest in the pension and welfare funds.

It all came to an end in 1971, after pensions had been reduced or denied, when Federal Judge Gerhard Gesell, in *Blankenship v. Boyle*, ruled the trustees of the fund were guilty of mismanagement and conspiracy in diverting the fund's money into the bank for the benefit of the bank and the union.[2]

He ordered the trustees to withdraw noninterest-bearing funds from the bank and awarded $11.6 million in damages to retired and disabled mine workers for the losses they had suffered. But it was not until 1976 that UMW President Arnold Miller proposed the UMW sell its 757,762 shares of the bank's stock and get out of the bank business, "where we didn't have any business being."

While unions show little interest in banking now, beyond repeated efforts to organize employees, they do have enormous liquid assets and a compelling interest in creating jobs with the funds. (A counteracting tendency has been to keep millions stashed away for strike benefits. Thus, when the United Auto Workers struck Ford Motor Company in 1976, the UAW had amassed $175 million in its strike fund, or enough to pay forty to fifty dollars a week to each striker for four months.) The unions' aggregate assets were estimated at $2.65 billion in 1969, with about 32 percent of it in cash. The assets, however, did not include over $35 billion in union-managed pension funds. (In comparison, the assets of Britain's trade unions totaled $320 million, while Canada was third in size with $220 million.)

The AFL-CIO has invested in bonds of the Federal National Mortgage Association, the Federal Intermediate Credit Bank, the Federal Land Bank, and FHA mortgages and notes in the YUC Cooperative Housing Society of Guyana and the Coracrevi Housing Project in Venezuela. It established its Mortgage Investment Trust (MIT) in 1964 "as a service to all affiliates . . . and to any qualified labor-management welfare, pension or retirement fund to provide them with a higher degree of security and reasonable yields and to create new union jobs and increased housing."[3]

Since then, MIT has grown to over $72 million in net participants' investments as of July 1, 1977. The Executive Council reported to the 1977 convention:

> During the past few years, the trust has channeled participants' monies into the construction of vitally needed low and moderate-income housing projects while continually safeguarding their investment. At present the

trust is financing the construction of 31 separate project loans located across the country representing $91 million in union-built housing.

MIT is a function of the Department of Urban Affairs, which has two other programs: the Human Resources Development Institute and the AFL-CIO Housing Committee. HRDI was established in 1968 to stimulate increased union involvement in federally sponsored man-power programs by offering technical assistance and guidance to state and local central bodies in major industrial areas. It is funded by the Manpower Administration, U.S. Labor Department. The staff assists AFL-CIO affiliates in the development, organization and management of housing projects. The housing committee serves as liaison with such national housing organizations as the National Housing Conference, the Foundation for Cooperative Housing, the National Association of Housing Redevelopment Officials, the National Urban League and others.

The manpower arm, HRDI provides labor with the support, training and technical assistance required to protect labor's interests. (The Comprehensive Employment and Training Act of 1973 allocated funds to local prime sponsors who were required to utilize a manpower advisory council including representatives of organized labor.) It does so by supporting central bodies in securing representation on CETA advisory councils, so they may influence the enforcement of standards on wages, working conditions and job security.

Representation on advisory councils, however, frequently amounts to little more than names printed on a letterhead. But HRDI conducts manpower seminars and training programs (in cooperation with the AFL-CIO labor studies center) to prepare labor representa-tives to take an active role in CETA programs. Can HRDI actually point to substantial results flowing from its activities? The 1977 report of the Executive Council noted HRDI was instrumental in the develop-ment of nearly 123,000 jobs and placed almost 50,000 individuals in those jobs since 1973. In two years, HRDI was involved in 385 training programs funded with $20,535,628, providing 10,677 training slots.

The Housing and Urban Development Department, meanwhile, has continued to assist affiliates in carrying out programs for housing senior citizens as Section 202 projects (long-term loans approved by Congress specifically for senior citizen housing). As recently as Oc-tober, 1976, six union-sponsored projects for the elderly had funds ap-proved by the Housing and Urban Development Department. They in-clude four projects of 100 units each, sponsored by the Chicago Joint Board of the ACTWU; the Laborers International Union, Jacksonville, Illinois; the Laborers, Columbus, Ohio; and the Greater Owensboro (Kentucky) Senior Citizens along with the Union Labor Housing Corporation (representing the Kentucky State AFL-CIO, Owensboro Council of Labor and Owensboro Building and Construction Trades Council). In addition, the Kentucky State AFL-CIO in Louisville sponsored a 250-unit rehabilitation project and twenty-five units are sponsored by the Evergreen Union Retirement Association, Eugene, Oregon.

The AFL-CIO Urban Affairs Department compiled a list of 127 union-sponsored housing projects, of which twenty-four were senior citizen housing projects. Since January, 1974, seven additional union sponsors were approved to build senior citizen housing.* Does this represent greater social commitment than management shows? The Clearing House on Corporate Social Responsibility listed fifty-five mutual insurance companies with $107.4 million invested in housing and ninety-nine stock insurance companies with $87.9 million in housing. Considering their assets, the insurance companies lagged behind labor.

As a rule, trustees of union assets are the most conservative of investors. Brandwen's philosophy of not throwing good money "into ratholes" may be considered representative of the trade union approach. Of the $600 million in union trust funds he administers, Duff Kennedy, president of Kennedy Boston Associates and Loomis and Kennedy (affiliates of the Boston Company), said that the trustees' "more conservative" approach called for a 50 percent investment in fixed income, such as real estate, and 50 percent in common stock equity, with no investments whatever in non-union projects.

There are, however, too many unions which turn over management of their pension funds to commercial bank trust departments or insurance companies without any further thought to the disposition of the funds. The president of a 20,000-member union with impressive assets shrugged off inquiries into what investments were being made with his local's pension funds: "We leave all that in the hands of the Prudential Insurance Company."

He appeared neither to know nor care what Prudential was doing with the workers' capital. Only the results counted. This attitude appears commonplace. Corporate Data Exchange revealed that at year-end 1976, 118 public and private union-related pension plans held $12.6 billion of common stock in 50 predominantly non-union firms.

Indifference, however, may be preferable to the options taken by some union trustees, which reflect little or no credit upon themselves.

---

* The labor-supported National Council of Senior Citizens fought for five years to have the Section 202 senior citizens' direct-loan housing program restored to the housing law after President Nixon's "moratorium." Work was started in 1978 on nine senior citizens' housing developments, to be built by union labor at a cost of $45 million.

An outstanding instance is the Central States Southeast and Southwest Areas Pension Fund of the International Brotherhood of Teamsters.

Half a million teamsters pour $400 million a year into the fund through employer contributions, but if pensions were paid to the teamsters entitled to them, there'd be no reason for repeated grand jury and U.S. Labor Department investigations or Congressional hearings.

But the $1.4 billion pension fund has not been concerned with paying out pension benefits; instead, its trustees have been siphoning million in loans to real estate ventures controlled by the underworld and stock swindlers. In 1976 the Labor and Justice Departments' investigations resulted in the resignations of all the trustees and the placing of management of the fund assets in the hands of Equitable Life Assurance Company. The resignations, however, did not remove the threat of legal action by the Labor Department under the 1974 federal pension law to bring about "reformation of fund practices and procedures."

There are other pension and welfare funds equally controversial, such as Amalgamated Local Union 355's United Welfare Fund, which made equally speculative and irregular loans to a company in which secretary-treasurer Bernard Tolkow had invested and to a Mafia-owned hotel in the Catskills.

In the public mind, these few exceptions exemplify what trade unions do with their members' capital. The picture is not accurate. One need only recall that New York City was bailed out of bankruptcy by pension funds when few banks were willing to take the risk.

The New York City municipal employee retirement systems' trustees agreed in 1975 to purchase up to $2.5 billion in city and Municipal Assistance Corporation (MAC) bonds through June 30, 1978, thus averting the first in a series of bankruptcy crises.

Granted, the service performed by the union trustees was made under duress, but it was effective in staving off bankruptcy. New York City's five pension funds were vindicated four years later when they sold more than $53 million of their Municipal Assistance Corporation bonds at a profit of nearly $1.5 million.

It was a risk the International Ladies Garment Workers Union did not take. The ILG invests only in U.S. Government obligations and gilt-edged bonds, and will not even consider corporate bonds for investments, according to Assistant President Gus Tyler.

In another area, labor's assets have been used to transform blighted acres of ghetto tenement housing in New York into massive low- and middle-income housing projects sponsored by labor cooperatives which provided the impetus, the planning and organization to realize the dreams of thousands of underprivileged families. This is not a recent development. Joseph G. Knapp dates the first significant housing development by labor as 1927, when the Amalgamated Clothing Workers started operating the Amalgamated Housing Cooperative.

> It was set up to take advantage of a New York State law passed in 1926 designed to encourage low-rental housing by providing certain tax advantages. Abraham E. Kazan was the manager of this enterprise, and he showed great abilities and leadership qualities in getting the project under way and established. Its basic plan was simple. The member residents were called upon to invest $500 per room in the Amalgamated Housing Corp. for the apartments they would occupy and then to pay a monthly rental to cover carrying charges on the amount borrowed to finance the enterprise.[4]

Kazan, who had earlier been managing the Amalgamated's credit union, managed the cooperative and its successor, the United Housing Foundation, retiring in 1966 as president emeritus of UHF.

The first Amalgamated Houses project, erected in the Bronx, was a small development, housing 303 families. Sidney Hillman, ACW president, favored restricting tenancy to the union's members. Instead, at the insistence of Kazan, Amalgamated Houses was opened to one and all in strict compliance with Rochdale principles. Donald D. Martin, UHF secretary, recalled that the dispute was so bitter that Hillman and Kazan "didn't talk to each other for years." One of the first families to move in was that of David Dubinsky, president of the International Ladies Garment Workers Union.

The principles adopted for Amalgamated Houses and adhered to since differ only slightly from the familiar Rochdale principles. The latter provide for open membership; one-member, one-vote; neutrality in politics and religion; patronage funds paid on the basis of the members' patronage; limited interest paid on share capital; cash trading; money set aside for reserves; constant education; and constant expansion.

Sidney Hillman, Jacob Potofsky (who succeeded Hillman as president of the ACW) and Abraham Kazan had a formula which worked, meeting the objective of the cooperative: to provide its members with good housing at the most reasonable price possible. Harold Ostroff, who makes a point of this objective, goes on to say:

> In time the original development quadrupled in size and, by 1965, the union had sponsored three additional cooperatives, which provided homes for 3,628 families. Since their inception, open membership has always been the first basic principle of cooperatives. One of the most encouraging aspects of the development of housing cooperatives has been that they create naturally integrated communities. More and more fre-

quently, people of minority groups discover the economic and social advantages cooperatives provide . . .

The 50,000 families living in housing cooperatives have demonstrated that, given the opportunity for participating in practical programs for self-help, the essential ingredient which has made cooperatives successful is the common bond of mutual ownership which exists between the members. This is particularly true in housing cooperatives where the members have made substantial investments in their homes.[5]

The housing shortage of the 1920s which prompted Hillman to undertake the first cooperative was followed by another shortage at the end of World War II, leading other unions to follow the Amalgamated's pioneer effort. The ILGWU took up the challenge:

The ILGWU Cooperative Village, completed in 1956 on Manhattan's lower east side, is a 1,672-family housing cooperative development. This same union undertook sponsorship of a second cooperative in the area known as the old Chelsea district, between 23rd and 29th streets and 8th and 9th avenues. Known as the Mutual Redevelopment Houses, the project was conceived as a walk-to-work community. Its location enabled many workers, particularly those employed in the garment industry, to get to and from work in a minimum time and with minimum discomfort. At the same time, its construction, of course, helped alleviate the accute shortage of decent housing for wage earners.[6]

As other unions became involved in cooperative housing to meet the needs of their members in the face of housing shortages in urban areas and ever-increasing rentals and property values, the United Housing Foundation was formed in 1951 as a membership corporation.

Many of the people behind United Housing were the same pioneers who helped develop the viability of cooperative housing. At United Housing's first meeting in July, 1951, Abraham E. Kazan was elected president, with Louis H. Pink, vice president; S. F. Boden, secretary, and Robert Szold, treasurer. Initial funds for the foundation were provided by the Edward A. Filene Good Will Fund in the form of a $10,000 loan.[7]

UHF (its operating arm is Community Service, which provides technical services to housing developments) has been responsible for providing 50,000 families with the benefits of cooperative living. Its largest effort to date has been Co-op City, a 300-acre project housing 15,382 families in 35 high-rise buildings and 236 town houses.

A great many union leaders are involved in UHF, since many unions are among the sponsors of UHF co-op housing developments. As might be expected, UHF officers and directors include prominent metropolitan New York labor officials. The president and a director in 1976 was Potofsky. Seven other trade unionists were on the board—a significant part of the total membership of seventeen, since some of the others had labor backgrounds. These are the men who have given so much to the cause of cooperative housing, which, it should be noted, goes far beyond housing as a way of life. As the UHF pointed out in its *Twenty Years of Accomplishment*:

> Cooperative housing as a way of life extends beyond buildings. It includes the development of a cooperative community, with shopping centers, pharmacies, optical dispensers, furniture store, insurance company. The approach is best typified by the statement of the purpose of UHF: "All that we do is directed toward utilizing the methods of cooperation to enable people to enjoy a better life and to achieve a better society!"

Another area in which union funds and initiative are being put to social use is in assisting banks owned by "minorities" (e.g., blacks and Puerto Ricans) by swelling their deposits with pension and welfare funds.

Such a program was adopted by the New York Central Labor Council in 1966, when President Van Arsdale appointed James Trenz chairman of the Civil Rights Committee's banking and business subcommittee. Trenz, who is president of Local 463, International Union of Electrical, Radio and Machine Workers, explained the rationale for the committee's work:

> It's a civil rights activity. We feel meaningful civil rights can be achieved by minority groups who can play an effective role in the economy as owners and employers in commerce and industry. And banks are at the center of business. We are trying to help the minorities establish businesses, be home owners, develop a minority middle class. The blacks and Hispanic employees can never become owners without capital. We are trying to supply the capital. We've passed the $3 million mark, the funds coming from pension and welfare funds and treasuries of local unions. The response of the trade unions has been fairly good, but we are still looking for more. And we're the only central labor council doing this.

It was a wise choice to make Trenz chairman of the subcommittee. Not only does his union have a 40 percent Spanish-speaking and black minority, but Trenz, in all he undertakes, is a gadfly who never takes "no" as an answer. He may be a bit shy in stature, physically, but not otherwise. But what has the Banking and Business Subcommittee really achieved? The answer can be found between the lines of the annual reports Trenz draws up.

The reports reveal wide swings in deposits made in four institutions, reflecting economic trends, but at its best the contribution of New York City labor amounted to about $3 million in as many as 105 separate accounts.

But it is revealing that more than one-third of the deposits in any year could be credited to the personal intervention of Harry Van Arsdale into the banking practices of IBEW Local 3, the Joint Industry Electrical Board, electrical industry members and Taxi Drivers Locals 3036 and 30261. That's exemplary of the way Van Arsdale leads the Central Labor Council.

Could New York labor do more for the black community? Unquestionably. Unions have the assets but not the inclination, apparently. Even so, their record puts to shame the response affiliates of the nearby Long Island Federation of Labor made when minority-controlled Vanguard Bank opened in Hempstead, New York.

Another area in which unions have been financially active to some extent (but not as widely as assumed) is in the formation of credit unions to enable members to secure low-interest loans.

The Credit Union National Association estimated that in 1975 there were 1,007 credit unions serving trade union members. While this is 4.53 percent of all credit unions in the nation, it is barely one-sixtieth of the number of local trade unions in the U.S. That, however, does not reflect a lack of interest on the part of unions. A number of years ago when the New York Newspaper Guild polled its members on forming a credit union, the lack of interest shown by members willing to invest (though most would borrow) persuaded Guild officers to drop the proposal.

Vivian Packard, research specialist for CUNA, estimated that assets of the credit unions sponsored by trade unions totaled $858,565,000 in 1974, or 2.33 percent of all credit union assets.

Overall, there were 29.4 million members of credit unions in 1975, enrolled in nearly 23,000 credit unions in the U.S. with aggregate assets of $36 billion. While there are unquestionably many trade unionists enrolled in credit unions not sponsored by labor organizations, there are only 1,098,188 enrolled in trade union credit unions, or 3.61 percent of total credit union membership.

The comparative lack of interest in credit unions may indicate workers have little need for credit. Or can it be that few have the funds to invest? Far more likely, the lack of interest reflects reluctance to become involved in business, finance or even cooperative movements. Trade union history is filled with numerous instances of financial failures.

One of the major successes, however, is the Union Labor Life Insurance Company, which opened for business in May, 1927, with an initial capital of $600,000—the investment of sixty international unions, six state federations, thirty-four city central labor bodies and 240 local unions. Fifty years later, ULLICO had assets exceeding $300 million and more than $3 billion of life insurance in force, so that it ranked among the twenty leading companies in the U.S. underwriting all forms of insurance.

The concept of a union life insurance company was brought before the 1923 AFL convention in Portland, Oregon, by Matthew Woll, president of the Photo Engravers, and George W. Perkins, president of the Cigar Makers. A committee appointed by AFL President Samuel Gompers reported favorably at the 1924 convention and plans to organize the company were approved by a conference of fifty representatives in the following year.

Chartered in Maryland, ULLICO began selling stock at the end of 1925. The charter provides for wide union control by guaranteeing repurchase of stock, requiring three-fourths of the directors to be labor officials, limiting board membership to no more than one member from a union and restricting the number of shares held by any one union.

Woll was the first president and Perkins the first secretary-treasurer. The first group policy, written in 1927 for a federal employees local union, was still in force fifty years later.

Licensed in forty-four states to offer group and individual policies in health, accident and life insurance, in addition to group pension contracts, ULLICO has shown consistent growth over the years, passing $100 million of insurance in force by 1945, $200 million by 1949 and $500 million by 1955. A merger with American Standard Life Insurance in 1957 boosted ULLICO's insurance in force over the $1 billion mark. A group pension portfolio was introduced in 1961. Holdings in pension fund contracts were valued at $150 million in 1976, when J. Albert Woll, AFL-CIO general counsel and son of ULLICO's first president, was board chairman.

There's but one other "union label" insurance company in the U.S.—American Income Life Insurance, with executive offices in Waco, Texas. While it was not organized by trade unionists or with union capital, Bernard Rapoport, board chairman and chief executive officer, determined AIL would capture the union market neglected by insurance industry giants. He won the confidence of unions by asking the Office and Professional Employees International Union to organize the company's workers—including his 800 field agents. Rapoport is an honorary member of OPEIU. With its slogan, A Union Label Company Serving America's Union Families, AIL has grown to over $116 million in assets and had more than $1.2 billion in life insurance in force in 1977. AIL's labor advisory board, composed of international union presidents, offers counsel on how the company can better serve unions and their members.

Notes

1. Thomas R. Brooks, *Toil and Trouble*, p. 153.
2. Vide Joseph E. Finley, *The Corrupt Kingdom*, chaps. 7 and 8.
3. Report of the AFL-CIO Executive Council, 1973, pp. 199–200.
4. Joseph G. Knapp, *The Advance of American Cooperative Enterprise: 1920–1945*, p. 182.
5. Harold Ostroff, "Labor Co-ops and the Housing Crisis," *American Federationist*, May 1969.
6. Boris Shishkin, "Organized Labor—Champion of Cooperative Housing," *Co-op Housing*, Winter 1964.
7. United Housing Foundation, *Twenty Years of Accomplishment*, p. 9.

14.
Union Democracy and Civil Rights

"You have several blacks in the graduating class," I said. "What would you do, Nick, if a supermarket refused a job to one of the apprentices?"

"Are you kidding?" he asked, incredulously. "We'd strike the store and I mean the whole damned chain." There was a flush of anger on his cheeks as he added, "And they damned well know it, too!"

Labor has come a long way since American unions systematically excluded blacks from membership with either an overt whites-only clause in the constitution of the union or a covert reference in the ritual. One can point to innumerable indications of a growing sense of brotherhood in many unions. But it is reasonable to start with the premise that historically racial prejudice was as pervasive in trade unions as in any institution of the United States. What more could be expected from any group of white males in a nation where racial prejudice has been as blatantly expressed, until recent years, as sexism? And yet, since unions tend to be pluralistic structures, labor has not been entirely racist in attitude.

Without minimizing the extent of racial prejudice still existing in unions, history shows that unions fought prejudice and, indeed, even opposed the institution of slavery long before the Civil War, and not only in the South (where there were few unions), but in the North, too, where their number, in comparison, was legion. As early as 1849 in Lexington, Kentucky, mechanics called for the abolition of slavery, resolving

> that the institution of slavery is prejudicial to every interest of the State, and is alike injurious to the slaveholder and non-slaveholder; that it degrades labor, enervates industry, interferes with the occupations of free laboring citizens, separates too widely the poor and the rich, shuts out the laboring classes from the blessings of education, and tends to drive from the State all who depend upon personal labor support.[1]

It must be recognized the poor white worker of the South was opposed to slavery primarily because the slave was a threat to the white man's job opportunities, wage scale and collective bargaining.

The competition of slave labor fostered the organization of unions, leading to democratic reforms which threatened the continuation of slavery. But in the North, the call for abolition of slavery sounded loudest of all from the wage earners who understood the parallel of their own struggle with that of the black slave. In 1830, the "Workingmen's Prayer" submitted to the Massachusetts State Legislature called for the abolition of slavery with this appeal:

> May the foul stain of slavery be blotted out of our fair escutcheon; and our fellow men, not only declared to be free and equal, but actually enjoy that freedom and equality to which they are entitled by nature.[2]

These sentiments gained currency among unions and workingmen's political parties in the decades before the Civil War, when the South fought for extension of slavery into the territories of the West, thus threatening further competition with free labor. When the war came, trade unionists flocked to the colors, volunteering in disproportionate numbers to defend the Union. The abolition of slavery appeared to offer as much hope to the wage slave as to the black slave.

The end of slavery did not signal any acceptance of freed black men by trade unions, despite a wave of organizing which saw unions flourish in the 1860s. On the contrary, unions were organized to protect the elite craft workers from the competition of unskilled hands as technological improvements were introduced in industry. This was not uniformly true of all organized labor. The Knights of Labor, for example, when organized in 1869, was open to all craft workers regardless of sex, race, creed or color, which may be one reason why so many craft unions withdrew from the Knights in 1886 to join the newly formed American Federation of Labor.

Blacks organized their own unions because they were excluded from so many white unions. Prejudice in some unions ran so deep that whites found working alongside blacks were expelled from the union, as in the Washington, D.C., bricklayers, while the National Typographical Union, without a color bar in its constitution, refused admittance to the Columbia Typographical Union No. 101 in Washington of a black printer, Louis H. Douglass, who had been hired by the Government Printing Office.

By the time the American Federation of Labor was organized in 1881 as the Federation of Organized Trades and Labor Unions of the United States and Canada (a name it retained until 1886), it was common practice for unions to limit membership to white males. But

Samuel Gompers, opposed to racial discrimination, could not control the federation's autonomous affiliates. His insistence that unions desiring to affiliate with the AFL must eliminate the color bar from their constitutions met with this reaction, Philip S. Foner relates:

> In late 1894, the National Association of Machinists and the National Machinists' Union amalgamated to form the International Association of Machinists. In March, 1895, James O'Connell, head of the amalgamated union, reported he had discussed the question of the constitutional ban with Gompers, McGuire and many other leading lights in the AFL, that they had suggested that the union remove the color ban from the constitution, transfer it to the ritual and then apply for membership in the federation. O'Connell was assured that rejection "would not stare us in the face." This is precisely what happened. The IAM removed the color ban from its constitution, transferred it to the ritual, applied for membership in the AFL and was allowed to affiliate. Thereafter, the union effectively excluded Negro machinists.[3]

The Machinists' pledge in the ritual bound members to propose only white men for membership. The pledge was not removed until 1947. The Boilermakers and Iron and Ship Builders Union, chartered in 1896, used the same device. For decades the AFL did not face up to the explosive issue, granting charters to all-black unions when the white craft unions turned them down. Autonomy could not be violated; human rights were. The black unions directly affiliated with the AFL could expect little or no help from the federation, since it had no voice in negotiations or the enforcement of contracts.

While the AFL did not come to grips with the problem until comparatively recently, some unions did far earlier. The United Mine Workers of America, for example, included in its constitution of 1890 the declared purpose, "to unite in one organization, regardless of creed, color or nationality, all workmen employed in and around the coal mines." But then, the UMWA is not a craft union. That is not to say there was no discrimination shown by white miners; there was, since blacks were used as strikebreakers in the southern coal fields.

Strikebreaking, however, merely compounded the basic problem of discrimination. When asked why blacks were not hired, mine operators said that white miners would refuse to work alongside a black. But it is indisputable that large numbers of blacks did join the UMWA because its constitution barred discrimination and its contracts provided superior wages and working conditions.[4]

Discrimination was rampant in the craft unions. The constitutions or rituals of twenty-seven unions barred blacks from membership as late as 1930, fourteen in 1943, but none after the Civil Rights Act of 1964. In others, black workers were kept out by tacit agreement or were disqualified by license laws inspired by white unionists, or other onerous conditions. In the industrial unions, however, it was difficult to exclude blacks without losing the bargaining unit. Obviously the Congress of Industrial Organizations, organized in the 1930s, could have no color bar. Nor did its leaders, including Philip Murray and Walter Reuther, believe in segregated unions. In other unions, such as the Amalgamated Clothing Workers and the ILGWU, blacks were being accepted as members shortly after the turn of the century.

By 1909, when the waist workers were organized by the ILG, the first blacks entering the needle trades were accepted as a matter of course, probably reflecting the views of the immigrant Jews who made up the greatest part of the membership. (They had known discrimination, too.) A decade later the blacks became a major factor in garment manufacturing. But even when black women were brought in to break a strike in Chicago in 1917, some 500 of them kept on working in the needle trades when the dispute was settled.

The ILG made no effort to bar the blacks from the industry; on the contrary, the union even organized the all-black shops with the result that employers were deprived of their cheap-labor market. Sterling D. Spero and Abram L. Harris[5] have recorded instances in which the ILG called strikes against employers who discriminated against their black workers.

Despite this policy, the ILG continued to deny blacks a voice in policy-making in the union and for years permitted conditions to exist that kept blacks in the lowest-paying jobs, Roy Innis and Herbert Hill, two articulate spokesmen for blacks, have repeatedly charged. Today, the ILG points with pride to Mattie Jackson of San Francisco, a vice president who is not only a black but a woman.

A black woman also served as a vice president of the Amalgamated Meat Cutters and Butcher Workmen of North America, a union representing retail food chain stores. She is Addie Wyatt, director of the Women's Affairs Department, which was created in 1972. When the union was chartered in 1897, blacks were already working in the meat industry, usually as strikebreakers. Too few remained in the Chicago stockyards after a strike to organize, but by 1917 the Meat Cutters organized not only thousands of blacks, but women, too, in keeping with a policy that was already "traditional." The tradition was further developed by the United Packinghouse Workers Union in the Chicago stockyards in the 1930s. (UPWU was merged into the Meat Cutters in 1968.)

The industrial unions organized the black workers long before there was a CIO, not primarily out of a sense of brotherhood, but to establish one wage scale and eliminate the competition of cheap labor.

The CIO could not and did not exclude blacks in organizing industrial plants where they represented a considerable portion of the work force. The CIO not only opened its doors to blacks, but the competition for members put pressure on AFL affiliates to lift their restrictions against the blacks. It would be shortsighted, however, to overlook the influence of civil rights organizations in this regard. An even more potent factor was the organization of the all-black Brotherhood of Sleeping Car Porters by A. Philip Randolph* in 1925. A former socialist, Randolph proved to be the gadfly who did more than any other labor leader to break down discriminatory practices in the AFL. Indeed, he was so unrelenting in his attack that at one point he demanded the AFL-CIO expel unions practicing discrimination and George Meany roared, "Who in the hell appointed you as guardian of the Negro members in America?"

By the time of the AFL-CIO merger in 1955, the pressure of migration, the civil rights movement and the absorption of millions of blacks into industry in a labor-tight market during World War II had brought about a more tolerant attitude in the labor movement.

Article II, Section 4 of the AFL-CIO Constitution states one object is "to encourage all workers without regard to race, creed, color, sex, national origin or ancestry to share equally in the full benefits of union organization."

Note the inclusion of "sex" in the current constitution. It was not until 1973 that the Executive Council recommended the constitution be amended by "adding the word, 'sex,' after the word, 'color.'" That, however, did not eradicate every trace of prejudice in the affiliated unions. The record is clear that racial prejudice still exists in some unions, as it does in social institutions outside the labor movement. Indeed, the recession of 1974–76 aggravated tensions for unions as blacks and whites competed for all too few available jobs.

Where does the AFL-CIO stand now on the civil rights issue? After all, there are about 2 million blacks who are members of its affiliates—or five times as many as belong to the National Association for the Advancement of Colored People. (Blacks make up 15 percent of the total union membership, or more than the proportion of blacks in the population.) The AFL-CIO position was clear in the controversy faced by the 1975 convention when the Kentucky State AFL-CIO introduced Resolution 224:

> RESOLVED: The AFL-CIO reevaluates its position on busing where it does not improve educational opportunities or quality education and to oppose this type of busing which accomplished nothing except unrest, worry, turmoil and the additional expense which should be used in hiring better

---

* Randolph died May 16, 1979.

teachers and in improvement of our system and be it further resolved that
the AFL-CIO opposes acts of violence or the violation of any law in the
process of seeking a solution to this busing issue and be it further resolved
that as Kentucky rates 49th in education, we respectfully request the
AFL-CIO to help alleviate this great problem and dissatisfaction where
there are no constructive results arising therefrom.

The resolutions committee called on the convention for nonconcurrence, but to reaffirm the stand taken in 1973, since the resolution
was blatantly racist. Delegate Leonard S. Smith of the Kentucky State
AFL-CIO, in supporting the resolution, revealed how thin the veneer
of racial tolerance remains in Kentucky:

> This is not a racial issue. I want to remind you this resolution passed our
> executive board by a unanimous vote, *including the black boy and a most
> respected boy* in Louisville, Ky., Jimmy Stewart. He is chairman of the
> Philip Randolph Committee, he is president of the State Building Trades.
> So I'll assure you it's not a racial issue.[6] [Emphasis added.]

The convention voted nonconcurrence on the resolution, but not
until after George Meany took the floor to explain the AFL-CIO continued to support busing "when it will improve the educational opportunities of children." The resolution opposed "forced busing," which
"accomplishes neither improvement of educational opportunities nor
quality education." Even a "most respected black boy" can see the difference in approach.

Meany, however, didn't appreciate the difference.

A month later, when the Massachusetts State Labor Council
adopted a similar resolution opposing busing, he threatened the council with disciplinary action, and the executive board of the council
voted to rescind the resolution adopted only two weeks earlier. Council
President Joseph Sullivan said union locals affiliated with the state
council "have a right to take any action they want" in regard to the
anti-busing stand.

The AFL-CIO has the necessary authority over labor councils and
does not hesitate to use it when its position is undermined by contrary
views. Its position on civil rights is, on the whole, commendable.
George Meany summed up that position in an unusually frank discussion in 1976, while presenting the Murray-Green Award to A. Philip
Randolph:

> We have never made any bones about the fact that there was discrimina-
> tion in the trade union movement; not to the extent . . . that it existed in
> the community at large, but we never tried to sweep it under the rug.

In 1940, when I became secretary-treasurer of the AFL, out of approximately 100 national unions which comprised the AFL at that time, twenty-three had a color bar in their constitution. When we merged in 1955, there were no unions with a color bar in their constitution. We took in two unions at that time that had been outside of both the AFL and CIO and we brought them into the family of labor despite the fact that they had a color bar in their constitution and we gave them two years to take it out. Well, they took it out and they are still part of the AFL-CIO.

Yes, there is racial discrimination in the ranks of labor, just as there is in many churches, but the widespread condemnation of segregated unions has not been matched by an equally broad attack on religion. What is truly appalling is the attitude of those union officials who contend discrimination is solely the result of employer decisions. "It's not our fault," said one high union officer. "The employer simply didn't hire *them*."

The "problem" didn't arouse concern in that union until the civil rights movement and the Civil Rights Act of 1964 forced the union to act. But even government intervention has failed to wipe out racial (and sexual) discrimination, the U.S. Civil Rights Commission declared on May 11, 1976. Its 291-page report conceded that bias was not as overt in the building trades and trucking unions as a decade earlier, but these unions were continuing "to restrict employment opportunities of minorities and women."

Robert A. Georgine, president of the AFL-CIO Building Trades Department, called the findings inaccurate and cited figures showing blacks accounted for 29 percent of construction apprentices.

It is pertinent to recall that unions, despite the popular stereotype, are not all guilty of prejudice. But the trade union movement not only has a degree of prejudice to overcome, but public opinion as well. Position papers will not overcome that public image. It is not enough for George Meany to declare, as he did before the Negro American Labor Council in 1962, that "when anyone tries to say that the trade unions are the chief barrier to the economic opportunities of Negroes in this country, I resent it and I reject it, for it is simply not true."

It will take decisive action by labor to eliminate racial prejudice wherever it exists, whether in the hiring hall or union elections, in collective bargaining or any social endeavor union members participate in. It is a challenge trade unionists must face squarely.

It is a role forced upon unions by their structure: democratic political institutions whose form is dictated by their functions. Of course, it is apparent too many unions have become oligarchies in which democracy is an illusion, but that is because of their unwieldy size, the heterogeneous membership and the high degree of apathy, not the structure of the institution. And the larger they become, the more unwieldy and less democratic.

While a high degree of public exposure will be essential to be convincing, it will not be enough to elect a few blacks or Chicanos or any
other minority representatives to high union office. The Executive
Council of the AFL-CIO in 1976 did not include a single woman and
had only C. L. Dellums of the Brotherhood of Sleeping Car Porters and
Frederick D. O'Neal of the Associated Actors and Artistes of America
on its board as representatives of the blacks.

Obviously, since few blacks are elected president of international
unions, few are elected to the council, which is usually limited to
presidents. Independent unions vary widely. There is, for example, the
National Alliance of Postal and Federal Employees, the oldest and only
black-controlled union in the country. In its sixty-three years, the
union hasn't excluded workers because of race, sex, creed, color or national origin, according to Mary Treadwell, public relations representative. Women constitute 25 percent of the 55,000 members; four
are on the national executive board, two of them officers.

Social reforms which would convince the public all unions are free
of prejudice must be more than highly visible token gestures. To be
convincing, action should involve the rank and file. Neither elections
nor resolutions can have the impact of testimony on behalf of civil
rights, either in Congress or Selma, Alabama, lobbying for Title VII of
the Civil Rights Act (the section owes its existence to the urging of the
AFL-CIO), or negotiating contracts with effective machinery to gather
and evaluate data on employment practices.

To be convincing, it will take such programs as the one adopted by
the Newspaper Guild in 1963, when the Human Rights Report at the
union's convention in Philadelphia declared:

> In order to improve the circumstances of an increasing number of
> minority-group people, who are now turned aside as "unqualified" for
> employment and promotion, we seek . . . a realistic, down-to-earth mean-
> ingful program, which will include not merely the hiring of those now
> qualified without discrimination as to race, age, sex, creed, color, na-
> tional origin or ancestry, but also efforts through apprenticeship training
> and other means to improve and upgrade their qualifications.

The attitude outlined by those words mirrors the convictions held
by the Guild since it was founded in 1933 by Heywood Broun. Indeed,
the union's constitution contains what is known as the Heywood Broun
clause (because Broun insisted it be included):

> Guild membership shall be open to every eligible person without
> discrimination or penalty, nor shall any member be barred from member-
> ship or penalized by reason of age, sex, race, national origin, religious or
> political conviction or anything he writes for publication.

The parallel between the report and the Broun clause is not coincidence. But what has the Guild actually done to put those beliefs into practice? It has opened newspaper jobs to blacks by going directly to newspaper management to urge they be hired. It has in its contracts prohibitions against discrimination in hiring or firing practices. It has worked with the National Urban League in developing a "skills bank" of minority workers. The union's Human Rights Department maintains a file of information on black candidates for jobs. The Guild has also circulated its own booklet, *Careers for Negroes on Newspapers*, outlining what the jobs are and how they can be found.

How effective has this Guild program been? That's difficult to evaluate, since the print and broadcast media have scrambled to entice blacks for several reasons: the civil rights movement, growing awareness of the "black market," enforcement of EEOC regulations and the Guild's nondiscriminatory policy. Even so, it's doubtful that more than 1 percent of the 40,000 working press is black. Two-thirds of the nation's newspapers have no minority employees, the F.E. Gannett Urban Journalism Center at Medill School of Journalism estimated in 1978, yet 4 percent of the reporters and editors on dailies are minority members, its survey showed, compared with 1 percent in 1968.

But the Guild has made an impression, according to Herbert Hammerman and Marvin Rogoff:

> The Newspaper Guild, AFL-CIO, has . . . introduced equal employment opportunity into the mainstream of everyday bargaining. The Guild . . . has adopted a basically decentralized equal employment opportunity approach. Certain equal employment opportunity requirements (such as equal pay for equal work among reporters, proper recognition of pregnancy disability, and hiring goals for minorities and women) must be met for locally negotiated agreements to receive Guild approval.
>
> Local unions are committed to uncovering violations, but the Guild does provide training and conferences to equip officers and committees to do their work. The Guild has, in fact, sent local negotiators back to the bargaining table to achieve parity for women's page and society reporters (most of whom are usually women) with general assignment reporters (mostly men). Local committees are likewise to review hiring standards for conformance to the formula set forth in *Griggs v. Duke Power Co.*
>
> Finally, after several successive convention rejections, the Guild has created its first national-level position to coordinate activities in human rights.[7]

The Newspaper Guild is not unique in its approach to the problem. Equally diligent efforts are being made by the International

Union of Electrical Workers, the United Auto Workers, the American Federation of State, County and Municipal Employees, the United Steel Workers, the Amalgamated Meat Cutters, the Utility Workers of America, the Transport Workers Union and the United Furniture Workers of America to give the black worker an equal opportunity to earn a living as an organized worker.

Far more convincing than public declarations or constitutional provisions to demonstrate concern over the minorities' plight were the concerted campaigns the entire labor movement mounted on behalf of the California farm workers and the Mexican-American employees of the Farah clothing plants in Texas and New Mexico. Nationwide boycotts, in which labor joined hands with intellectuals, young people, the churches and prominent writers to force California growers and Farah to submit to representation elections, demonstrated that labor did give a damn about what was unquestionably the most oppressed ethnic class of workers in the country.

The Amalgamated Clothing and Textile Workers now represent Farah employees in five plants in collective bargaining, while the United Farm Workers have been winning a significant proportion of elections in the California grape and produce fields. Both campaigns took organization, manpower and millions in funds—all of which were forthcoming from the AFL-CIO and its affiliates, so the Chicano could win *dignidad*. It is doubtful that many for whom the taste of California iceberg lettuce became bitter had ever met or known a Chicano, but the boycott persisted for years.

Unions deserve credit for the first nationwide boycotts, obviously, but in the light of their neglect of the farm worker who remained "exempt" from collective bargaining, the laurels belong to Cesar Chavez, the Mexican-American farm worker from Yuma, Arizona, whose persuasive drive won unstinting labor support. Chavez has been characterized variously as saint, fiend, radical or racketeer, but a single meeting with him convinced the author that Chavez is primarily a humanist who believes intensely in helping mankind attain *dignidad*. And isn't that the essence of trade unionism?

Labor has had no charismatic black leader to ignite an equally militant drive on behalf of oppressed Southern black workers since the death of Martin Luther King Jr., but the AFL-CIO has thrown all its forces behind the Amalgamated Clothing and Textile Workers to organize the sixty-three J. P. Stevens plants in the Carolinas. In announcing a nationwide boycott, George Meany characterized Stevens as "the No. 1 labor lawbreaker in America."

It's no coincidence that blacks make up the bulk of the lower-paid, blue-collar workers at Stevens; this allows a parallel to be drawn with the campaign mounted on behalf of the Chicanos. If anyone ever needed help from the labor movement, it is the black worker in the "right-to work" states of the South.

The inescapable fact is blacks and other minority group members do not have equal employment opportunities. There are frequent reminders in the press that unions are to blame. (Even in the non-union shops?) But it makes good copy, since unions are popularly assumed to be beyond reproach. While unions cannot be given absolution in toto, they have moved too slowly to escape constant criticism, even when the employer is clearly to blame. When Braniff Airways was ordered in November, 1976, to begin paying $1.1 million in penalties to minority workers, the district court judge noted the International Association of Machinists and the International Brotherhood of Teamsters were also defendants, since "their combined practices had discriminated in both hiring and promotion."

There's reason enough for the existence of the Coalition of Black Trade Unionists, as well as similar regional coalitions, notably in Chicago, Detroit and New York. Each works within the labor movement to advance the interests of black workers in the hope of attaining a realistic role in decision-making within the movement.

The national CBTU, comprised of 3 million black members in forty-five unions, does not focus solely upon internal union matters; employment is a much larger issue, as it is for the regional conferences. William Lucy, president (he is international secretary-treasurer of the American Federation of State, County and Municipal Employees), denounced the "fundamentally racist" policies of President Ford. In 1975 Lucy told the Joint Congressional Subcommittee on Economic Growth, "If the nation accepts the President's plan for a depression decade, half a generation of black youth will reach their mid-20s without ever having a secure and productive job."

But, it should be added, Lucy was equally critical of Ford's predecessor in the White House ("There's no way black unionists are going to remain neutral in this election") and in no way did he spare the AFL-CIO either. "It's obvious the AFL-CIO is not doing its job for black workers. The federation may consider the problems of poor blacks," Lucy said, "but it doesn't understand those problems."

There was some reason to believe black workers would make appreciable progress economically during the Carter Administration, since Carter clearly owed his election to a heavy black vote in the South. But that hope soon faded, as the NAACP made apparent at its 1977 convention.

The black worker needs job opportunities far more than he needs token representation on the executive boards of international unions or the AFL-CIO. Unemployment statistics for blacks have far more relevancy than the number of blacks elected to union office. That is not to suggest that if more blacks were employed and earning incomes equivalent to whites (rather than 62 percent of the median income of white families) they would win a more representative voice in the hierarchy of organized labor.

They would still remain a minority in union membership (and thus in officers elected), as they remain a minority of the total population. The solution, integrated membership and leadership, must come from an enlightened membership freeing itself from the bondage of prejudice through the awareness that bigotry is as destructive to whites as it is to blacks.

That is no evasion. Innumerable instances can be cited of well-integrated unions whose policies as well as officers reflect an enlightened attitude on racial matters. Indeed, so much progress has been made in integration that the Black Trade Unionists Leadership Committee of the New York Central Labor Council published a bicentennial booklet[8] listing biographies of prominent black trade unionists and extolling their contributions to the movement and to society. Some of them are nationally prominent and are leaders in the trade union movement.

But the handful of black trade union leaders could be expanded. The Amalgamated Meat Cutters, for example, had two black vice presidents, as well as Charles Hayes, director of organization. And Addie Wyatt, also a black and director of the Amalgamated's Women's Affairs Department, was honored by *Time* on January 5, 1976, as one of twelve "Women of the Year." Black officers are also encountered on the local, state and national levels in many other unions. Among them are the American Federation of Teachers, American Federation of State, County and Municipal Employees, International Union of Electrical, Radio and Machine Workers, United Auto Workers, Service Employees International Union, International Brotherhood of Electrical Workers, National Maritime Union and the Retail, Wholesale, Department Store Union.

Where unions could more effectively show their intentions were praiseworthy would be in the appointment of blacks to staff positions—a step which requires only a will to act. The Communications Workers of America acted while Joseph Beirne was president. His orders were to recommend black women for staff vacancies, or justify the alternative choice to his satisfaction. Blacks, however, were not only the preferred choice; the same order applied to Indians and Mexican-Americans. Beirne's successor, Glenn Watts, is considered to be even "more civil-minded" than Beirne and so "reverse discrimination" continues to be the policy of CWA.

The United Furniture Workers of America found a simple device for placing blacks in top posts, through adoption of a convention resolution in 1970 calling for representatives at large from each of four geographic regions, leaving it to the general executive board to make nominations of blacks in those areas with predominantly black membership.

The growing number of black staff members, shop stewards and officers on union rolls invites two reactions: Why aren't there more? And, what difference does it make, so long as blacks are locked into lower-paying, less desirable jobs under collective bargaining agreements? There's validity to the second objection. One might cite a federal appeals court verdict of October, 1975, finding that 2,700 black workers at the United States Steel Fairfield Works in Birmingham, Alabama, were the victims of a seniority system negotiated by the United Steel Workers and U.S. Steel. (Yet, William B. Gould, who has been severely critical of the treatment of blacks in the nation's white unions, "commended" the USWA "for bowing to the dictates of the law, albeit a decade after Title VII became the law."[9])

The damage discrimination does to the black worker is obvious; the damage to the white worker is less visible, but Harry Fleischman, race relations director of the American Jewish Committee in New York, has defined the danger to the white worker. Fleischman pointed out the price that whites pay in discriminating against blacks, as he urged them both to combine their forces and fight for full and fair employment, and to share in the advantages of social welfare programs. Generally overlooked, this aspect of intolerance becomes patently obvious in his observation that "white building trades workers will benefit along with blacks by a program to build at least a million housing units annually for lower-income families."[10]

His statement requires no demonstration, yet it has proven virtually impossible to convince a high proportion of white workers that they cannot be free so long as black workers remain chained in slavery, which is what racism amounts to. The thought of achieving a working-class consciousness in the face of blatant discrimination is an obvious incongruity. Such "gestures" as contributing funds to the National Association for the Advancement of Colored People are hardly more than palliatives.

Organized labor has come to the aid of the NAACP. In October, 1976, the National Education Association pledged $50,000; the AFL-CIO pledged, in a cooperative movement with the United Auto Workers, another $800,000 to help the NAACP raise collateral so that a bond could be posted in appealing a court judgment of $1.25 million in Mississippi. The judgment arose from a suit filed by twelve white merchants in Port Gibson, who charged the association had been involved in a 1966 boycott aimed at eliminating employment and voting discrimination.

Labor has a long way to go before the United States can be said to have a unified black-and-white working class. But how far has it come to date? Perhaps it would be best to hear from spokesmen for the blacks:

Frederick O'Neal, international president of the Associated Actors and Artistes of America (4A) and president emeritus of Actors Equity Association, is fearful the role of blacks in the labor movement is viewed from a poor perspective. As one of the few blacks to sit on the Executive Council of the AFL-CIO, O'Neal is convinced more attention should be paid to the role of blacks in the labor force. "It's more important to have blacks working," he said, "than to worry about the number of blacks holding high union office."

O'Neal is convinced that once the economic problem is resolved, primarily through on-the-job training and continuing education, recognition in the labor movement will follow. But he does concede it will take more than a black constituency to elect a black as an international president. "I keep telling them," he said, "they have to come to meetings and be active in the union. We have to educate our people."

O'Neal's conviction that jobs and a living wage are more important to the black than union office is amply borne out by the experience of black paraprofessionals trained by the United Federation of Teachers in New York. An episode related by Velma Hill, chairman of the UFT paraprofessional division, sums up the impact of the program:

One incident I witnessed was typical of the change in attitude that had taken place in New York City. Last December I was in a debate that had nothing to do with the UFT—the subject was women's liberation.

Of course, the subject of unions came up and as invariably happens in New York City, one of the speakers or someone from the audience would begin to recite pieties about the "racist UFT" or the "racist Shanker." Some fellow paraprofessionals had come to the meeting with me, and one of them, Patricia Jones, rose to speak. Many people in the audience probably stereotyped her as a good militant who would repeat the usual line about the UFT, only with greater zest and bitterness.

"I used to be a domestic," she said. "I earned $50 a week and worked like a slave. It was a degrading job. Then I became a paraprofessional, joined the UFT and began to fight for a better life. Albert Shanker not only helped that fight, he led it. Now I earn a decent salary. I have paid vacations, sick leave, health insurance and other benefits. I also study so that some day I can get a college degree.

"My whole life has changed. You call it racism. Well, if that's racism"—and she raised a fist clenched gently, in mock imitation of the militant salute—"then that's the kind of racism black people need."

The UFT people in the audience burst into applause. The rest sat in stunned silence. Their simplistic world of "heroic black militants" and "racist union leaders" was shattered—and by someone they could not dismiss as a spokesman for the "system."[11]

Unfortunately, this effective appraisal is likely to have limited effect and will not counter the reiterated stereotype of unions as racist institutions. William B. Gould's *Black Workers in White Unions*, a scholarly work which nearly founders under the weight of its ponderous judicial citations, is likely to be accepted as an authoritative survey of prejudice in U.S. unions. It is difficult not to think of Gould as a racist after reading his conclusion:

> The dreariness of this picture is compounded by the fact that when black trade unionists are elected [to high office in unions] they are often those who are all too acceptable to a conservative white leadership. Under such circumstances, a racially balanced executive board means little if anything for changes in union policy on the issue of race.[12]

It is difficult to see how Gould could have come to any other conclusion, for he started with the belief that

> while the unions purport to adopt a moral stance which is a notch above the country's, they have struggled against adhering to the requirements of new civil rights legislation. More than any other institution, trade unions are the focal point of racial discord in our society . . . A principle obstacle to a more progressive labor movement in the United States is its unwarranted self-satisfaction and smugness about organizing new categories of workers. The effect is to disregard the interests of those who need protection most—the significant number of the poor who are members of racial minorities.[13]

But it remains for the spokesmen for the A. Philip Randolph Institute to have the last word on blacks and trade unions. Bayard Rustin, president, and Norman Hill, executive director, should be acceptable as authorities on the relationship of the civil rights movement and organized labor.

The institute, founded in 1964, acts to achieve the goals of the civil rights movement through a political approach, organizing and educating blacks to register and vote in elections, while simultaneously developing black community leaders with the support of trade unions. Not only is the black worker assisted in finding and keeping a job, but the labor movement itself is supported by the institute as an instrument for attaining dignity for *all* exploited workers.

Rustin's thoughts on the subject are well known since publication of his article, "The Blacks and the Unions," in the May, 1971, issue of *Harper's*. In that magazine, he outlined the recognition, first uttered by Martin Luther King Jr., that blacks are mostly working people who need what labor needs, "and they must fight side by side with unions to achieve these things." They are, indeed, fighting side by side, Rustin contended, pointing out the percentage of blacks in trade unions is higher than the proportion of blacks in the population. While he conceded the entire labor movement cannot be exonerated "of any possible charge of wrongdoing," Rustin stressed that finding work was far more difficult for blacks than making progress in most unions. In an overall assessment of labor's attitude toward black workers, he wrote:

> How ironic that in this period when the trade union movement is thought to be conservative, its social and economic policies are far and away more progressive than those of any other major American institution. Nor—again in contrast to most of the other groups officially concerned with these rights—is labor's program merely in the nature of a grand proposal; there is also an actual record of performance, particularly in the area of civil rights.[14]

Eight years later Norman Hill sat behind his desk at the A. Philip Randolph Institute's headquarters and updated the picture in his habitually gracious manner. Overall, he declared, he would not hesitate to say organized labor is making "progress" in handling the problem of race relations, but it was apparent Hill considered the problem far from resolved. On the most highly publicized area of racial discrimination in unions—the building and constructions trades —Hill's observations were revealing:

> Less than two percent of the enrollment in the building trades' apprenticable crafts were blacks in the late 1960's, but now it's almost 20 percent. I'd say we were making some progress, although we had expected a decline in progress, since the building trades have been the hardest hit by the slump in the economy.

But there is a difference between apprenticeship and journeyman's status, it was suggested to Hill. What proportion of blacks are remaining in the craft after apprenticeship?

"The retention rate has gone up to 75 to 80 percent," he said. "That compares with a normal rate of 50 percent."

The last bastion of "white supremacy," the building trades, has been the target of savage criticism focused upon the unions rather than the employing contractors. Hill pointed out that the building trades are the least unionized of all the crafts, with the unions concentrated chiefly in urban areas. The criticism appears to be misdirected.

Impatient with generalities, Hill doggedly stuck to specifics in discussing the labor movement's contributions to the institute and its programs:

• Financial support comes from "all segments of the union movement."

• George Meany's testimony persuaded Congress to include the critical Title VII in the 1964 Civil Rights Act, despite the opposition of President Kennedy and his brother, Robert. (Meany testified before the House Judiciary Committee that the labor movement wanted "legislation for the correction of shortcomings in its own ranks.")

• The International Association of Machinists, which did not remove its "lily white" clause in its constitution until 1947, finally set up a civil rights department in 1977.

• The AFL-CIO has one black serving as a regional director. He is Walter Waddy, director of Region 3, covering Delaware, Washington, D.C., Kentucky, Maryland, Ohio, Pennsylvania, Virginia and West Virginia.

• The United Steelworkers, unlike most unions, has made civil rights infractions part of the regular grievance machinery. (USWA has one black, an international vice president, on the executive board.)

These particulars, obviously, cannot be summed up with any generalities, but Hill and Rustin, in a joint paper, did sum up labor's attitudes on civil rights:

The labor movement, like every other American institution, is not without a record of racial discrimination. Nonetheless, it is today the most integrated segment of American society. The labor movement not only provided the crucial political muscle that was necessary to enact the civil rights legislation of the 60's, it was far out in front of other institutions in its willingness to set its house in order . . .

The myth of union racism, nonetheless, remains very powerful. Unions, to be sure, play a role in the problem of job discrimination in the United States, but we should see that role in perspective. The overwhelming majority of hiring done in this country is done by employers. Of the charges of job discrimination by the Equal Employment Opportunity Commission, 85 per cent are brought against employers and the other 15 per cent is divided between employment agencies and trade unions. Despite this, the lion's share of public attention to the problem is focused on discrimination by unions. If we are serious about combatting the problem of black unemployment we will keep this in perspective and remember that the union movement has fought harder, longer and more effectively than any other institution to improve job opportunities for minority members.[15]

217

Notes

1. Philip S. Foner, *History of the Labor Movement in the United States*, vol. 1, pp. 263–64.
2. Ibid., p. 266.
3. Ibid., vol. 2, p. 348.
4. Sterling D. Spero and Abram L. Harris, *The Black Worker, the Negro and the Labor Movement*, p. 356.
5. Ibid., pp. 337–38.
6. *Proceedings of the Eleventh Constitutional Convention of the AFL-CIO*, 1973, pp. 263–64.
7. Herbert Hammerman and Marvin Rogoff, "Unions and Title VII of the Civil Rights Act of 1964," *Monthly Labor Review*, April 1976, p. 36.
8. Walter G. Davis, "Afro-American Labor Leaders of New York City."
9. William B. Gould, *Black Workers in White Unions: Job Discrimination in the United States* (Ithaca, N.Y.: Cornell University, 1977), p. 396.
10. Harry Fleischman, "How to Combat Racism and Bigotry," *Crisis*, December 1975.
11. Velma Hill, "A Profession with Promise," *American Federationist*, July 1971, p. 22.
12. Gould, *Black Workers in White Unions*, p. 426.
13. Ibid., p. 15.
14. Bayard Rustin, "The Blacks and the Unions," *Harper's*, May 1971, p. 80.
15. Bayard Rustin and Norman Hill, *Seniority and Racial Progress* (A. Philip Randolph Institute, n.d.), p. 3.

15.
Unions and Sexism

American women began to assert their right to work in coal mines on Dec. 3, 1973, when two mothers each put on overalls, a helmet with light, steel boots and other gear and went down into Mine 29 at Beth-Elkhorn Corporation in Jenkins, Ky. . . . A spokesman for the Bethlehem Steel Corporation, of which Beth-Elkhorn's a subsidiary, says, "Right now we have 88 women working in six coal divisions. At least 80 of them are working underground. The United Mine Workers of America reports that of the 148,000 miners in the country today, 207 are women.

—*New York Times*
February 22, 1976

If blacks have suffered at the hands of white racists, women's lot has been no better; indeed, they have been treated as chattels far longer than were black slaves. Unions have not only discriminated against women, both black and white, but for too long dismissed them as unlikely prospects for organizing. (How soon we forgot the militancy of the "girls" who struck New England textile mills 150 years ago!)

Labor has also forgotten that women have proven on many occasions to be militant organizers—even on behalf of unions solely composed of men. Undoubtedly the best example was "Mother" Mary Jones, who fought for her "boys," the mine workers, when she was a white-haired old woman. It took her "shoot and be damned" attitude for women to claw their way into the ranks of the labor force and unions. Their progress hasn't approached the advances made by the civil rights movement on behalf of black workers—yet. If anything, the outlook for women is more dismal than that of blacks.

Despite the Equal Pay Act of 1963 mandating equal pay for equal work, women earn only 57 percent of men's wages on the average. Forty years earlier, the gap was 58 percent. The gap remains despite the increased number of women in the labor force. Why? Women account for nearly two-thirds of the clerical, service and sales employees; only 15 percent of them are professionals, and when they do the same work as men, they're still paid less. For example: female editorial assistants performing the work of male rewrite men on newspapers work for substandard wages.

Women do not represent a small fraction of the labor force, nor is it true they work only for short intervals on jobs suitable for women only. Over 41 percent of the labor force, or 39.3 million workers in 1977, were women. The Bureau of Labor Statistics estimated a year later that 50.1 percent of women sixteen years and over were either working or looking for work. That compares with 43.2 percent just eight years earlier. As for part-time jobs, that illusion has no foundation; three out of four women in the labor force were working full time, and an even greater proportion of unemployed women were looking for full-time work.

The outlook for improvement in job status and earnings for women in the next decade is dismal, according to the Conference Board, whose projections indicate the vast majority of women will still be employed in "traditionally female," low-paying jobs.

In sheer numbers, the increasing proportion of women in the labor force presents problems for unions as well as the business community. And for government as well, where women held slightly more than 35 percent of white collar jobs.

It wasn't always that way. Not only was there a time when it was (almost) universally believed "women's place is in the home," but comparatively few women worked outside their homes before the Industrial Revolution. Cottage industries, or home work, enslaved them every bit as much as their bondage to their generative functions.

While most histories of the United States (written by men) give the impression bands of misogynists conquered the wilderness to carve out the original thirteen states, there are a few references which make it clear that women were also involved—and not solely as childbearers. Philip S. Foner, for example, cites an advertisement in the *New York Weekly Journal* in 1734 in which maid servants thought it "reasonable we should not be beat by our Mistresses Husband(s), they being too strong, and perhaps may do tender women Mischief."[1] The first mention of women in John R. Commons' history of labor refers to female weavers in Pawtucket, Rhode Island, who struck with the men in an attempt to resist a reduction in wages and an increase in hours in 1824; this was followed a year later by the first strike in which women alone participated, when "the tailoresses of New York" struck for higher wages.[2]

Other strikes by women followed swiftly. About 400 cotton mill operatives—all of them women and apparently organized into their own trade union—struck in Dover, New Hampshire, in 1828, but it's not clear why the strike was called, nor whether it was successful. Six years later, they struck once more in protest against a wage reduction.

Female factory workers struck Pennsylvania cotton mills in 1845 and won a ten-hour day, but at a reduction in pay from the former twelve-hour rate. This early evidence of union activity among women should not excite surprise.

The "mother" of Women's Lib, Simone de Beauvoir, tells us the first women's associations in France "dated from 1848, and at the beginning these were associations of industrial workers." The parallel may be extended, for in the U.S. and in France, women were exploited by their male employers and by male trade unionists. Not only did they work for wages vastly lower than men did, but women were regarded by trade unionists as unfair competition, since they would work for sweatshop wages. "Only when women have been integrated into the life of trade-unionism have they been able to defend their own interests and cease endangering those of the working class as a whole," de Beauvoir wrote in 1953.[3]

There is a strong temptation to rewrite that thought in the future tense after contemplating the role women play in most U.S. unions now—even in those where women represent an overwhelming majority of the members. And the lot of more than 34 million women in the labor force who remain unorganized is patently worse. Far from being integrated into unions, women workers are still dependent upon men to defend their interests. Consider these relevant observations:

- There's not a single woman on the AFL-CIO Executive Council. (Mrs. Shirley G. E. Carr, however, is executive vice president of the Canadian Labour Congress!)

- Of 885 delegates to the AFL-CIO's 1975 convention, only twenty-two were women.

- In major unions where women outnumber men, the top officers are predominantly males. The Amalgamated Clothing Workers, for example, with half a million members, of whom 75 percent are women, has no more than a 2 percent female leadership, according to Joyce Miller, one of five female vice presidents. The International Ladies Garment Workers, with close to 500,000 members, of whom 80 percent are women, has but one woman vice president, Mattie J. Jackson of San Francisco. It was not until mid-1977 that the first woman, Belle Horenson, was named to be manager of a New York City local (Children's Dressmakers Local 91).

- The only woman to lead a nationally known union is Kathleen Norris, elected president of the Screen Actors Guild in 1976. Alas, SAG is only an affiliate of the Associated Actors and Artistes of America (4A), and not an international union in its own right.

- The United Auto Workers estimates 15 percent of its 1.49 million members, or 200,000 approximately, are women, and about 14 percent of the top local offices are held by women, but fewer than 10 percent of its bargainers are female. The Amalgamated Meat Cutters and Butcher Workmen has 110,000 female members, or more than one out of five members, but the international's officers include but one woman, Addie Wyatt, a vice president. The Communications Workers of America's membership is 60 percent female, but its executive board also has only one woman member, Vice President Dina Beaumont.

• The list could go on much further, but it would only indicate that the 4.5 million women in the trade union movement (and the 34 million other unorganized women) have little voice in determining either their role in the labor market or their unions.

Considering that women constitute more than half the population of the country, and more than 50 percent of them are employed; that the Nineteenth Amendment was ratified in 1920; that women now make up 44 percent of the nation's college students; and 46 percent of the nation's poverty-level families are headed by women—considering these factors, why do women have so little voice in determining trade union policies?

It is hardly enough to say there's as much prejudice against women in the male bastions of trade unions as there is in every other institution of society. Where women outnumber men in local unions, the officers are still predominantly male.

Asked why this is so, a high-level officer of an international whose members are predominantly women replied that because of the burdens of children and homes, women "cannot consistently follow political careers." But they can, of course, be breadwinners, because they must. In broad terms, women are still regarded as the second sex because, under the oppressive burden of educational and social traditions shaped by patriarchal societies through the ages, they have been treated as inferiors. Just how difficult it has been to escape that pervasive tradition can be seen in the struggle to ratify the Equal Rights Amendment.

So far, women have not overcome the oppression of the past, chiefly because of their failure to recognize what their common goals are. For example, some of the most articulate opponents of the Equal Rights Amendment have been women. There are too many differences among them (as there are among men, obviously) to expect any sense of unity or class-action movement.

If there are few class distinctions between men, there are many among women. Working-class women, we are told by Rosalyn Baxandall, Linda Gordon and Susan Reverby, "have often been alienated from the feminism of more prosperous women whose focus on sexual equality seemed irrelevant or shallow."[4]

One of the most articulate spokeswomen for her sister trade

unionists, Olga Madar, retired vice president of the United Auto Workers and the first president of the Coalition of Labor Union Women (CLUW), succinctly summed up cause and effect in a blunt declaration to the 1976 convention of the Amalgamated Meat Cutters:

> Your leadership and members are endowed with the same cultural and religious attitudes about the role of girls and women that permeates the other sectors of our society. The result has limited the effective participation of females in our society . . . and this is particularly true in the most important aspect of an individual's responsibility in a democratic society, and that is limiting the participation of women in their role as citizens.

Overcoming the cultural and religious mores about the role of women in society will be no easier in trade unions than overcoming racial prejudice — not as long as sexism permeates every sector of society. Yet, there is CLUW to take into account, as well as Olga Madar, who spoke her piece boldly and defiantly to a union which is doing much to remove discrimination from its practices. But CLUW is not an innovation. There was its forerunner, the National Women's Trade Union League, established in 1903 by women of the United Garment Workers, the Retail Clerks Association, the Shoe Workers, Textile Workers and the Amalgamated Meat Cutters. NWTUL's stated purpose was to give the working women of all the trades an organization to express the hopes and aspirations of women, to make their protests effective and to organize the unorganized workers.

It was effective for decades, in assisting striking women and children, in organizing the needles trades, in lobbying for social legislation and publicizing the "intolerable conditions that had driven the women to revolt," according to Ellen Rosser and Erwin Kelly. Their brief tribute to the women pioneers of the labor movement has preserved the stirring words of Margaret Drier Robins, president of NWTUL from 1907 to 1922:

> "Our day's work is in the main directed to the immediate aspects and demands of the struggle, but we cannot act wisely nor fully understand the meaning of the hours in which we live, unless we keep in mind the underlying cause for these conditions and the fundamental principles of justice. Today, as yesterday, the spirit must be born to see the vision, to hold it, to live and die for it. To release and set free this spirit so that it may achieve its purpose foretold in the hidden heart of man—to show the path of freedom, to bring hope, faith, courage to those held in bondage and crushed under the weight of wrong—and to give them the message, 'To you, too, has been given dominion over life,' this is our task."[5]

The National Women's Trade Union League was but one of the

predecessors of CLUW. Over 100 years ago the Workingwomen's Association, under the guidance of Susan B. Anthony, suffragist pioneer, maintained an uneasy truce with the National Labor Union because the latter was unwilling to support women's suffrage. (It did, however, advocate equal pay for equal work—a breakthrough for women, but adoption would have relieved male workers of the burden of low-wage competition from women.)

Other trade union women's organizations flourished and declined during that century's span, including the Working Women's Protective Union, the Working Women's Union, the Ladies' Federal Labor Union of Chicago, and scores of single-employer shops organized by their women employees . . . with little or no help from their brother trade unionists.

They formed their own unions for the very same reason that black male workers did: They were excluded from the white, male, craft unions with few exceptions. In the early 1800s, women organized unions of shoe binders, tailoresses, cordwainers, umbrella sewers and bookbinders. Girls and women in the New England cotton mills not only organized "societies" or unions, but called strikes which frequently lasted until the workers were starved into submission.

These early predecessors of CLUW, it should be noted, had far more than a single consequence. While women have been absorbed into previously male-only unions, including even the rail brotherhoods, their welfare was not significantly improved. The women's movement, encompassing far more than working conditions and wages, permeates all facets of society. CLUW, in perspective, must be considered only one manifestation of the women's liberation movement. Other organizations playing roles in the movement include the National Organization of Women (NOW), the League of Women Voters, the Women's Legal Defense Fund, the Equal Rights Advocates, the Women's Campaign Fund, Women Office Workers, Women's Action Alliance, and the newly organized National Women's Studies Association, founded by more than 500 women in January, 1977, at the University of San Francisco.

No matter what CLUW's impact may be, women trade unionists are an essential feature of the women's liberation movement. CLUW was founded in 1974, when 3,000 women delegates representing fifty-eight unions met in Chicago and adopted a "Statement of Purpose," whose main points were:

> The Coalition seeks to encourage our leadership and our movement into policy-making roles within our own unions and within the union movement in all areas.

> Whenever or wherever possible, CLUW urges women to seek election to

public office or selection for governmental appointive office at local, county, state and national levels.

It is a far cry from being a revolutionary cause; i.e., it will not create a class of working women who will threaten either the political structure or the trade union movement. But it will, Miss Madar believes, improve the lot of women. She told the Meat Cutters:

> Yes, we will shake up the establishment of our unions sometimes, and in some cases, and in some unions more often than others, because it will be the women and those unions who are doing it . . . All we are doing is assuming our rights and responsibilities as members of our union. We will fight for equal opportunity and, in the process, we will strengthen our union. We will not do it at the sacrifice of others, but in the long run, it will be better for others.[6]

CLUW has resisted efforts to radicalize its program. Attempts during the second national convention in Detroit in 1975, chiefly by left-wing organizations, to open membership to all women, rather than trade unionists alone, and calls for "more militant" programs, were decisively rejected by 1,000 delegates from sixty unions in forty-three states. Miss Madar, who was reelected president (she was succeeded in 1977 by Joyce Miller, ACTW vice president), asked the left-wing dissidents to leave the coalition. Although CLUW decided to pursue a moderate course, including lobbying for legislation and sponsoring "educationals" designed to train women for union leadership, Miss Madar conceded some confrontations with labor leaders lay ahead. "We're not going to get a woman on the board of the AFL-CIO tomorrow," she said. "There will be and there is conflict."

That conflict was apparent during the 1975 convention of the AFL-CIO, when delegate Stanley L. Johnson, representing the Illinois AFL-CIO, filed a resolution calling for more blacks and women on the Executive Council. His Resolution 215 concluded:

> Therefore, be it resolved that this convention supports a new approach, in that new additions to the Executive Council be specifically geared to correcting the gross imbalance relating to race and sex; and be it further resolved that the traditional Executive Council nomination of international presidents be expanded to other international union officers in order that fair and reasonable representation may be quickly established.

The resolution was referred to the Executive Council for review, but Johnson tried again, with a resolution which would have put the convention on record as calling for the appointment of blacks and women to the Executive Council. This, too, was referred to the council for review. Whereupon, CWA delegates introduced a resolution calling for the creation of a new standing committee, a Committee on Women, by amending the constitution:

> The Committee on Women shall have the responsibility of providing guidance and information in order that women may obtain equality, ensure their full integration in national development, and make full contribution to peace.

This resolution, too, was shelved by the Committee on Constitution, which proposed in its stead another constitutional amendment:

> The Committee on Civil Rights shall be vested with the duty and responsibility to assist the Executive Council to bring about at the earliest possible date the effective implementation of the principle stated in this Constitution of non-discrimination in relation to any member because of race, creed, color, sex, national origin or ancestry.

That was moderate enough to meet with no opposition from the male delegates (at least none that appears in the record), but not before a few critical remarks were made. Glen Watts, CWA president, had this to say:

> It is a sad commentary on us that only 22 or 23 delegates to this great convention are women . . . a great deal that we and they have done over the years has prevented women and minorities in our ranks from being as assertive as they should be.

Delegate Myra Wolfgang, Hotel, Restaurant and Bartenders Union, supported the substitute resolution, but warned:

> Now, let me assure you, Mr. President, gentlemen of the convention and the 22 women delegates, that the foot that is in the door is not encased in a ballet slipper hiding twinkletoes. It is a shoe that is a marching shoe, and it tends to march jointly with the men of the labor movement to address itself to the problems of millions of unorganized women of this country.[7]

Six months after adoption of the resolution, George Meany named four women to the AFL-CIO Civil Rights Committee to expand the scope of its work, so it could participate in helping women workers. The four, who were termed "knowledgeable about the problems of women workers," were Dina Beaumont, CWA vice president; Sandra Feldman, AFSCME vice president; Joyce Miller, ACTWU vice president; and Louise Smothers, director of women's affairs for the American Federation of Government Employees. The nineteen other committee members were men.

Slow to move? Not necessarily, when compared with nationwide conditions oppressing women. This is a country in which:

- No woman judge sits on the Supreme Court bench.

- Only two women were state governors in the seventies decade.

- Only one woman represented a state in the U.S. Senate and only sixteen women sat in the 435-member House of Representatives.

- Only thirty-five of the required thirty-eight states had ratified ERA by 1979, three years short of the extended deadline of June 30, 1982.

- There were only 685 women serving in state legislatures in 1977, or 9.1 percent of the total membership of the fifty houses.

- There were only three women's banks in the nation, and one, Western Women's Bank, was headed by a man.

- It was not until 1972 that the national service academies opened their doors to women.

- Despite a 22 percent increase in the number of women holding management posts in business in the decade of the sixties, there are still five times as many men as women in managerial positions.

Such citations could be continued indefinitely. However dismal the picture nationally, women are making progress in the labor movement—at least white women are! The AFL-CIO, which amended its constitution in 1973 to give women equal rights, is male-dominated, although 25 percent of the members are women. But they hold less than 5 percent of the key leadership posts. Black women fare far worse, despite 4.6 million in the labor force. There may be 4.8 million women trade unionists, but few are blacks or Hispanics.

But there are signs that our sisters are battering down the brothers' resistance. The AFL-CIO has not only endorsed ERA but recognized that women have become so significantly large a part of union membership that their participation in union activities must be encouraged. The AFL-CIO Executive Council recommended at the 1975 convention that affiliates should

1. Reaffirm their commitment to the equality of women, especially equal opportunity for women in the work place.

2. Continue to combat discrimination at the bargaining table by seeking to eliminate all wage differentials based on sex; provide for sickness and accident benefits for pregnancy and maternity leave paid on the same basis as any other disability; job posting and upgrading; and supporting expansion of applicable state laws which now protect only women to protect men.

3. Urge Congress to pass fully adequate child care legislation.

4. Encourage full participation of women in all union activity.

5. Endorse the Equal Rights Amendment as a clear statement of commitment to the principles of equality of the sexes and urge all affiliates to work for ratification of ERA in the remaining state legislatures.[8]

Both the 1973 and 1975 conventions gave their endorsements to ERA, but George Meany followed up on these actions by urging state AFL-CIO presidents in December, 1976, to mount intensified campaigns for ratification in those states whose legislatures have not yet done so.

With an endorsement of ERA from the AFL-CIO, one might imagine women would not have too much difficulty in gaining ratification in the required number of state legislatures. After all, the proposed amendment is so innocuous that that male bastion endorsed it:

1. Equality of rights under the law shall not be denied or abridged by the United States or by any State on account of sex.

2. The Congress shall have the power to enforce, by appropriate legislation, the provisions of this article.

3. This amendment shall take effect two years after . . . ratification.

Endorsement of CLUW, however, is far more controversial than ERA. A resolution presented at the AFL-CIO 1975 convention by a delegate from the Arkansas AFL-CIO was not adopted because the Constitutional Committee pointed out CLUW affiliates include "many who are members of unions that are not affiliated with the AFL-CIO." But the committee added:

The committee's recommendation in no way should be construed as critical of CLUW. The committee shares President Meany's observation that the organization of CLUW is clearly in the trade union tradition that people with common problems and common goals should work together in a common organization. The AFL-CIO, many of its affiliates and state and local central bodies, are now cooperating and will continue to cooperate with CLUW on programs of common interest where there is an identity of purpose. But formal endorsement, because of CLUW's structure, is not possible. The motion, Mr. Chairman, is for non-concurrence with Resolution No. 187 and I so move.[9]

The flaw in CLUW's structure which made endorsement repugnant was that among its members were National Educational Association delegates, as Mary Ellen Riordan, American Federation of

Teachers delegate, pointed out a moment later as she supported the recommendation of non-concurrence. While she endorsed CLUW, Miss Riordan appeared fearful this could connote an inferred endorsement of NEA; that simply wouldn't do!

While the differences separating NEA and AFT (and therefore the AFL-CIO) do not appear to be reconcilable, it is precisely that sort of jurisdictional dispute that keeps the labor movement from attaining unity—and effectiveness. The capriciousness of the reasoning contrasts with CLUW's organization, which is to unite women in a common cause without regard to union affiliation.

In declared principle, the AFL-CIO appears to be reconciled to the eventual integration of women into the hierarchy of unions. But it is inescapable that foot-dragging, to be overcome only by the persistence of women, will be the rule. George Meany was reputed in 1977 to be considering appointment of a woman to the Executive Council, but was unable to find a candidate.

However, what is more important is that women, black and white, gain the equal employment opportunities guaranteed to them by Title VII of the Civil Rights Act of 1964. Unfortunately, the Equal Employment Opportunity Commission's record of enforcement has been far from exemplary. It will take strong union advocacy to help women attain parity. There are several international unions whose work in this aspect has been noteworthy.

The program adopted by the American Federation of State, County and Municipal Employees appears to be effective in combating both sexual and racial discrimination. The union devoted the entire March, 1974, edition of its *AFSCME Leadership Letter* to spelling out the facts of illegal discrimination, including provisions of the law and how to comply with them. AFSCME told its locals:

1. If there are discriminatory provisions in the contract, take the initiative to reopen the contract for negotiations. As new contracts are negotiated, make sure they do not contain provisions which are unlawfully discriminatory.

2. The local should file a grievance through the normal procedures, if the problem is within a grievable area.

3. File a charge or bring a complaint to the proper agency. The vast majority of cases will come under two federal laws. Title VII of the 1964 Civil Rights Act covers discrimination in every aspect of employment. Locals should first file a complaint with the nearest office of the federal Equal Employment Opportunity Commission. Then the complaint should be filed with the state or local agency that enforces a law prohibiting sex discrimination in public employment, if there is such a law in your area.

Employees who work in certain schools, colleges and hospitals and who have a complaint concerning equal pay for substantially equal work are covered by the Equal Pay Act. Contact the nearest office of the Wage and Hour Division of the Department of Labor to file a complaint.

These "suggestions," the leadership letter pointedly remarked, apply not only to "female employees" the locals and councils represent, but also to "their own employees."

Well, of course, the comment is bound to be made, AFSCME is an extraordinary union led by a maverick, Jerry Wurf (who can "walk on water," according to the *New York Times*), and neither the union nor its international president is representative of trade unionism. True enough, but consider the far more representative International Association of Machinists, which bragged about its policy toward women in a leaflet published in 1976, *A Salute to 116,544 Women in the IAM*.

The first sister, Nellie T. Burke of Wilkes-Barre, Pennsylvania, to become a "brother" in the IAM was initiated into Local 210 in 1904, seven years before the IAM constitution was amended to admit women to membership.

A lace mill operative, Sister Burke became a machinist one day when some machinery broke down. She repaired it because the machinist was away. Promoted to assistant machine fixer, Nellie asked for a raise and got it. But when a dispute arose, she went to the union and asked to become a member. In March, 1904, the *Machinists Monthly Journal* reported:

> Miss Burke was admitted and the Journal offers congratulations both to the young woman and to the lodge at Wilkes-Barre. The Journal hopes also that Miss Burke will attend her local regularly, for if she does, it will result in the making of every one of her fellow members a thorough gentleman.

By 1911, the IAM had about 100 sisters in the union and on the recommendation of William O'Connell, the union's third president, delegates to the 1911 convention approved an amendment to the constitution admitting women to membership. Half a century later women account for an eighth of the total membership. But of the 116,544 women members, only 10,000 are journeymen; the rest, production workers or specialists.

The IAM turned to its research department to learn that six women were business reps of districts or locals in 1976; sixty-five were presidents of their locals; 198 were financial secretaries of locals and 272 were recording secretaries. Hundreds of others were vice presi-

dents, trustees, committee members, shop stewards or delegates.
But the IAM's eight-page leaflet in praise of women doesn't have
the impact of the union's stated policies regarding women members. Its
program was adopted in convention in Los Angeles in 1972, the year
Title VII of the Civil Rights Act was extended to cover public
employees. The two major points of the program are:

Contract clauses prohibiting sex discrimination and securing equal pay
for equal work.

Support for women fighting sex discrimination under grievance procedures, Equal Pay Act (1963), Equal Employment Opportunities Commission, Office of Federal Contract Compliance and state law.

Other points call for increased organization of women, increased
representation by women as officers and staff, contracts and legislation
providing maternity leave, day care centers and training programs for
women, and a more active role for women in political action programs.
The IAM, however, is hardly likely to have an overwhelming
number of women as members, but the American Federation of
Government Employees does, and the union is on record as being the
champion of women employees of the federal government. AFGE said
in a recent leaflet, *Women's Place Is in the AFGE*, "AFGE is the way to
go. It is the union where women have an equal voice, where they can
be part of both the leadership—and the action."
Since its membership of 300,000 is half female, AFGE could hardly take any other position, and that is fortunate, for if discrimination
against women is rampant in any workplace, it is in the federal government. While women hold more than 35 percent of white collar government jobs, they still hold less than 3 percent of the top-paid
"supergrade" positions, according to the U.S. Civil Service Commission. Similarly, while federal and postal unions, representing more
than half the government employees, estimate half their members are
women, few of the women are represented in most elected, appointed
or top staff jobs of the unions.
When the employer discriminates against women workers, it is all
too easy for the male-dominated union to wink at the practice and
blame management. But it is difficult to believe that American
Telephone and Telegraph for innumerable years could have discriminated against women and blacks in employment practices without the
tacit compliance of the Communications Workers of America. In 1973,
the EEOC ordered AT&T to pay $15 million in back wages and $23
million in pay increases to blacks and women—mostly women—who
had been discriminated against for many years, and to hire and promote more members of either minority.

Of course CWA knew; how could it fail to, with 55 percent of its 500,000 members women? CWA Vice President Morton Bahr, recalling contract negotiations prior to the consent decree, said efforts had been made in 1971 to remove sex differentials from the contracts with a union demand that women "clerks" be reclassified as "craftspeople." In negotiations with New York Telephone, CWA was more successful, although Bahr conceded "we didn't make a big thrust" to open up craft jobs to women.

As dismal as the discrimination pattern has been in AT&T, once women began demanding craft jobs, as framemen, for example, CWA did try to open them up to women. Bahr recalled: "Joe [Beirne] moved quickly."

Even so, CWA early in 1977 announced that upgrading the status and wages of jobs traditionally considered women's work would be a major contract demand in negotiations with Bell later in the year. CWA President Glenn Watts, in making the announcement, said he believed it would be the first time a union would make sex discrimination a key element in national contract bargaining with a major industry. There was no strike, and when the contract terms were revealed in August, they called for significant improvements for women workers. Indeed, until forty-eight hours before the deadline, AT&T had insisted that pay increases for clerical workers and operators—jobs held mostly by women—could not match those of all other jobs, i.e., men's jobs, but would have to be lower. Union negotiators contended women would be treated equally with men—or there would be a strike. CWA won that point. But they also won additional pay increases for operators and service representatives (mostly women) and, for the first time in a major industry, included in the contract paid maternity leave for six weeks as a disability benefit.

How does one gauge the effectiveness of a union's concern for the welfare of the woman member? By the number working in jobs at pay levels equal to those of men? Or by the number of women officers on the local or international level? (Only one woman sits on the executive board of CWA; there are no blacks.) The Amalgamated Meat Cutters has a Women's Affairs Department headed by a black woman. It is a full-fledged department of the union, but in its first two years of operations, Vice President Addie Wyatt expanded her home-office directive into the field by organizing women's committees in thirteen locals and three districts.

Efforts to raise women's consciousness (in the trade union sense) at the grass-roots level brought quick response. It was in that period that Emma Beck of Local P-500, Chicago, was elected president of the Chicago Area District 12 Women's Committee and named the first woman member of the Packinghouse Negotiating Committee. In those two years the Women's Affairs Department lobbied for ERA, took part in a civil rights conference in New Orleans and in a legislative conference and helped write the constitution of CLUW. But more pertinent, the department brought the message to women members at a conference of seventy delegates from eight districts and thirty-one locals that "true equality and fuller participation of women" was now possible.

True equality would be even more of a reality if the women who work to support 13 percent of all American households (46 percent of all poverty-level families) were able to turn over their children to child care centers during their working hours. In this area, the Amalgamated Clothing and Textile Workers Union has been a pioneer and sponsors more child care centers, probably, than any other union.

The problem of child care is not only national in scope, but of vital importance to the women who must work. In fact, a (Louis) Harris survey late in 1975 indicated "another 11 percent of all women would come into the work force if more child day-care centers were set up," while public support for the day care center rose from 56 to 67 percent of the entire adult public between 1970 and 1975. But the children need the centers every bit as much as their mothers do. Joyce Miller of the ACTWU, in a study of the problem, pointed out there is no national commitment to children:

> The infant mortality rate in the United States is higher than in 12 other major developed countries; five million children suffer from malnutrition; vast numbers of handicapped children receive no services; retarded children live in situations which amount to "institutionalized child abuse;" child abuse and neglect is growing as a problem among all social and economic groups; teenage alcoholism is rising along with drug abuse; one of every nine children enters juvenile court before the 18th birthday; and suicide is the second leading cause of death for young Americans between ages 15 and 24.[10]

The ACTWU started its child care center programs in Chicago and Baltimore and extended the concept throughout its jurisdiction, claiming to provide care for more children than any other private agency in the nation.

While the union's Chicago Joint Board has published a booklet explaining why it is involved in day care centers, there's at least one answer that appears to be overlooked: Since there's no national commitment to meet the demand, unions must step in to satisfy it.

In a positive vein, Amalgamated President Murray H. Finley has explained why the program was first undertaken in Chicago while he was manager of the Chicago Joint Board:

> One of the reasons our union has become involved in the establishment of day care centers is because industry encouraged women to enter the work force, but did nothing to meet the problem of caring for the children of the mothers they encouraged to work.

> The union is not providing an opportunity so mothers can leave the home. Women in the garment industry have to work and they have no choice. Their only choice is what kind of care their children get. In most cases, working mothers have no choice today in the quality of care for their children. We intend to give our members a choice.[11]

In the ACW's Baltimore region, the first center was opened after vice president Sam Nocella came back from a trip to Europe impressed by "the effectiveness of European day care centers." This resulted in the development of the Verona, Virginia, center in 1968. Today there are at least six such centers in operation in Verona; Baltimore, Maryland; Chambersburg, Hanover and McConnellsburg, Pennsylvania; and Winchester, Virginia, serving 1,400 children aged two to six.

The child day care centers are funded by employer contributions under union contracts, but it is relevant that that was not the way the program was initiated. Finley has recalled that the employers "were thinking in dollars and cents figures, and not in terms of children or workers' welfare. They refused." And that was why "the union decided to go ahead on its own . . ."

The clothing workers have not been alone in their endeavors on behalf of working mothers and children, for other unions, ranging from the Seafarers in Ponce, Puerto Rico, to the Newspaper Guild in Vancouver, British Columbia, have undertaken similar programs. But this hardly scratches the surface; what is needed is broad commitment in which the federal government provides funds to the states so they may meet federal standards and safety and health requirements.

A wide range of unions has lobbied for such legislation to provide not only child care centers but early childhood education. While this represents AFL-CIO policy, the American Federation of Teachers has performed exemplary service in campaigning for passage of a comprehensive child care bill in Congress.

Neither Congress nor the courts has been sympathetic to women's rights. On December 6, 1976, the Supreme Court ruled that company disability plans excluding payment of compensation to women for absences due to pregnancy did not violate federal laws against sex discrimination. It was the International Union of Electrical Workers that acted as a plaintiff against General Electric in bringing the case to the Supreme Court.

Intensive lobbying for legislation to require companies to include pregnancy as one of the risks in disability insurance was the only course open to the unions, the IUE declared. Obviously, trade union women still have difficult times ahead. But will legislation or court decisions enable them to overcome discrimination? An intense study of women's participation in trade union locals provides some of the answers. Barbara M. Wertheimer and Anne H. Nelson, who developed courses for women trade unionists for the metropolitan office of the New York State School of Industrial and Labor Relations, sought the answers in seven unions in New York City with memberships of more than 50 percent women. Their report,[12] they conceded, was descriptive, not analytical, yet the findings indicated the obstacles women must overcome before they attain equal status as trade unionists.

Among the observations made by union leaders (usually males) and women members in surveys that shed some light on the obstacles: Women were reluctant to run for union office or to participate in union affairs because they have the burdens of family responsibilities, or are disinterested, or are fearful of braving the streets of New York at night. Others are accustomed to seeing men take charge and feel they lack the capacity of leaders. (It is no wonder that only eighteen locals out of ninety-two had women presidents.)

Of course, it is not entirely the indifference of women that keeps them out of leadership posts. Much blame can fall on the shoulders of their husbands, who saw their machismo threatened by women activists. And the men who dominate the unions can also share in the blame for deterring women from striving for leadership posts. They have as stereotyped an image of women, it must be acknowledged, as most women have of themselves.[13]

Following the year-long study, the ILR Metropolitan Office embarked on an extensive Trade Union Women's Studies program as the first step in an education and leadership training ladder for women. It led to a year-long college-credit program with courses geared to developing "the skills and insights of women unionists."

Based on the study's conclusions, it is apparent this program can turn out proficient women trade union leaders:

> We have found women union members devoted and dedicated. We have found them able and tireless. They believe in labor unions and want to work within and through their unions to help—for they are helpers—and to lead—for they are leaders—in carrying the labor movement forward to new levels of achievement that will mean a better life for all Americans.[14]

Notes

1. Philip S. Foner, *History of the Labor Movement in the United States*, vol. 1, p. 26.

2. John R. Commons, ed., *History of Labour in the United States*, vol. 1, p. 156. (Incidentally, one of the authors, Helen L. Sumner, was a woman.)

3. Simone de Beauvoir, *The Second Sex*, p. 117.

4. Rosalyn Baxandrall, Linda Gordon and Susan Reverby, *America's Working Women: A Documentary History 1600 to the Present*, pp. xvii–xviii.

5. Ellen Rosser and Erwin Kelley, "From Silent Hardship to Militant Protest to Power," *American Teacher*, December 1976, p. 15.

6. Proceedings of the convention of the Amalgamated Meat Cutters, 1976, p. 1.

7. Proceedings of the AFL-CIO convention, 1975, p. 442.

8. Report of the AFL-CIO Executive Council, 1975, pp. 219–20.

9. Proceedings of the AFL-CIO convention, 1975, p. 375.

10. Joyce D. Miller, "The Urgency of Child Care," *American Federationist*, June 1975, p. 3.

11. *A Union-Sponsored Day Care Center*, Amalgamated Clothing Workers of America, September 1972.

12. Barbara M. Wertheimer and Anne H. Nelson, *Trade Union Women: A Study of Their Participation in New York City Locals*.

13. Ibid., p. 98.

14. Ibid., p. 158.

16.
Labor and the Arts

For years, Saul Solomon, attorney and administrator of pension and welfare funds, enjoyed his hobby: painting canvases of idyllic scenes which brought nature into his home and office. Whenever he could, he would buy paintings that brought him the same pleasure.

It was an avocation that delighted him to such an extent that it occurred to Solomon to share his interests with others who, very likely, had never been exposed to the arts. And where better to start than with the teamsters who were covered by the funds he was administering—the Teamsters Joint Council 16 and Management Hospitalization Trust Fund, as well as Teamsters Local 816's pension and welfare funds.

Some eleven years later, Solomon recalled, he had another motive in mind: It would be a project which would "help change the image of the Teamsters Brotherhood."

A more unlikely constituency for the arts is probably difficult to imagine. But teamsters are not necessarily beer-guzzling Archie Bunkers who are fiercely loyal to corruption-prone "union bosses" modeled after Dave Beck or his successor, Jimmy Hoffa. Teamsters—and that includes their leaders—are people of infinite variety. And that includes artists and would-be artists.

At any rate, Teamsters Joint Council 16, persuaded that the program would be good for the council's image, gave its consent in 1965 and the Teamster Art Center was launched. Eleven years later no one would consider the venture ill-advised. On the contrary, the reaction of the joint council, the rank and file and the press had been one of unstinting praise.

Each Monday and Thursday from 7 to 10 P.M., in a loft at 205 West Fourteenth Street, New York City, a professional artist and a professional sculptor hold classes for members of the fifty-seven unions affiliated with the council. And each year an art exhibition is mounted for three days, meriting wide notice in the newspapers, radio and television. The council, led by John O'Rourke's successor, Joseph Treretola, and the Teamster Art Center, directed by Solomon, are delighted with the results.

Members who attend the classes pay only for the materials used. The art center obtains the supplies at wholesale and does not add the usual retailer's mark-up.

Is there sufficient interest among the 175,000 men and women of the fifty-seven locals to justify the project? In the first year, Solomon recalled, thirty-five members signed up for the classes. In the first eleven years, over 500 became painters or sculptors. Is this any sort of activity for a union to be sponsoring? Solomon thinks so, and so does Joe T. (as Treretola is known).

"We are enormously proud of the work of our members, most of whom never painted, sketched or sculpted previously," said Joe T. at the eleventh annual art exhibition.

Solomon, the man who remained closest to the art center, summed up his own and the members' participation simply:

> As for the member, he finds that painting or sculpture is self-fulfilling. He takes his work home, shows it to his family, his neighbors and friends and puts it on display in his home.
>
> As for me, I know I have helped enrich many lives and I am getting satisfaction out of it, sharing my love for the arts with them.

He pointed out that for many retired members the newly acquired interest has proven to be "a lifesaver," providing an appealing occupation for idle hands, consuming many hours fruitfully.

How do members learn about the art center? Each local publicizes the program through its own publication and notices are posted in the shops and garages—just as similar notices alert the membership to other services available, Solomon pointed out. (It would be odd indeed if New York's teamster locals offered their members little or nothing beyond an art program. And, no matter what the public image may be of the brotherhood as "corrupt," Teamsters Joint Council 16 does have a Social Services Department supported by fourteen union trust funds through employer contributions of one-half cent an hour per employee each month. The Teamsters Joint Council No. 16 and Management Hospitalization Trust Fund maintains two Teamster Centers—at Montefiore Hospital and Medical Center and at Long Island Jewish Hospital and Medical Center—where members covered by contracts may obtain diagnostic examinations, professional counseling regarding health problems and treatment requiring surgery for specific conditions, including cancer, heart disease, respiratory ailments, etc.)

An even more extensive cultural program is sponsored by the National Union of Hospital and Health Care Workers, a division of the Retail, Wholesale and Department Store Union. (But it does not teach its members to paint or draw or sculpt.) "After all, a union is more than bread and butter," remarked Moe Foner, executive secretary. "Why not expose the member to culture? It's an ingredient in his life. And a good union does not have to be dull. It should be concerned with all the needs and interests of its members."

In its impressive, fifteen-story headquarters on West Forty-third Street, New York City—the Martin Luther King Jr. Labor Center—the union built a gallery directly off the lobby on the first floor. Opened in the spring of 1971, the gallery houses painting, sculpture and photographic exhibits open to the membership and public without charge. A member of the union's Retirees Division watches over the exhibit and coaxes visitors to sign the guest book. "This is the only permanent art gallery in the labor movement," the union boasts.

The exhibits are not restricted to union members, but are open to all serious artists who want to show their work. Toward the end of 1976, for example, Sheila Solomon, sculptor, had a score of her works on view. A resident of Setauket who is teaching sculpture at the State University at Stony Brook, she won a Creative Artists Public Service Grant for Sculpture. Earlier in the year, Louis Stettner had an exhibit of photographs on display in Gallery 1199, stressing people on the job. Stettner is a professor of art at Long Island University and a columnist for *Camera 35*.

Outside the gallery hang two paintings. On the right is the massive and famous *The Strike*, by Robert Koehler, the first painting to depict industrial strife. First exhibited in 1886, it has been widely publicized. To the left hangs *Elegy*, by Harvey Dinnerstein, a painting inspired by civil rights workers.

It would be strange indeed if the gallery were the only indication of an interest shown in culture by Local 1199. But this is not the case. The union has produced two widely acclaimed documentary films, *Like a Beautiful Girl* and *I Am Somebody*. It has also produced a long-playing record of Dr. King's speeches to Local 1199 members.

(Dr. King often referred to Local 1199 as "my favorite union." He and his family have been closely identified with hospital strikes. His widow, Coretta Scott King, is honorary chairman of the National Union of Hospital and Health Care Workers.)

In the field of the arts, the union has published a book of poems, *Talking with My Feet*, written by one of its organizers, Marshall Dubin, after the 1959 and 1962 hospital strikes in New York. In a foreword to the fifty-five-page book, Ossie Davis said:

> It would be well if those of us in the Labor Movement who have grown weary and cynical—who can no longer dream we "saw Joe Hill last night"—would take a good long look at Marshall Dubin. He just might be the Joe Hill of our times.

Talking with My Feet consists of "memories of a very real strike in a mythical institution herein called Suffren Hospital," Dubin wrote. One of the poems, "Harry Decides," merits wider distribution, since it recognizes the tremendous contribution made by Harry Van Arsdale in winning other hospital strikes:

> The Stewardship of Labor is my pride;
> Yet I'd be less than true
> Did I not candidly admit
> A sad decline among us these past years.
> Oh, we have wealth enough and status too.
> The mighty seek my counsel;
> His Honor helps me putting on my coat.
> And yet the smell of decadence is in the air.
> Sloth, corruption and timidity have done their work;
> Minorities, the natural allies of our cause,
> Grow daily more estranged.
> The mighty Giant of Labor now
> Takes his tea and crumpets near the fire,
> Fearing cold.
> Yet, there's a different path to take.
> Salvation still, can I but point the way
> Suffren, Suffren—the word's a magic ring.
> I'll seize it now!

The last poem in the book, "Where Is the Union?" sums up the story of the two major hospital strikes:

> Where is the Union now, friend,
> At the Strike's End?
> Inside my heart, friend.[1]

District 1199 does not have an in-house theater, but it does bring theater to its members, presenting plays in the Godoff Auditorium at union headquarters. The program for the winter of 1976-77 included three shows: an evening with Ossie Davis and Ruby Dee, "America's favorite stars of stage, screen, TV in a program of dramatic readings and poetry"; the Labor Theater productions of *The Wobblies*, by Stewart Bird and Peter Robilotta, and *Singly None*, a play with music telling the "story of American working people as told by John L. Lewis."

Theater, arts, LP records and motion pictures, however, can be considered only part of the package of services the National Union of Hospital and Health Care Workers offers its 100,000 members in seventeen states, most of them blacks in the urban centers (whites in the suburban and rural areas), but all of them with a history of poverty because hospital workers were "exempt" from collective bargaining until Local 1199 came along.

The former "wards of the city, who can take care of themselves to-day," according to Foner, number more than half of the membership (Local 1199 in New York accounts for 70,000 of the 100,000 members), but they depend on a Personal Service Department to handle their health and welfare problems through referrals or information. The union holds indoctrination courses for new members, awards scholarships on the basis of financial need, sends 200 children to camp each summer, has a Retirees Division (providing preretirement training and a program of year-round activities) and has even sponsored a housing project.

The 1199 Plaza, a 1,600-family cooperative, was built under the auspices of the union in 1973 on the East River Drive of New York to provide desperately needed housing for union members. Undoubtedly there would have been further construction, except, as Foner exclaimed, "Housing is dead in New York."

Obviously, it takes such broad concern for the members' well-being to include the arts and theater among the union's services. The Labor Theater, which stages plays at Local 1199, however, is not an arm of the union, nor, incidentally, is it a theater group sponsored by a union.

It is a theater group that presents drama with labor themes to audiences of working men and women with the cooperation of a handful of unions. Yet, the Labor Theater in New York is one of the very few (Chicago and San Francisco have their own groups) concerned with plays about and for workers. And that is lamentable, if one recalls the Federal Theater created during the Depression to alleviate unemployment among actors or the labor theater created by the Communist Party in the same era to serve as a weapon against capitalism.[2]

Between the federal and left-wing theaters, the American audiences were exposed to considerable drama, some with social significance and some which brought instant success to a new generation of aspiring playwrights. But it was the Communists who realized that "drama is a weapon," a slogan yet to win much support from the trade unionists who could make good use of such a weapon. (The memory of seeing the ILGWU production, *Pins and Needles*, in the 1930s still remains vividly alive. There was reason enough for the union to revive the show in June, 1978.)

The Labor Theater of the Seventies was formed in 1972 by a group of writers, directors, actors and labor educators. Their spokesmen, Bette Craig, executive producer, and C. R. (Chuck) Portz, artistic director, appear to have been inspired by Emanuel Fried, playwright (off-Broadway, *The Dodo Bird*), to "do something with meaning and content that's about workers and worth doing." Craig does not think of herself as a trade unionist, but as a theater person. She has worked for the Amalgamated Clothing Workers and is a member of Actors Equity. Portz, a member of the National Association of Broadcast Employees and Technicians, was pursuing a master's degree in labor studies at Rutgers University in 1976.

Their choice of productions for the Labor Theater since its founding shows their inclinations: *Waiting for Lefty* by Clifford Odets; *The Dodo Bird* by Emanuel Fried; *Union Maid* by Bette Craig and Jolly Robinson: *200 RPM* (Revolutions per Minute) by Charlotte Brody and Si Kahn; *Working Out Way Down* by Craig, Portz and Gene Glickman; *Singly None* by Portz; *Mother Jones* by Terry Uppenberg; and *The Wobblies* by Bird and Robilotta.

The casts are composed mostly of professional actors, usually members of Actors Equity who are glad to have a chance to practice their professions, even in an Actors Equity Showcase Production. This means their expenses are paid, but they receive no salaries.

"Workers come to see our plays. Obviously, it's blue-collar workers who pack the hall. We usually play to a full house," Craig said. The house is frequently a union hall.

Some of New York's unions have been quick to welcome the Labor Theater by sponsoring productions in their own halls, by contributing services, such as printing posters, or by making cash contributions. The unions that have been of assistance include the United Mine Workers, United Auto Workers, District Council 37, AFSCME, Local 1199, the ILGWU, Local 3 of the Bakery and Confectionery Workers, the Furriers Joint Council, the Retail, Wholesale and Department Store Union, and the ACTWU.

The thirty-member advisory board included twenty-three who were trade union representatives in 1976—an overwhelming indication of labor support, and yet, with as many as three (in one instance five) representatives from a single union, it was surprising how few of New York City's many unions showed support for the Labor Theater. Indeed, only sixteen unions had members on the board of directors and one suspects many were to a large extent "letterhead names."

How long the Labor Theater can survive without foundation support is questionable. That it merits support can be seen in the few reviews the press has given its productions. The support, however, should come from organized labor. But that is a vain hope, as the story of *I Paid My Dues* amply illustrates.

I Paid My Dues, a musical, started out when the Union Label and Services Trades Council of Greater New York attempted to organize a workers' chorus; it failed because secretary-treasurer Harry Avrutin's appeal for funds met with apathy. His second attempt, a labor version

242

of *America Sings*, did get off the ground when he and Eric Blau, stage and screenwriter (*Jacques Brel Is Alive and Well*), teamed up to develop a show "written for the people, the working people and all the people," in Blau's words.

In the first project, Avrutin served as chairman of Labor/Arts, apart from his duties with Union Label or as secretary of Central Labor Council. *I Paid My Dues* was a fully professional show about the contributions of the American worker. It was intended to be "politically informative and poetically written in language as close to educated street language as possible," Blau said. "The music is powerful, stirring and joyous; the dialogue is very tough, witty and wise. Staged very simply with a minimum of sets and props," he explained, "it was designed to tour nationally and was conceived with the flexibility to play in any union hall, concert stage, ball park or street corner."

Blau and Avrutin agreed to act on their concept and met with Stuart White, who formed a syndicate to raise $150,000 for the production. Blau and Henry Fleischman did the research, working more than three months on histories and anthologies. *I Paid My Dues* shaped up as a medley of songs expressing labor involvement in America's problems for 200 years, starting with Colonial times. David Frank, composer-conductor, developed the music, arranging old, familiar tunes to give them contemporary sounds, and original songs were added, with lyrics by Blau and music by Frank.

Labor/Arts Inc., with the assistance of Actors Equity, the American Federation of Musicians and the International Alliance of Theatrical Stage Employees, staged *I Paid My Dues* twice in 1976 at the Electchester Theater and eleven times at the Astor Place Theater —because District Council 37, AFSCME, bought out the house for the eleven performances. One more performance was given in Washington for delegates to the Eighteenth National AFL-CIO Conference on Community Services and then the show went into limbo. There was no money forthcoming from union sources to underwrite the national tour that had been planned. Nor were there many press reviews aside from the labor press, which hailed it as superb, spellbinding and "nothing short of great."

Labor/Arts, which seeks to act as a "catalyst," according to Avrutin, has been responsible for other innovations, including an exhibit of arts and crafts by union members and a round of concerts by the 129-member New York Philharmonic, which enabled trade unionists to hear a series of three concerts for only $6. The response to the concerts was overwhelming. Trade unionists will support the arts when the price is right. Unfortunately, not enough is being done in this area by unions.

The failure of *I Paid My Dues* is an indictment of union leaders, who failed to use the powerful propaganda weapon they had in the play. Fortunately, however, there is a tradition in some unions of using the arts as an educational instrument (for their own members usually)—the ILGWU may be cited as an example—and there is a methodology available for others interested in trying the same approach. A handbook, *Exploring the Arts*, by Barbara M. Wertheimer, outlines programs for unions:

> Traditionally, workers have shied away from arts, partly because of the high-cost image and aura of exclusiveness they presented. . . . One of the big challenges for unions is how to stimulate millions of members and win them away from the easy chair and television to live programming. . . . Unions must keep pace with the changing need of their membership, and they must respond to new demands with the rapid growth in the numbers of white collar, technical and professional workers and the influx of younger, better educated members to labor's ranks.

> Can a program to explore the arts help to meet this new challenge? Yes, and in several ways. It encourages the individual member and his family to use their increased leisure as participators in rather than spectators of the cultural scene. At the same time, such a program strengthens ties to the union through developing a new membership service. It can build leadership within the union through the training of interested, active rank and file to plan, organize, and follow through as members of an arts committee or as teacher-assistants.[3]

How did such a handbook come to be written? In response to demands from trade unions already involved in an experimental program, Labor Explores the Arts, launched in 1966 by the Metropolitan Center of the State School of Industrial and Labor Relations with Local 169, Amalgamated Clothing Workers; Local 1199, Hospital and Drug Employees Union (as it was then known); and District 65, then affiliated with the RWDSU. The handbook provides a permanent record for reference of what was discussed in the workshops on the arts.

New York City, however, is but one center of union activity in the arts, concentrated there because of the ready availability of resources; the pattern is repeated throughout the United States.

The AFL-CIO Community Services Department is responsible for involving trade unionists in the arts, as might have been assumed from the sponsorship of Labor/Arts in New York by the Central Labor Rehab Council. The nationwide program is a logical extension of the community services program, in keeping with the pledge made at the founding convention of the AFL-CIO of "active support to programs which help create and develop aesthetic values in youth and adults." It was a pledge that the AFL-CIO kept when labor supported the legislation creating the National Council for the Arts and Humanities more than a decade ago. (Two union presidents served on the first National Council for the Arts.) By 1968 the AFL-CIO had established its Council of Professional Employees—since upgraded to full departmental status—to represent professional artists in affiliated unions, while CSA embarked on its first demonstration arts projects in Buffalo, Louisville, Minneapolis and New York City in the same year.

In 1974, CSA, the National Endowment for the Arts and the Pennsylvania Council on the Arts started a pilot program in statewide union/arts liaison that demonstrated the commitment of the labor movement in developing union participation in the arts. The program's goals, as outlined by Paul Stackhouse Jr., full-time CSA liaison representative with the Pennsylvania council, are:

1. To develop a network of national and community leaders interested in helping union members and their families become active participants in the arts.

2. To stimulate activities which mine the rich heritage of labor-related artworks . . . and bring them to the attention of the public.

3. To motivate the development of programs by arts and educational institutions which are oriented toward the arts needs of union members and their families in a non-patronizing manner.

4. To assist local, regional and state union groups to develop arts programs, either alone or in cooperation with other groups and institutions.

These goals not only testify to labor's concern for the expression of artistic, creative talents in the union rank and file, but are the basis for a series of diverse programs across the state of Pennsylvania realizing that concern. Among them have been:

• Marionette shows in a Bethlehem public housing project and Lehigh County Prison

• A "beer and ballet" lecture/demonstration by modern dancer Dan Wagoner in Blawnox

• A performance by Wagoner and his dance ensemble in Pittsburgh

• Two other modern dance performances by Kathryn Posin in Etna and New Kensington

• An exhibit of painting by steelworker Henry Fiore in Pittsburgh

• Performances of Brecht's *The Measures Taken* by the Shaliko Company in the Allentown-Bethlehem area

• The Labor Theater production of *Singly None—an Evening with John L. Lewis* in Johnstown, Uniontown and Pittsburgh

The effects have been discernible in the community outside the union area, as might have been expected. Because a school district president attended the statewide CSA Institute in June, 1975, and because he had the interest of his home community in mind, the Nancy Houser Dance Company opened a two-week residency at the Salisbury Township School District in March, 1976. And a series of theater-arts workshops was planned for the Lehigh County Prison by the Lehigh County Labor Council.

Encouraged by these ventures, labor and the community were emboldened to continue with the arts. Erie Labor Council secured a matching grant of $500 from the Pennsylvania Council on the Arts to present a Memorial Day concert by the Erie Philharmonic Ensemble. The Northampton County Labor Council raised several thousand dollars to present a week-long series of performing arts events during Bi-Centennial Labor Week in Bethlehem. Theater workshops for Steelworkers and Mineworkers locals in Ebensburg were sponsored by the Cresson Lake Playhouse, and a photography exhibit focused on "workers on the job" was undertaken by the Philadelphia AFL-CIO Central Labor Council.

The Pennsylvania programs are not unique but exemplary of what CSA is doing in the area of the arts. The growing chain of Labor agencies offers CSA its finest opportunity for involvement in the arts, education and other areas, since their functions as nonprofit organizations are spelled out as manifold in the incorporation papers. The United Labor Agency, enrolling the Cleveland AFL-CIO Federation of Labor, the United Auto Workers and the International Brotherhood of Teamsters, produced the play, *John L. Lewis, Disciple of Discontent*, in September, 1977, in the Music Hall of Cleveland's Convention Center. Written by James A. Brown, the play starred Robert Lansing, a past vice president of the Screen Actors Guild who has appeared in television and other stage roles.

Ben Shouse, chairman of the agency's cultural arts committee, said the play was commissioned to give working people a chance to see what unionism was in the past, while Mel J. Witt, a former coal miner heading both the agency and the Cleveland Federation of Labor, said the purpose was "to expose our members to the richness of the theater and to labor history."

In a review in the *Cleveland Press*, Tony Mastroianni wrote:

> The performance is a tour de force and a great deal more. This is a performance of consummate skill as well as seemingly limitless energy . . . While it is a message work, it doesn't fail to be theatrical, entertaining and informative.

The extensive involvement of the AFL-CIO in the arts should

evoke no surprise, since among the affiliates are the Associated Actors and Artistes of America (4A), the American Federation of Musicians and the International Alliance of Theatrical Stage Employees and Moving Picture Operators.

The 4A includes among its nine national affiliates Actors Equity Association, which has launched many a stage, screen and TV star on a career. Its Equity Library Theater, working on an annual budget of $134,000, presents eight productions a year, each with a different cast, crew and producer, while the Equity "showcase" productions, Frederick O'Neal, president emeritus, explained, "enable actors to keep their hand in, much like athletes keep in trim, by performing (for little or no wages) in plays presented at either no admission charge or at which contributions are asked."

The American Federation of Musicians, zealously devoted to pro-moting "live music," has long made it a practice to offer scholarships to young musicians at annual summer workshops. Its Music Performance Trust Fund brings "live music" to communities across the nation—no inconsiderable contribution, in addition to offering employment to musicians who are chronically unemployed, reflecting the inroads made by juke boxes, television, records and radio. In Baltimore, the Trust Fund, in cooperation with the Labor Agency for Community Service and the Baltimore Symphony Orchestra, brought music appreciation courses and demonstrations of symphony orchestra instruments to the public schools under a two-year, $30,000 grant.

Music, as well as theater, films, panel discussions and exhibits, were used by the Women's Performing Arts Coalition in "Women in the Performing Arts Past and Present," presented to observe International Women's Year at a festival in New York's Lincoln Center in October, 1976. The coalition was made up of members of Actors Equity, AFTRA and the Screen Actors Guild. But the nonprofessional unions have also brought workers to music through the purchase of large blocks of tickets so that members may attend symphony concerts. This is not only a service to the members, but to the community, since support is created for community orchestras.

The United Steel Workers, for example, sponsored tours by the Pittsburgh Symphony Orchestra, bringing music to steel towns that had never heard a performance by professional musicians. Orchestras, however, are but a single facet of a nation's culture. There are museums, theaters, operas and art galleries which fail to attract enough devotees to keep themselves afloat financially. And yet, the needle trades unions have found a tremendous response whenever tours to these cultural centers have been arranged for union members. The ILG noted its members responded avidly to such tours—even when the member had to pay for the tour, according to Assistant President Gus

Tyler. In a single year, 20,000 members signed up for tours and trips arranged by the union "as part of their educational exposure." Similarly, as part of its legislative program, the ILG has sponsored tours to Washington that go far beyond sightseeing.

The ILG has long been committed to making use of theater to help the members become aware of their environment and their role in it. Morgan Y. Himelstein recalled the ILG Educational Department had mimeographed two short plays in 1933 for presentation by amateur groups in the union. Both *All for One* and *In Union There Is Strength* pointed up the advantages of belonging to a union—in this case, of course, the ILG.

The ILG organized Labor Stage in 1936, not only to educate but to entertain—an important ingredient of theater frequently overlooked. Labor Stage's greatest achievement, *Pins and Needles*, did entertain, to the extent that the musical was performed more than 1,100 times in New York before it closed. It was a box office hit and even forty years later one can recall hearing:

> Sing us a song with social significance,
> Or you can sing till you're blue.
> Let meaning shine from every line,
> Or we won't love you.

The ILG has remained devoted to the use of theater—as an educational device—and several of its locals are still producing plays for amateur union groups across the country. One example of contemporary vintage is in Baltimore, where the Education Department of the Upper South Department of ILG started with choral singing and blossomed into *The Work I've Done*. A group of twenty-five union members was trained in four-part harmony and developed a repertory of songs expressing the concerns of unions. They began to sing at banquets, summer schools and conferences, union label shows and city fairs, senior citizen centers and hospitals.

Martin Rader, director, expanded the program to theater, drawing his material from the singers' views about a wide range of subjects—work, love, family, neighborhood, religion, race, good times and sickness—in taped colloquies. Out of some sixty hours of tape he wove a spoken text interspersed with songs selected by the troupe members. Jerry Breslaw, education director of the department, commented, "Thus was born *The Work I've Done*, a vital expression of workers' perceptions, concerns and dreams."

Since October, 1974, *The Work I've Done* has been presented at least once a month. The docu-drama is constantly revised in response to the feelings and interests of the cast and the exigencies of performances.

A fifteen-minute version with a cast of three is available for lunchtime performances, while the full, fifty-five-minute, ten-voice version plays evenings. Neither requires scenery, props nor special lighting. No charge is made for the services of the troupe, which is an amateur company. However, the cast is reimbursed for lost time when they perform during work hours and the ILG requires payment for travel expenses and that the troupe be fed. Breslaw was candid in explaining the motivation for the ILG's involvement in this program:

> *The Work I've Done* is a product of the education policy of the Upper South Department of the ILG, which stresses the involvement of the membership in union-related processes. The goal is to get ILG members to become attached to the union during nonworking hours. . . . Add to this the fact that there are creative people who work in the shop but lack suitable outlets for their self-expressive impulses, and a labor arts program becomes a natural.

One other aspect of the arts, the motion picture, has not been fully exploited by unions, but understandably, considering the tremendous expense involved in producing a single film. However, it is a capital expenditure which may be recovered through rental fees. Considered as an educational tool, the film can be remarkably effective. What would be far more remarkable would be to consider the production as a work of art. Not many Hollywood super-stupendous epics can pretend to that stature. Motion pictures about unions are rare and hardly ever flattering to labor.

The film, *Harlan County U.S.A.*, was the only American film screened at the New York film festival in 1976. Produced by Barbara Kopple, the 103-minute film is a documentary on a coal miner's strike in Harlan County, Kentucky, involving the United Mine Workers. Richard Eder of the *New York Times* called *Harlan County* a "fascinating and moving work," while *Newsweek* hailed it as a "passionate and often suspenseful hit that emerged as the surprise hit of the recent New York film festival." It remained for the usually dyspeptic John Simon to remark in *New York* magazine, "It takes vision and determination to conceive, shoot and put together a *Harlan County U.S.A.*, even if it is not done particularly well."

Harlan County U.S.A. opened in New York, January 26, 1977, at Cinema II on a two-week trial run, but proved to be so popular it was still playing a month later. In that time could it have failed to sway even one viewer to show more sympathy for the miners' hardships, more understanding for the need of a miners' union?

Union Maids, another labor documentary, produced by Julia Richart, James Klein and Miles Mogulesco, and distributed by New

Day Films and Distribution Co-op, was screened in New York at the same time, after being seen in Chicago, Boston and San Francisco. While Vincent Canby of the *New York Times* hailed it as "one of the more moving, more cheerful theatrical experiences available in New York this weekend," few labor officials seemed aware of its existence.

The documentary may or may not be shaped into an art form, but certainly it can be as effective a tool for labor as it has been for industry. And to some extent, unions have made use of the motion picture in educational areas. Some have been produced by unions, including, in recent years, *Listen*, a documentary on the hazards of industrial noise, produced by the United Papermakers International Union; *Overworked and Underpaid*, produced by AFT Local 189 filmmakers and historians; *Testimony—Justice vs. J.P. Stevens*, produced by the Citizens Committee for Justice for J.P. Stevens Works; and *Why We Boycott*, National Farm Workers Service Center.

Also, *Solzhenitsyn—The Voice of Freedom*, AFL-CIO Education Department; *Contract, Contract*, Textile Workers Union of America; *The People vs. Willie Farah*, produced by the Amalgamated Clothing Workers; and *Walk the High Iron*, produced by the Ironworkers Union in cooperation with the Bureau of Indian Affairs.

But most of the films are produced by independents aiming for general audiences, but with particular interest, at times, for workers and their unions. The AFL-CIO Film Catalog lists more than 200 films available in 16 mm from the AFL-CIO Film Library in Washington.[4] They have been selected, of course, for showing to union audiences. The rental fees are nominal—as low as $3 for such COPE films as *Do It*, or *The Phoney Issue, the Real Issues and You*. The theatrical unions should be delighted with the use of motion pictures as educational tools.

Unions spearheaded the drive to reopen the long-neglected Astoria Television and Motion Picture Production Center in New York, thus helping create jobs not only for their own members but for actors and others as well. The mammoth studio had been held as surplus property by the federal government since it was used during World War II by the Signal Corps as the Army Pictorial Center.

New York locals of the International Alliance of Theatrical Stage Employees and Moving Picture Machine Operators and the 4A raised $45,000 to renovate the studio, which was leased from the government for the production of *The Wiz*, a $10 million Universal Studios film. With a cast of 300 and a $340,000 set, *The Wiz* pumped some money into New York's dying economy and appeared to set an example to other movie producers.

Overall, it must be conceded, unions have made inadequate use of the arts, either to improve the cultural welfare of their members or as a propaganda tool. But there are indications of an awareness of the potential. The Communications Workers of America, which neglected the field, has set up the Beirne Memorial Foundation with an initial appropriation of $100,000 to be used to encourage arts and education.

One other group deserves at least a mention here, even though it is only a quasi-union, and that is Artists Equity Association of New York. While it does not negotiate labor contracts for its members, Artists Equity does help pictorial artists and sculptors to negotiate individual contracts with galleries. In every other respect, however, Artists Equity resembles the benevolent societies which preceded trade unions.

Founded not in the Colonial days but within the past forty years, Artists Equity has over 900 members who pay $20 a year in dues; hold regular membership meetings; elect officers; have a welfare fund which helps all artists, whether members or not; subscribe to a Blue Cross-Blue Shield group insurance plan; and engage in an active legislative program designed to protect reproduction rights, to obtain tax deductions for contributions to museums and to secure a voluntary checkoff on federal income tax returns to fund the arts and education.

It does sound like a union program! And it does demonstrate that even among artists, in union there is strength.

Notes

1. Reprinted by permission of Local 1199.
2. For the story of both the Left-Wing Theater and the Federal Theater, vide Morgan Y. Himmelstein, *Drama Was a Weapon.*
3. Barbara M. Wertheimer, *Exploring the Arts.*
4. *Films for Labor*, publication no. 22, AFL-CIO Pamphlet Division.

17.
The Future
of Trade Unionism
in the U.S.

I could not understand what was going on in the crowded Hotel Biltmore ballroom I had entered an hour late. The suave speaker on the platform was demonstrating locks, but clearly this was no hard-sell sales pitch, since he was pointing out flaws in one lock after the other on the table before him.

"What's going on, Sid?" I asked the man beside me. "I don't get it."

"We've had a rash of complaints from members about house burglaries. That man is from the New York Police Department's Crime Prevention Bureau. He's telling shop stewards what to do about security at home."

Is that the function of a union? To spend two hours of the shop stewards' conference discussing the type of lock to install on one's apartment door? Sid Heller, president of Retail Clerks Local 888, thought so, and from their eager questions, the shop stewards appeared to agree with him. The question, however, should be rephrased to feel its full impact: "What role *can't* the union play in the member's life?" That should narrow down the options considerably.

But there is no limit in actual practice, as may be seen from the instructions Local 888 gives its 250 shop stewards who represent 16,000 members:

The Steward can help his members and strengthen the union, too, if he lets them know what services the union offers outside the shop. The union can help with many out-of-shop problems. A member's claim for unemployment compensation has been denied. A mother needs a day nursery that has a place for her child. These are real problems even though the contract can't help solve them. Our community services program trains "union counsellors" to help members with these out-of-shop problems. If you have a member with out-of-shop problems, call the union office. We may be able to help.

Ideally, Local 888—or any union—should try to cope with the

problems of its members, no matter what they may be, whether in or out of the contract, in or out of the shop. As a union, it has an obligation to do so, whether the motive is altruistic or self-protective. After all, unions were formed to fill a void in the social structure by offering services no other institution does—at least, not to as broad a spectrum of the population.

"Of course," is the most frequent response. "That's self-evident, but labor leaders don't seem to realize it." (Again, that dichotomy dividing members and leaders into separate entities!)

But unions do not rely upon the benevolence of detached strata of leaders. Elected union officers invariably grow old, retire and die, but the unions endure. Harry Van Arsdale once observed that when he was a young man, he thought that "no matter how bad the leaders may be," the unions would survive.

"I still think so today," he added.

Trade unions have survived despite a long roll call of malefactors who destroyed themselves, but not their unions. Labor will continue to produce its own leadership from one generation to the next, because it is the union that develops its leaders, not leaders who engender unions. And the unions will survive in the future despite a host of new problems confronting the labor movement.

The challenges are many, including widespread, long-term unemployment, urban decay with a concomitant attack on public employee unions, demands for recognition of blacks and women, industrial diseases, repeated defeats of labor's legislative goals, persistent inflation eroding real wages and, oddly enough, the growing acceptance of the welfare-state concept.

The implied peril to union loyalty was tersely expressed in London by a harried Trades Union Congress official who took a few moments from preparing the agenda for the 109th annual TUC to explain why there was no community services department in England's labor movement. "With so many [government] social workers around," he said patiently, "we have no need for anything like your AFL-CIO community services."

Acceptance of the welfare-state concept in the U.S. is not far behind England's experience. A Ford Foundation study by two Columbia University sociologists concluded late in 1975 that "social services in the United States should be expanded—as they have been in Europe—to help the entire population gain better living standards." While that is a goal the labor movement can endorse with enthusiasm, the welfare state will seriously attenuate what should be the strongest bond of allegiance between member and union: community services.

Another challenge looms in the adoption of national planning, an inevitability if the United States is to break the "self-corrective" features of the economy that counter prosperity and recessionary cycles with disturbing frequency.

But who does the planning will determine to what extent the welfare state will be realized. Planning will come; the alternative could well mean the decline of our mixed economy. Dr. Robert L. Heilbroner is convinced economic planning will come within a few years, but not because labor demands it; businessmen will. "And demand it they will," Heilbroner said, "for without more planning, it is difficult to believe that capitalism will last out the century. It may not."[1]

Will organized labor be content with the role of having a representative on an advisory board furnishing advice to the Council of Economic Advisors when economic planning becomes a reality? That was all labor was entitled to under provisions of the much-vaunted Full Employment and Balanced Growth Act of 1976.

A third challenge already here is the decline of metropolitan urban centers. Labor is almost compelled to adopt a forceful role in dealing with the urban crisis. Brought about by the exodus of jobs and workers from the nation's metropolitan areas, the urban crisis threatens both areas, the workers' livelihoods and their spirits. ("Runaway shops" are a symptom, not the problem.) Public employee unions still negotiate contracts with those centers but ratification of the agreements will increasingly depend upon the approval of emergency financial control boards rather than rank and file ballots. That's unfortunate, since public employees represent the strength of labor in coming years. Government employment more than doubled in the twenty years ended in 1975, the Conference Board estimated in a "Road Map of Industry" report on July 5, 1977. The trend will continue, with or without a welfare state. But public employee unions, Thomas R. Brooks has suggested, are already in much the same position as unions in the private sector were in the 1930s:

> Today, public employee unions are experiencing a similar period of discouragement. Public workers are being laid off, though not in such great numbers. But the shock is as grave—given the widespread conviction that public employment was tantamount to total job security. Public employees are being forced to subsidize public services through reduced wages and benefits as well as by job cutbacks.[2]

It is no longer enough to depend on political activity at the level of COPE to win political "clout." Yet, labor is not prepared to form its own political party. Witness George Meany's reaction to the idea of forming an American Labor Party. Asked on a television talk show why the AFL-

CIO did not foreswear the Republican and Democratic parties, he said:

> No, because then we would be telling the people that we want to run the country and we don't want to run the country. All we want is a decent share for the people who work for wages. That is all we want . . . If we wanted to run the country, we would have a labor party, and we don't have a labor party and never had a labor party.[3]

What are the alternatives? There are promising ones being considered by a bloc of progressive labor leaders who are aware of the troublesome problems confronting unions. Sol Chaikin, ILGWU president, has spoken out for a national incomes policy which would result in the redistribution of wealth to benefit "the people at the bottom." William Winpisinger, who became president of the International Association of Machinists in 1977, is equally dissatisfied with labor's programs. "Wimp" has little use for the lethargy of aging leadership and believes it is time to involve workers in humanizing working conditions. He also advocates a rededication of the labor movement to its forgotten goal of redistribution of the nation's wealth. Even the Defense Department budget, upon which so many IAM members depend, is not sacred to him, for "Wimp" would like to see it trimmed so more funds would go into resolving social problems.

With Chaikin and Winpisinger on the AFL-CIO Executive Board, David J. Fitzmaurice, IUE president, would like to see a "crusade" by labor to satisfy, rather than deride, the demands of antiestablishment elements among the younger, more educated workers.

A major irritant to Meany, Jerry Wurf, AFSCME president, has been abrasive in criticizing AFL-CIO leaders, angering them by advocating arbitration to resolve labor disputes, by calling for improved productivity by workers and an overhauled national tax structure, by making alliances with independent unions and by urging development of a social contract to stabilize the economy. He has also had the audacity to point out new directions for labor:

> The strange thing is that, unlike all the rest of the world's labor movement, ours is not an adversary of the system in terms of direction and philosophy. It is not socialistic; it wants to be part of the system. Yet, it can't develop the kind of social contract that is helping to relieve the frustrations and promote the survival of governments abroad.[4]

The federation is far more likely to endorse the views of Lane Kirkland, as he expressed them on Labor Day of 1976:

> Our interests relate to the best interests of working people. We have no vi-

sionary world, no utopia, that we're working toward, but we do have building blocks, and to the extent that we can develop it, we're trying to get the blocks in place . . . We're interested in a more humane society in which everybody has his chance.[5]

Having "no visionary world, no utopia," in the face of an unstable economy, what can organized labor do short of becoming an adversary of "the system?" Certainly, continue to bargain for "more," even if that means a guaranteed annual wage and a job for life. But it must go far beyond these building blocks to attain the society Americans once dreamed of but now consider unattainable. The better life means more than job security and prospects of more pay.

It means decent housing, a work place and environment safe and healthy to work and live in, a government responsive to the needs of the people rather than special interests, regulatory agencies which oversee rather than protect those interests, industry which can develop alternative sources of energy without destroying mankind, assurances that cycles of recession and prosperity need not continue and above all, a socially progressive outlook in a pluralistic society with tolerance for the rights of all its minorities.

Is that the sort of world for labor to fight for? Can there be any doubt? Isn't that what "a union is all about," the path trade unionism has taken to achieve "that more humane society in which everybody has his chance?" So much more could be achieved in the face of the problems confronting labor merely by building more blocks on the traditional community services foundation. By extending that solid base, the labor movement could be certain of sufficient loyal support—in the ranks and in the public mind, as well—to meet the challenges of the future.

There are indications that the labor movement is broadening its horizons to show greater concern for the community. For example, consumer protection, affecting the non-union worker as well as the lodge brother, has become the concern of sixteen international unions in recent years.

They are members of the Consumer Federation of America, a 225-member lobby in Washington whose executive director, Carol Tucker Foreman, became assistant secretary of the Department of Agriculture for food and consumer services in 1977. Sixteen international unions are members of CFA; where are the others? Their participation would not only lend weight to CFA's lobbying efforts in Washington, but, more to the point, would go far in convincing their members that unions really do "give a damn" about their welfare.

Protecting the member's pocketbook, however, does not threaten his job, but protecting the environment would, most union people are convinced. There has been far from adequate movement by unions to join forces with environmentalists, who now have a more powerful lobby in Washington than labor does, but beginnings have been made by some AFL-CIO affiliates and the United Auto Workers. A five-day conference at the UAW's Reuther Educational Center at Black Lake, Michigan, in May, 1976, assembled 300 delegates of 140 labor, environmental, civic, religious and racial organizations. The major unions in attendance were the UAW, the International Association of Machinists and the United Mine Workers. That type of involvement tends to bring unions into the social structure, overcoming the prevailing notion that unions seek to subvert social patterns.

Leonard Woodcock, then UAW president, pointed up the absurdity of that notion in his keynote address:

> There is today more than ever a common cause between union members and environmentalists, between workers, poor people, minorities and those seeking to protect our national resources. It is in times such as these that the corporate tactics of trying to make workers and communities choose between jobs and ending pollution can be most effective . . . If we had a full-employment economy in America today, corporate polluters would have a far more difficult time with environmental blackmail.

All too often, unions succumb to the threat of corporations to close down plants rather than conform to environmental guidelines. What too many unions fail to see is that a clean environment would not only save lives, but jobs as well. Man is as much an endangered species as the Galapagos tortoise, the Florida sandhill crane or the Zapata sparrow. Environmental-protection and pollution-abatement projects would create jobs, not destroy them. Not only would 6,000 premature deaths be averted and $20 billion a year saved if the air were cleaned up, but 300 U.S. firms in the air equipment industry could expand operations and job requirements significantly.

If the impact of clean air on workers' lives remains in doubt, and that is apparent, the fault, at least in part, lies with the environmentalist who fails to present a convincing case. Peter Harnik, coordinator of Environmental Action, speaking at the UAW conference, said:

> I realize now that we've been a little myopic in some of our efforts to get our story across. We spend a couple of years studying up on something like solar energy, and we have expected people to accept our conclusions on our say-so, just on the basis of a few sentences of explanation. We realize now that we have to be far more coherent.[6]

Not only more coherent, but more relevant! The environmentalist's message speaks of endangered fish and bird species in the

Galapogos Islands, rather than the worker in the plant or the myriad of jobs in the making. Solar energy is a two-word message threatening the loss of construction jobs on nuclear reactors. But some unions have already seen the job opportunities inherent in solar energy. Sheet Metal Workers Local 55, for example, built a solar testing center on the roof of its Mineola, Long Island, headquarters, paying for the solar unit with contributions from the Ford Foundation, the New York State Energy Resources and Development Administration and four banks.

The project was undertaken to train sheet metal workers to work on solar systems. The rooftop unit was built by fifty apprentices who volunteered their labor, according to Murray Liebowitz, director of training. A by-product of the project was a 50 percent saving in heating 4,000 square feet of the building's classrooms during 1976–77.

There are jobs in alternative sources of energy, as well as in clean air and water, but it will take a massive educational program to convince unions, environmentalists and industry this path would furnish the economy with the stimulus it needs for decades to come.

Improving the quality of life might aptly describe the fundamental purpose of the community service activities program of the AFL-CIO. It is a program which could well be extended within as well as without the plant gates, not only to carry out that purpose more effectively, but to foster stronger ties of loyalty in the membership and engender a pro-union spirit in the community. One obvious new direction for this purpose would be through job enrichment. The UAW signed a contract in 1976 with Chrysler Corporation calling for labor-management cooperation in a job enrichment program and improved worker participation in job design. The union had already made inroads in that direction earlier, notably at General Motors, Rockwell International, Harman International Industries and Dana Corporation's Edgerton, Wisconsin, plant.

The impetus for these programs comes as much from management as labor in efforts to cope with poor productivity, slowdowns, sabotage and absenteeism, all of which are so prevalent as to indicate worker dissatisfaction with working conditions.

One job enrichment program which appeared for a time to show promise was in the National Quality of Work Center's quality-of-working-life experiment at Rushton Mining Company, a small, independently owned, 235-worker mine in central Pennsylvania. Twenty-seven top-paid volunteers worked in mid-1973 in an experimental section of the mine after being trained to work autonomously without a foreman's supervision. The foreman remained responsible for safety alone. The value of the experiment became apparent a year later in the reactions of labor and management, Ted Mills, director of the center, noted.

One of the volunteer miners focused on the satisfaction he gained from working without supervision: "It's like you feel you're somebody, like you feel you're a professional, like you got a profession you're proud of." And a section foreman said the crew respected him because of what he knew, not because he was a boss. Warren Hinks, mine president, saw a new concept of mine management evolving which pointed to an improved safety record, lower production costs and improved productivity.[7]

The Rushton experiment was one of many designed to improve the quality of work by giving the worker a sense of satisfaction through having a voice in determining his working conditions. In gaining that tool for the member, the union will take a large stride toward securing what most Americans want: improvement in the quality of life. While many surveys appear to indicate workers are satisfied with their jobs, as many others indicate overwhelming disssatisfaction. Surveys frequently fail to focus on specifics, taking the vague approach of asking: "Are you satisfied with your job?" Satisfied? Yes, for any job is preferable to unemployment, usually the only alternative.

But when the Research Department of the Allied Industrial Workers of America surveyed its members in February, 1973, reaching them through a full page of the *Allied Industrial Worker*, the question was pointed: "How much of the time are you satisfied with your job?" The breakdown of the responses was revealing:

Most of the time: 28 percent
A good deal of the time: 19 percent
About half the time: 29 percent
Occasionally: 13 percent
Hardly ever or never: 11 percent

What did AIW members want improved on the job? Better health and safety practices were named by 79 percent of the respondents as "very important." Also important were better contingency protection (71 percent); more pay (56 percent); improved fair employment practices (58 percent); and more opportunity to do interesting and satisfying work (68 percent). Similar results disclosed in other surveys confronting workers with distinct choices led Harold L. Sheppard and Neal Q. Herrick of the W.E. Upjohn Institute for Employment Research to conclude that "one thing is clear from the comments of these men and women: Something must be done, and fast, not only for the benefit of the individual worker, but also for general society."

The best-known study on humanizing working conditions is *Work in America*, carried out by a special panel for the Department of Health, Education and Welfare at the direction of then HEW

Secretary Elliot L. Richardson. The most pertinent finding of the task force was the conclusion that "if the nature of work is dissatisfying (or worse), severe repercussions are likely to be experienced in other parts of the social system. And significant numbers of American workers are dissatisfied with the quality of their working lives."[8]

Too many unions scoff at this, ascribing any plans for humanizing work conditions to the ulterior motives of increasing productivity (the "speed-up") and higher profit margins, recalling the infamous Frederick W. Taylor's "scientific management" time studies. The AFL-CIO, in what must be considered a "position paper," devoted seven pages of the January, 1974, edition of the *American Federationist* to debunking "the illusion" of worker discontent, only to follow it up in the July, 1977, issue with a scholarly work by Jack Barbash, again seven pages in length and much to the same purpose.

Not only unions, but workers, too, are critical of job enrichment. American auto workers exposed to work organization programs in Sweden found their own assembly line experience in Detroit superior in some respects to working in autonomous groups at Saab-Scania or Volvo. Detroit was preferable, one American said, "because you don't have to think all the time," and another added, "You can do the work without paying much attention to it." Professor Elizabeth Douvan of the University of Michigan found in these responses clear and appalling "evidence for the stultifying and dehumanizing nature of the assembly line."

Studs Terkel summed it up in the first paragraph of *Working*:

> This book, being about work, is, by its very nature, about violence—to the spirit as well as to the body. It is about ulcers as well as accidents, about shouting matches as well as fistfights, about nervous breakdowns as well as kicking the dog around. It is, above all (or beneath all), about daily humiliations. To survive the day is triumph enough for the walking wounded among the great many of us.[9]

It is that daily humiliation which makes extension of community service activities into the plant, the office, the power plant and the mine shaft, not only desirable, but essential, particularly because of the simultaneous crises the economy is confronting, and the tremendous toll sociey is paying for the inept manipulations of shortsighted politicians of both major parties.

Clearly, labor should think in new directions if it is to muster strength in numbers adequate to meet the challenges of the future. The traditional collective bargaining approach has failed to inspire unswerving loyalty in the membership or to improve the public image of unions; a new approach is needed to meet the pressures coming from the rank and file as well as the public. "What have you done for me lately?" is far more likely to continue as the cry of the rank and file rather than any sense of being oppressed by "the system" that's at the root of the problems.

"The system" could also be modified if unions were represented on corporate boards of directors, but thus far only the UAW has espoused the heresy of codetermination. "The system," however, does not appear to draw any of the anger the worker feels, either because of unemployment, underemployment or dissatisfaction with working conditions which do not change fast enough "to keep up with the rapid and widescale changes in worker attitudes, aspirations and values," in the words of *Work in America*. But the anger is there and finds outlets in assaults on family members, neighbors and fellow workers, and in self-inflicted injuries. The anger resulted in a substantial number of deaths, murders and suicides, the Congressional Joint Economic Committee concluded in a study released October 30, 1976. It found that at least 26,000 deaths from the stress-related diseases of stroke, kidney and heart ailments, at least 1,500 of the suicides and 1,700 of the homicides during 1970–75 were related to increased unemployment.

Nor did the anger appear to spill over in the direction of union leadership; it did show up in a marked apathy that kept the rank and file from voting in elections, strike ballots and contract ratifications in meaningful numbers. The 1976 election of David J. Fitzmaurice as president of the International Union of Electrical, Radio and Machine Workers was typical. At a cost of $300,000 to mail and tabulate ballots for 285,000 members, the IUE determined Fitzmaurice polled 42,925 votes and his opponent, William Bywater, received 34,461 votes. The number of members who mailed in valid ballots was 77,418 or 27.16 percent of those eligible.

Tallies in the heated race for president of the United Steelworkers early in 1977, which saw Lloyd McBride, administration candidate, win with 328,861 votes, against insurgent Ed Sadlowski's 249,281 votes, revealed 40 percent of the union's 1.4 million members had taken the trouble to vote. But that was considered extraordinarily high, compared with other union elections. Usually a tenth of the International Association of Machinists' membership votes for officers.

Apathy may be a misnomer, for it's not indifference, but lack of confidence labor shares with the rest of society in the leaders of the nation's major institutions, as (Louis) Harris polls indicate annually. (Only 27.5 percent of eligible voters cast ballots for President Carter in 1976.) There's a critical need to rekindle confidence in the labor movement's leadership, since it will take massive grass roots participation to make union "clout" effective in lobbying, in voting, in representation on boards of directors of community institutions, to meet the critical years ahead. Labor needs more "live bodies" than the Committee on Political Education has been able to persuade to register and vote, and one way to do it is Samuel Gompers' way—"organize, organize, organize"—and George Meany was aware of this.

Early in 1977, Meany said he saw organizing as "an essential obligation of the trade union movement," in addressing a conference for organizing directors and officers of forty-one unions. That appears to contrast with an earlier, apparent indifference to the small number of union members. He said it didn't "mean a thing" to him, while Kirkland shrugged he'd "never been concerned about what proportion of the working force is organized at any given time."[10] Organizing, however, remains a function of the autonomous members of the AFL-CIO; the federation itself only assists on request.

Amendments to the National Labor Relations Act would remove many obstacles from organizing, but rekindling a spirit of militancy and the missionary zeal of earlier days will require labor to move in new directions, including organizing by the AFL-CIO on the scale of the CIO of the 1930s. Asked about "new directions" at a press conference in February, 1976, Meany replied:

> The federation over the years has been moving in new directions, but always with the same objective—the objective of building up the standards of the people we represent . . . Well, we are just in to everything. We are in the field of education. Who would have thought that 20 years ago we would have an educational set-up right outside the city of Washington. And of course, that's only one. That's the AFL-CIO Labor Studies Center.

> We are, of course, moving in the field of collective bargaining and in the legislative field. Actually, we are trying to keep pace with the development of the American economy, with the American society. But, always with the idea of building up the standards of life and work for those who work for wages. Of course, not just on-the-job, but we are interested in them as citizens. We are interested in them as consumers. We have a very active Community Services department that works with the various agencies, in the welfare field and private agencies, like the American Red Cross. So the field is certainly widening all the time. But the simple objective, of course, remains.[11]

He might have added the AFL-CIO is also represented in the U.S. delegation to the International Labor Organization, but the U.S. had already served notice it intended to resign in view of the politicization of the ILO. Overall, one couldn't quarrel with Meany's directions. But there's serious doubt labor is getting the message across to the member who's indifferent or hostile to the union which compels him to pay dues but leaves him dissatisfied with his returns. That's what gives weight to the "compulsory unionism" concept. If the member is ignorant of the value of being a member, the fault lies in the lack of communication. The gap can be closed by the labor press, which can overcome the prevailing notion that no one listens to the members, no one cares about their problems and nothing is being done to resolve those problems with all the alacrity of a grievance procedure.

There are scores of publications, ranging from four-page mimeographed leaflets to professionally written and printed magazines, but most of them suffer from the same fault—failure to involve the rank and file member, because they are devoted to reporting the pontifical declarations of the labor hierarchy.

The best known labor publications are the *AFL-CIO News* and the *American Federationist*. The former is a weekly newspaper of eight to sixteen pages and a circulation of 140,000. The latter is a monthly magazine of some literary pretensions. Its circulation is 110,000. Considering the cost of publishing each—over $300,000 for the *AFL-CIO News* and $204,000 for the *Federationist*—it's questionable whether either is worth the cost in view of the minute fraction of the membership reached. If millions of AFL-CIO members never read either one, where do they get their information about labor from? We find the answer in the Kraft opinion poll of 1967:

> The entire area of communications emerged as one of the most interesting sections of the poll. For, though members by and large read their union journals, they appear to rely generally on television, daily papers and magazines—in that order—as their most trusted sources of information.[12]

A fair proportion of members looking to union sources of news as "helpful" deserves better treatment. The critical need to improve the labor press becomes obvious in light of labor's deep-seated conviction that the "commercial press" is hostile to labor. Indeed, trade unionists are inclined to blame labor's poor image on "labor-busting" stories and editorials in the press. The rationale is that newspapers are owned by corporations who are anti-union because they must negotiate with unions.

Lane Kirkland summed up labor's attitude on this score at the 1975 convention in San Francisco in what can be considered a fair evaluation of journalists' sins of omission and commission.

He saw "ignorance" on the part of the reporter, something he attributed in part to the failure of education to include trade union history in school texts, but he also saw an unwillingness to learn, "to be confused by the facts," while the coverage of contract negotiations appeared to consist chiefly of news about "the fist fight, the walkout, the heated exchange." Kirkland condemned newspaper editorials for their "sins of commission":

Every union proposal is a "demand," every management proposal is an "offer." Every strike is a strike against the public interest. Never mind that the function of collective bargaining is to resolve disputes. Forget that 98 per cent of all negotiations do not end in strikes. Forget that what makes collective bargaining work, what keeps both parties trying to resolve their differences is the strike weapon. Forget the fact that union negotiators are elected officials—elected by the workers to represent them. Forget the contracts are voted on by the members. Forget the underlying democratic structure of the labor movement. Forget all that. And just ask yourself one question: "Who elected the editor to be guardian and judge of the public interest?" That does not mean newspapers should not editorialize on labor-management relations. They should. But they should be honest with themselves and their readers, and state openly the reasons they are on management's side . . .[13]

A veteran newsman finds it difficult to disagree, beyond entering a feeble demurrer, "There are exceptions." But it is equally true, alas, that the labor press is just as prone to errors of omission and commission. If the commercial press is anti-labor, the labor press is anti-management.

The former may be illustrated quite easily. Over 140 years ago, workers were complaining they were being maligned in print. "We are charged," said the workingmen of Woodstock, Vermont, "with being deists and infidels. On [the] one hand, it is alleged we are under Masonic influence—on the other hand, it is said as confidently we're anti-Masons. We are charged with being Agrarians and Levellers, and that we intend to use the guillotine."[14]

In the early 1900s, it was commonplace for newspapers to treat the unions as enemies of society, Philip S. Foner recalled.

Throughout the period 1900-14, the newspapers castigated labor as an un-American element—"How many of the most active leaders of labor unions are of American blood?" asked The New York Journal of Commerce rhetorically—pictured it as an unchained beast ready, if given the opportunity, to pounce upon a helpless public; and portrayed labor unions as one with thuggery, dynamiting, and the employment of all forms of and variety of terror. Labor's favorite weapons were referred to in The New York Times as "the bludgeon, the bullet, the dynamite cartridge," and the terrible boycott. Its record was one of "outrages and oppression, of riot and bloodshed, of cruel boycotts, of defiance of the law."[15]

The press has not improved noticeably in recent years. The dean of American labor columnists, A. H. Raskin, is the culprit who tagged trade unionists as "Archie Bunkers," using the stereotyped and denigrating image of the working man developed by the most popular TV program of the decade.

The labor press does not merit higher marks, despite the wide range of publications of local unions, city and state labor councils and international unions. If they share a fault, it is that uniformly they trumpet in praise the declarations of their union officers as infallible dogma, without recognition of their proneness for fallibility. It is difficult to deny there's more than an element of truth in the assessment B. J. Widick has made of the labor press:

> The state of the labor press is so sad that knowledgeable labor leaders and labor intellectuals seldom bother to read it. For reliable reports the *Wall Street Journal* and *Business Week* have become almost required reading, along with *The New York Times*.
>
> It is no lack of talent that keeps labor from having its own first-rate press. There are many good journalists and writers still working for the labor press. But they are hobbled by the concept that union papers must be solely "house organs," without any freedom of the press which labor demands in other newspapers. The sole purpose of the labor press is to reflect the policies of the dominant leadership, and to defend them against all criticism, with no pretense of presenting both sides.[16]

"Both sides" refers not only to election campaigns within unions, but to labor-management disputes. If the labor press sees no pressing need for objectivity, then the "house organ" will remain just that. But it has a far more urgent mission to accomplish: to tell the rank and file member what the union does, not what the union leader says. What it does, day in, day out, to serve the members and the community can be critical because it does make a difference in collective bargaining. Negotiating a contract with a union backed by solid public support, as the Communications Workers of America has long recognized, is quite different from negotiating with a union condemned by the public, whose elected representatives may have to intercede in the negotiations.

Keeping that in mind, CWA had little difficulty in getting news coverage when it decided to intervene in a pending rate case on behalf of its members and the community. Vice President Morton Bahr said the CWA would appear before the New York Public Service Commission when the New York Telephone Company filed for a 12.7 percent rate increase in 1976.[17] Union intervention in such a case helps establish in the public mind the concept of a union concerned with the public welfare. It is an example worth emulating, whether intervention is effective or not.

The labor press should be enlisted as a strategic weapon in creating a large and enthusiastic following for the trade union movement. Less emphasis placed on reporting speeches and position papers and more emphasis on investigative reporting and the reactions of the rank and file would be a distinct improvement. "Feedback," almost lacking, for example, in letters to the editor of most labor publications, should be an essential ingredient in determining policy and closing the gap between the union and its members.

The future of the labor movement might well be better charted if more labor papers sought out and printed the reactions of the rank and file to the declarations from Olympus; at least, then, what the worker wants, needs and would fight for would be known. Their photographs, rather than six to twelve close ups of the presiding officer in each edition, would also help close the gap between member and union.

More imaginative reporting would enliven and give perspective to labor news. Objectivity, in which management is given "equal space," is not essential, but management positions should be presented without distortion, if only to add credibility to the response. Perspective is essential, however, to give any account meaningful content. For example, the popular misconception that unions are "strike-happy" is responded to with data showing the low percentage of work days lost in strikes:

> Work stoppages in the nation's offices and factories dropped dramatically in 1972 and 1973 when labor unions found generous pay pacts difficult to squeeze past federal pay controllers. Indeed, the 27 million work days lost to strikes in each of these years was the lowest since 1966.[18]

Why not go one step further and point out the time lost was less than the time lost because of illness or injury attributed to industrial hazards? The Labor Department said so in the *Monthly Labor Review* of February, 1975:

> Of the nearly six million injuries and illnesses reported (in 1973), 97 per cent were injuries. Two out of three injuries did not cause workers to lose work time. Nevertheless, 28 million work days, amounting to some 114,000 work years, were lost. About 6,200 injuries and illnesses resulted in death.

That kind of story has "impact," not only in polishing up labor's public image, but in awakening a positive reaction among the rank and file and the public, as well, in labor's efforts to save lives. A similar story, which received all too little space in the press, went far in persuading the rank and file their union did, indeed, "give a damn" about them. The International Association of Heat and Frost Insulators and Asbestos Workers and the Johns-Manville Company donated $250,000 each to start research programs at Mount Sinai Medical Center to find an effective treatment and means of early diagnosis for mesothelioma.

Mesothelioma is an invariably fatal form of cancer caused by exposure to asbestos fibers. Extremely rare in the general population, mesothelioma is an industrial hazard accounting for 7 percent of the deaths among asbestos workers. Because of past exposure, 70,000 workers may die of cancer in the next four decades.

The research grant for Mount Sinai, according to Andrew H. Haas, asbestos workers' president, represented what could be done "in a spirit of labor-management cooperation to reduce and ultimately eliminate the needless tragedy of job-related illness."

It was a most unlikely area for labor-management cooperation. But there are indications unions are looking to even more unlikely areas to improve the welfare of the member. The ILGWU, for example, has undertaken a series of unlikely seminars for garment industry executives to show them how to use new assembly-line techniques to cut costs. If the industry can overcome its antiquated production methods and increased competition from imports, the jobs of 376,750 ILG members will be saved. Actors Equity insisted that Manhattan Plaza, twin forty-five-story apartment towers, had to be open not only to performing artists, but "support personnel" as well, and that includes stage hands, radio and television sound effects persons, ushers, electrical workers and television broadcast engineers. "We felt that to lend credibility to the concept that it is a performing artists' facility we had an obligation not to be elitist," said Donald Grody, Actors Equity executive secretary. "And it reflects good trade unionism."

That is the message that calls for a continuous barrage of stories; not one-time shots, such as the drive accompanying the campaign to amend the National Labor Relations Act in 1977, or the brilliant coup the AFL-CIO staged in inviting Aleksandr Solzhenitsyn to address the federation after President Ford refused to see him. (The public reaction was gratifying; labor's image was enhanced. But it was damaged when the AFL-CIO vetoed the appearance of a Soviet trade union delegate at the 1977 convention of the International Longshoremen's and Warehousemen's Union; it was a needless display of the power the AFL-CIO has in having a visa denied to a visitor to an independent union.) What is needed is more public display of labor's altruistic spirit—enough to overcome the anti-labor antics of the $5.5-million-a-year National Right-to-Work Committee and the disparaging picture of labor being spewed forth by the Advertising Council in its giveaway booklet, *The American Economic System.* The two paragraphs of the twenty-page booklet devoted to the unions are a tongue-in-cheek put-down:

Many American workers belong to labor unions. When the United States was just a few years old, workers began to join together to bargain with employers for better wages and working conditions. These were our first labor unions, on a very small scale, to be sure.

The American labor movement became an important force in our economic system after the Civil War. The Knights of Labor had 700,000 members in the 1880's. In 1886, the American Federation of Labor (A.F. of L.) was formed and later came the Congress of Industrial Organizations (C.I.O.). In 1955, the A.F. of L. and the C.I.O. joined forces and became what is now our nation's largest labor organization. Today, about one-fifth of all workers belong to labor unions.[19]

And that's it! There is no further mention of the labor movement or the role it plays in the American economic system. The disparagement of unions is not likely to convince anyone who has gone to school beyond the sixth grade, but it is an indication of the contempt for unions being instilled in impressionable minds.

Labor has the skill and talent to mount an adequate response. The AFL-CIO has not only a publications department, but a public relations department as well. They are extensive operations accounting for more than $900,000 of the AFL-CIO's annual budget. AFL-CIO staff members showed what they were capable of in preparing the pamphlet, *Unions in America*, for distribution to public schools at no cost in celebration of the bicentennial.[20] But again, it was a one-shot deal sparked by the National Endowment for the Humanities.

However, there are unions that have become aware of the need for ongoing programs of public exposure through institutional advertising. The American Federation of State, County and Municipal Employees, for example, was plastering the nation's publications in 1976 and 1977 with advertisements attacking indifferent, hostile or incompetent public employers the AFSCME deals with. Of course, such an ad program is prohibitively expensive for most unions, but the question must be asked: Can they afford not to spend the money? The International Ladies Garment Workers Union, for example, spends $2 million a year broadcasting its union label song, which seeks to halt the export of American jobs. But the song, "Always look for the union label, it says we're able to make it in the U.S.A.," has had an impact on millions of minds. The only other ongoing public relations program functioning all year 'round is that of the AFL-CIO Union Label Department, which promotes union-made goods and services with publicity releases, advertising and exhibits of union-made products that are extolled as "best" in quality—something the public, including union members, does not believe.

Can it be the efforts to improve labor's image are being misdirected? That there is a breakdown in communications between union and member? A letter to "Problem Line" in the Long Island newspaper, *Newsday*, which has never been sympathetic to organized labor, illustrates this aptly:

> Q. I have been working as a part-time shoe salesman for two years, earning $2 an hour plus 4 per cent commission. I have also been paying $1.50 union dues for which I supposedly receive benefits. Must I continue to pay the dues and what benefits come from these payments? Am I entitled to an hourly wage increase?—R.M., Valley Stream.

"Problem Line's" answer is not relevant beyond the suggestion that R.M. obtain a copy of the union contract, but the lack of communication between the union and R.M. is a real problem—one which business manager Jack Maltz quickly solved on reading the letter.

Clearly, it isn't enough to provide services; the member and the community must be informed of what is being done. And the need for more services and more information will increase as pressures mount on the labor movement. Can labor meet the challenge? It must, if human rights are to endure; there's no other spokesman for workers. One of the human rights spelled out by Article 23 of the Universal Declaration of Human Rights, adopted by the United Nations on December 10, 1948, is: "Everyone has the right to form and to join trade unions for the protection of his interests."

Does labor have the vitality to meet the challenges? Almost two decades ago, George W. Brooks declared he was not pessimistic about the future of the labor movement, but was troubled over "the danger to our long-run prospects for new leadership and vitality," as well as the factors that "withdraw from local unions more and more control over their own affairs."[21] While the weaknesses of local unions have since been augmented, new leadership has appeared on all levels and unions are meeting the challenges. Unions will not "run out of ideas or imagination or courage," we can agree with Brooks. They will solve the problem of creating a militant membership through extended and adequately publicized services to the community.

Notes

1. Robert L. Heilbroner, "The American Plan," *New York Times Magazine*, 25 January 1976, p. 40. Vide Heilbroner, *Business Civilization in Decline* (New York: W. W. Norton, 1976).
2. Thomas R. Brooks, "Public Unions: Parallels to the 1930s," *American Federationist*, December 1976, p. 9.

3. Transcript, "Dick Cavett Show," 19 December 1974.

4. *New York Times*, 1 September 1975, p. 5.

5. Ibid., 5 September 1976, sec. 3, p. 4.

6. Ibid., 9 May 1976, p. 27.

7. Ted Mills, "Altering the Social Structure in Coal Mining: A Case Study," *Monthly Labor Review*, October 1976, pp. 3–10.

8. *Work in America*, pp. xviii–xiv.

9. Studs Terkel, *Working*, p. xiii.

10. Haynes Johnson and Nick Kotz, *The Unions*, pp. 175–76.

11. Transcript of Meany's press conference, 20 February 1976.

12. Alexander E. Barkan, "The Union Member: Profile and Attitudes," *American Federationist*, August 1967, pp. 1–6.

13. Excerpts from Kirkland's speech as reported in *American Federationist*, December 1975, pp. 1–6.

14. *New York Workingmen's Advocate*, 31 July 1831, cited in John R. Commons, ed., *History of Labour in the United States*, vol. 1, p. 293.

15. Philip S. Foner, *History of the Labor Movement in the United States*, vol. 3, p. 52.

16. B. J. Widick, *Labor Today: The Triumphs and Failures of Unionism in the United States*, p. 107.

17. *New York Times*, 7 December 1976, p. 25.

18. *Wall Street Journal*, 12 June 1974, p. 1.

19. *The American Economic System . . . and Your Part in It* (Advertising Council, n.d.), pp. 4–5.

20. AFL-CIO publication no. 153.

21. George W. Brooks, *The Sources of Vitality in the American Labor Movement*, p. 47.

Bibliography

Basic Training Manual for Union Counselors, The. AFL-CIO Department of Community Services, 1974.

Baxandrall, Rosalyn; Gordon, Linda; and Reverby, Susan. *America's Working Women: Documentary History 1600 to the Present.* New York: Vintage Books, 1976.

Beauvoir, Simone de. *The Second Sex.* New York: Alfred A. Knopf, 1953.

Bok, Derek C., and Dunlop, John T. *Labor and the American Community.* New York: Simon & Schuster, 1970.

Boulding, Kenneth E. *The Organizational Revolution.* New York: Harper Bros., 1953.

Brooks, George W. *The Sources of Vitality in the American Labor Movement.* New York State School of Industrial and Labor Relations, Cornell University, 1960.

Brooks, Thomas R. *Toil and Trouble.* New York: Delacorte Press, 1971.

Butler, Lawrence N. *Why Survive? Being Old in America.* New York: Harper & Row, 1975.

Careers for Negroes on Newspapers. Newspaper Guild, n.d.

Carter, Richard. *The Doctor Business.* New York: Doubleday & Co., 1958.

Clague, Ewan; Palli, Balraj; and Kramer, Leo. *The Aging Worker and the Union.* New York: Praeger, 1971.

Commons, John R., ed. *History of Labour in the United States.* New York: Macmillan, 1958.

Community Services and Rehabilitation Counselors Handbook. New York Central Labor Council, AFL-CIO, Community Services and Rehabilitation Committee, 1966.

Cook, Alice H. *Labor's Role in Community Affairs.* New York State School of Industrial and Labor Relations, Cornell University, 1955.

Cormier, Frank, and Eaton, William J. *Reuther.* Englewood Cliffs, N.J.: Prentice-Hall, 1970.

Davis, Walter G. *Afro-American Labor Leaders of New York City.* New York Central Labor Council, AFL-CIO, Black Trade Unionists Leadership Committee, 1976.

Denisoff, R. Serge. *Great Day Coming: Folk Music and the American Left.* Urbana, Ill.: University of Illinois Press, 1971.

Drucker, Peter F. *The Unseen Revolution.* New York: Harper & Row, 1976.

Finley, Joseph E. *The Corrupt Kingdom.* New York: Simon & Schuster, 1972.

Fitch, John A. *Social Responsibilities of Organized Labor.* New York: Harper Bros., 1957.

Flexner, Eleanor. *Century of Struggle.* New York: Atheneum, 1974.

Foner, Philip S. *History of the Labor Movement in the United States.* New York: International Publishers Co., 1975.

Hamilton, Alice. *Exploring the Dangerous Trades.* Boston: Atlantic Monthly Press, 1943.

Hapgood, Hutchins. *The Spirit of the Ghetto: Studies of the Jewish Quarter of New York.* New York: Schocken Books, 1966.

Harbrecht, Paul P. *Pension Funds and Economic Power.* Twentieth Century Fund, 1959.

Himmelstein, Morgan Y. *Drama Was a Weapon.* New Brunswick, N.J.: Rutgers University Press, 1963.

Industrial Hazards. Scientists Committee for Occupational Health, 1971.

Job Development Project Final Report: Demonstration of Union-Based Selective Placement Program for Disabled Workers. Washington, D.C.: Department of Health, Education and Welfare, 1970.

Johnson, Haynes, and Kotz, Nick. *The Unions.* New York: Pocket Books, 1972.

Justin, Cornelius, and Impellizeri, Mario E. *Mirage of Private Pensions.* Manhattan College School of Business, n.d.

Kane Hospital—A Place to Die. Pittsburgh: Action Coalition of Elders, n.d.

Knapp, Joseph G. *The Advance of American Cooperative Enterprise: 1920–1945.* Danville, Ill.: Interstate Printers & Publishers, 1973.

Law, Sylvia A. *Blue Cross: What Went Wrong?* New Haven: Yale University Press, 1974.

Lens, Sidney. *The Crisis of American Labor.* Cranbury, N.J.: A. S. Barnes & Co., 1961.

Lerner, Gerda. *Black Women in White America.* New York: Vintage Books, 1973.

Lester, Richard A. *As Unions Mature: An Analysis of the Evolution of American Unionism.* Princeton: Princeton University Press, 1958.

Levinson, Charles, ed. *The New Multinational Health Hazards.* Geneva: International Chemical and General Workers Federation, 1974.

Nelson, Anne H. *The Visible Union in Times of Stress.* New York State School of Industrial and Labor Relations, Cornell University, 1969.

Occupational Epidemic: The Ralph Nader Task Force Report on Job Health and Safety. Center for the Study of Responsive Law, 1972.

Organized Labor: Source Materials for the Study of Labor in America. United Federation of Teachers, 1976.

Proceedings of the Eleventh Constitutional Convention of the AFL-CIO and Report of the Executive Council. 1973.

Proceedings of the Twelfth Constitutional Convention of the AFL-CIO and Report of the Executive Council. 1975.

Project Rehab Final Report: Demonstration of a Labor Rehabilitation Liaison Service. Washington, D.C.: Department of Health, Education and Welfare, 1968.

Rayback, Joseph G. *A History of American Labor.* New York: Macmillan, Free Press, 1966.

Readings on Labor Education. Institute of Management and Labor Relations, Rutgers University, n.d.

Reed, Louis S. *The Labor Philosophy of Samuel Gompers.* Port Washington, N.Y.: Kennikat Press, 1958.

Reynolds, Bertha Capen. *Social Work and Social Living.* National Association of Social Workers, 1951.

Rogin, Lawrence, and Rachlin, Marjorie. *Labor Education in the United States.* Institute of Labor Education at the American University, 1968.

Schnapper, M. B. *American Labor: A Pictorial, Social History.* Washington, D.C.: Public Affairs Press, 1975.

Scott, Rachel. *Muscle and Blood.* New York: E. P. Dutton, 1974.

Sexton, Patricia, and Sexton, Brendan. *Blue Collars and Hard Hats.* New York: Vintage Books,1971.

Spero, Sterling D., and Harris, Abram L. *The Black Worker, the Negro and the Labor Movement.* Port Washington, N.Y.: Kennikat Press, 1966.

Stellman, Jeanne M., and Daum, Susan M. *Work Is Dangerous to Your Health.* New York: Vintage Books, 1973.

Taft, Philip. *The AFL in the Time of Gompers.* New York: Harper Bros., 1957.

———. *Organized Labor in American History.* New York: Harper & Row, 1964.

Tartell, Lottie Haid. "Education in the Amalgamated Clothing Workers of America." Master's thesis, Columbia University, 1949.

Terkel, Studs. *Working.* New York: Avon Books, 1975.

"This Is the AFL-CIO." AFL-CIO publication no. 20, 1975.

Tunley, Roul. *The American Health Scandal.* New York: Harper & Row, 1958.

Tyler, Gus. *The Labor Revolution.* New York: Viking Press, 1966.

Weiner, Hyman J. *A Group Approach to Link Community Mental Health with Labor.* New York: Columbia University Press, 1967.

Wertheimer, Barbara M. *Exploring the Arts.* New York State School of Industrial and Labor Relations, Cornell University, 1968.

——, and Nelson, Anne H. *Trade Union Women: A Study of Their Participation in New York City Locals.* New York: Praeger, 1975.

Why Labor Staff? New York: AFL-CIO Community Services Activities, New York, n.d.

Widick, B. J. *Labor Today: The Triumphs and Failures of Unionism in the United States.* Boston: Houghton Mifflin Co., 1964.

Work in America. Report of a Special Task Force to the Secretary of Health, Education and Welfare. Cambridge, Mass.: M.I.T. Press, 1973.

Index

Johnson, Dr. Herrick, 39
Johnson, Keith W., 169
Johnson, Lyndon, 6
Johnson, Dr. Maurice, 59
Johnson, Michael, 112
Johnson, Stanley L., 225
Jones, Bill, 146–47
Jones, Casey (John Luther), 43
Jones, Mother Mary, 31, 219, 242
Jones, Patricia, 214
Jones & Laughlin Steel Corporation, 72
Joy, James, 67, 132
Junior Sons of '76, 35

Kahn, Si, 242
Kaiser, Henry J., 162
Kaiser Health Plans, 162
Kane Hospital, 111
Karth, Joseph E., 148
Katz, Edward M., 188
Kaye, Bess, 133
Kazan, Abraham E., 194–95
Kechler, Ken, 148
Kehoe, John (Black Jack), 35
Kennedy, Duff, 192
Kennedy, Edward, 153
Kennedy, John, 217
Kennedy, Robert, 217
Kennedy Boston Associates, 192
Kerr-McGee Corporation, 40–41
Keuchler, Charlie, 1
Keyes, Thelma, 165
King, Coretta Scott, 239
King, Martin Luther, Jr., 210, 216, 239
King, Thelma, 61–62
Kirkland, Lane, 148–49, 181, 256, 263–64
Klein, James, 249
Knapp, Joseph G., 193–94
Knights of Columbus, 26
Knights of Labor, 31, 35–36, 42, 171–72, 202, 269
Koehler, Robert, 239
Kopple, Barbara, 249
Kraft, John, 5, 7, 265
Krasner, Al, 79–80
Kronberg, Shirley, 113–19

Labor/Arts Inc., 243–44
labor agencies, 101, 141–45, 154, 158, 246–47
labor banks, 187–90, 196–97
labor colleges, 168–69, 173
labor education and labor studies, 61, 73–74, 165–84, 191, 235, 242, 263

Labor Education Association, 167, 178
Laborers International Union, 43, 54, 191
Labor for Peace, 21–22
Labor Health Institute, 163
labor press and publications, 42–43, 51, 60–61, 68, 73, 86–87, 89, 99–100, 102, 112, 136–38, 141, 154–55, 176, 182–83, 196, 209, 229–31, 260–61, 264–67
Labor Rehab. *See* Central Labor Rehabilitation Council
Labor's Community Agency, 142, 144
Labor Studies Center, 73
Ladd, H. Landon, 168
Ladies' Federal Labor Union, 224
LaGuardia, Fiorello H., 158
Lansing, Robert, 246
Lasko, Stan, 1
Laundry and Dry Cleaning Workers, 21
League of Women Voters, 224
Lee, Ernest, 149
Legal Aid Society, 118
legal services, prepaid, 53–54, 87
Lema, Charles, 72
Lemeraro, Anthony, 72
Levine, Louis L., 123, 125, 128, 141, 162
Levinson, Charles, 77
Lew, Sid, 125, 141
Lewis, John L., 24, 83, 189, 240, 245–46
Liebowitz, Murray, 258
life insurance, 197–98
Lincoln, Abraham, 188
Lingg, Louis, 37
Lions Club, 32
Livolsi, Frank, 141
Long, John E. (Buddy), 109
Long Island Federation of Labor, 142, 197
Long Island Lighting Co. (LILCO), 1
Long Island Railroad, 166
Loomis and Kennedy, 192
Lucy, William, 211
Ludlow Massacre, 39

McBride, Lloyd, 262
McCart, John A., 71
McCarthy, Dr. Eugene, 48
McCarthy, Sen. Eugene J., 3
McCormick Harvester, 36
McGuire, Peter J., 17–18, 203
MacKenzie, John R., 178
McMahon, Charles, 26
McManigal, John, 72
Madar, Olga, 223, 225
Maintenance union, 114
Maltoni, Dr. Cesare, 77

Maltz, Jack, 270
Manson, Dr. Julius J., 165–66
Manufacturer's Hanover Trust, 187
Marshall, Ray, 149
Martin, Donald D., 194
martyrs and violence, 22, 31, 35–42
Mastroianni, Tony, 246
Mazzocchi, Anthony, 26, 40–41, 63, 66, 75
Meany, George, 21–22, 71–72, 97, 137, 139, 149, 169, 178, 181, 205–07, 210, 217, 226, 228–29, 255–56, 263
Meany Center for Labor Studies, 167, 177–79
Mechanics' Union of Trade Associations, 170
Medicare and Medicaid, 6, 80, 93–95, 103, 114–15, 152, 182
Memorial Day battle, 40
mental illness, 127–28, 152, 154, 157–58
Metallic Lathers union, 146
Metal Trades union, 160
Metal Workers Federation Union of America, 16
Micale, Frank, 60
Michelson, William, 48, 50, 159
Midwest Research Institute of Kansas, 61
Miller, Arnold, 68, 70, 148, 190
Miller, Jeffrey M., 43
Miller, Joyce D., 85–87, 221, 225–26, 233
minimum wage laws, 19–20, 47, 64, 113, 182
Mintz, Copal, 54
Mire, Joseph, 174
Mobil Oil, 4
Mogulesco, Miles, 249
Mollie Maguires, 35
Molloy, Dan, 103
Molofsky, Sol, 47, 50
Morbidelli, Nello, 60–61
Mortgage Investment Trust (MIT), 190–91
Morton, William, 72
Mossberg, Walter, 60
motivation of union leaders, 1–2, 23–29, 47, 50, 52, 62, 84–87, 99, 101–02, 107, 109, 113, 116–17, 122, 124, 133–34, 136
Mount Sinai School of Medicine, 59
Municipal Assistance Corporation, 193
Municipal Employees Union, 48
Murray, Philip, 24, 26, 83, 204
Murray-Green Award, 135, 206
Muste, A. J., 173

Nader, Ralph, 74–75
National Alliance of Postal and Federal Employees, 208
National Association for the Advancement of Colored People (NAACP), 54, 94, 205, 211, 213
National Association of Broadcast Employees and Technicians, 102, 242
National Association of Housing Redevelopment Officials, 191
National Association of Letter Carriers, 92, 104
National Association of Machinists, 203
National Association of Manufacturers, 64
National Bank of Washington, 189
National Civic Federation, 148
National Coal Board, 69
National Consumer Center for Legal Services, 54
National Council for the Arts and Humanities, 244–45
National Council of Senior Citizens (NCSC), 54, 85, 90, 93–95, 192
National Council on Alcoholism, 98, 100, 154
National Council on Crime and Delinquency, 98, 100–01
National Education Association, 54, 213, 228–29
National Endowment for the Arts, 245
National Endowment for the Humanities, 269
National Foundation, 11
national health insurance plan, 45, 152–53, 160
National Health Service, 152
National Housing Conference, 191
National Institute for Occupational Safety and Health (NIOSH), 57, 61, 77–78
National Institute on Alcohol Abuse and Alcoholism, 98, 154
National Institute on Alcohol and Drug Abuse, 98, 155
National Labor Party, 3
National Labor Relations Act, 5, 39, 263, 268
National Labor Relations Board, 36, 83
National Labor Union, 224
National Machinists' Union, 203
National Maritime Union, 102–03, 156, 158, 164, 184, 212
National Organization of Women (NOW), 224
National Quality of Work Center, 259
National Recovery Act, 28
National Right-to-Work Committee, 268

Quill, Michael, 123

Rader, Martin, 248
Railway Labor Act, 28
Randolph, A. Philip, 205–06, 215–17
Rand School of Social Science, 173, 177
Rapoport, Bernard, 198
Raskin, A. H., 4, 265
Rayford, Norman, 41
Republic Steel, 40
Retail, Wholesale and Department Store
Union, 21, 146, 212, 238, 242, 244, 253
Retail Clerks International Union, 15–16,
25, 79, 158, 223
retired workers, 25, 79–96, 128–29, 241
retirees clubs, 25, 79–80, 84–85, 88–90, 93
Reuther, May, 175
Reuther, Victor, 173
Reuther, Walter, 40, 42, 84, 94, 107, 173,
204
Reuther Education Center, 175, 258
Richardson, Abbott, 72
Richardson, Elliot L., 261
Richart, Julia, 249
Riordan, Mary Ellen, 228–29
rituals and ceremonies, 32–36, 201, 203
River Rouge fight, 40
Robbins, Guy M., 128, 132, 134
Robilotta, Peter, 240, 242
Robins, Margaret Drier, 223
Robinson, Henry, 72
Robinson, Jolly, 242
Rockefeller, David, 148
Rockefeller, John D., 32
Rockefeller, Nelson, 147
Rockefeller family, 39
Rockwell International, 259
Romanko, Michael, 72
Romney, George, 6
Roosevelt, F. D., 188
Rosenstein, Irving, 180
Rotary International, 32
Rubin, Jay, 113, 117, 119
Rushton Mining Center, 259–60
Rustin, Bayard, 215–17

Sadlowski, Ed, 180, 262
safety. *See* occupational safety and health
Salvation Army, 11, 154
Sampson, Michael, 125
Samuels, Sheldon, 71, 73
Sass, Frank, 72
Schaak, Capt. Michael J., 37
Schlossberg, Joseph, 176

scholarship programs, 51, 175, 181, 241
Schwab, Eugene, 37
Schwartz, W. H., 14
Scientists Committee for Occupational
Health, 61
Scott, Rachel, 62, 74
Screen Actors Guild, 53, 221, 246–47
Seafarers International Union, 156, 234
Selikoff, Dr. Irving, 59, 61, 77
Seman, John J., 72
Service Employees International Union,
21, 71, 88, 111, 118, 212
sexism. *See* women's rights
Shanker, Albert, 52, 108, 183, 214
Sheehan, John J., 71
Sheet Metal Workers International Associa-
tion, 20, 92, 259
Shell Oil, 75
Sheppard, Harold L., 260
Shoe Workers union, 223
Shouse, Ben, 246
Silberman, Laurence H., 75
Silkwood, Karen G., 40–41
Simon, John, 249
Slaiman, Donald, 21
Smith, Hilda, 173
Smith, Leonard S., 206
Smothers, Louise, 226
Socialist party, 3, 148, 173
Social Security, 13, 27, 47, 82, 90, 93, 95,
103–04, 114, 129, 131, 153, 162, 182
Society of the Plastics Industry, 59
Solomon, Saul, 237–38
Solomon, Sheila, 239
Solzhenitsyn, Aleksandr, 268
songs of workers, 41–44, 84
Sottile, James, 166
Southern New England Telephone Co.,
164
Southern Pacific Railroad, 43
Sovereign Sons of Industry, 35
Spies, August, 37
Stackhouse, Paul, Jr., 245
Steinberg, William R., 92
Stettner, Louis, 239
Stevens, J. P., Company, 210, 250
Stewart, Jimmy, 206
Sullivan, Dave, 21
Sullivan, Joseph, 206
Szold, Robert, 195

Taft, Philip, 19
Taft, William Howard, 148
Taft-Hartley Act, 6, 54, 83, 182

196–97, 240, 254
Vanderbilt, William H., 32
Vanguard Bank, 197
Vento, Bruce Freank, 148
Vietnam War, 6, 8, 21–22, 63
Viglietta, Virginia, 121
vinyl chloride. *See* polyvinyl chloride
violence. *See* martyrs and violence.
Vivert, Frank, 132
Vladeck, Stephen C., 162

Waddy, Walter, 217
Wagner Act, 28, 35
Wagoner, Dan, 245
Wagoner, Dr. Joseph, 78
Waldbaum's, 165
Wall Street Journal, 77, 266
Ward, Captain, 27
Ward, Martin J., 138
Waters, Jerry, 121–23, 128, 132, 156
Watts, Glen, 89, 212, 226, 232
Western Electric, 124
Western Women's Bank, 227
West Virginia Black Lung Association, 70
Wharton, Hunton P., 177
White, Stuart, 243
Widick, B. J., 21–22, 174
Wiggers, James, 72
Wilensky, Harold, 174
Wilson, William, 148
Wilson, Woodrow, 148
Winpisinger, William, 256
Witt, Mel J., 246
Wodka, Steven, 40
Wolfgang, Myra, 226
Wolfson, Arthur, 80
Wolfson, Theresa, 177

Woll, J. Albert, 198
Woll, Matthew, 198
Women Office Workers, 224
Women's Action Alliance, 224
Women's Campaign Fund, 224
Women's Legal Defense Fund, 224
Women's Performing Arts Coalition, 247
women's rights and sexism, 18, 36, 107,
    139, 170, 201–02, 204–05, 207–09, 212,
    214, 219–36, 254
Women's Trade Union League, 172
Woodcock, Leonard, 148, 258
Workers Bank, 189
Workers Defense League, 108
Workers Education union, 167
workers' schools. *See* labor education
Workingman's Institute, 172
Workingmen's Party, 3, 170
Working Women's Association, 224
Working Women's Protective Union, 224
Working Women's Union, 224
Work I've Done, The, 248–49
Workmen's Benevolent Association, 35
Workmen's Circle, 28–29
workmen's compensation laws, 13, 47, 65,
    134, 175
Works Progress Administration (WPA), 173
World Health Organization, 77
Wurf, Jerry, 230, 256
Wyatt, Addie, 204, 212, 222, 232
Wysocki, Bernard, Jr., 77

Yablonski, Jock, 148
YMCA, 11, 137
YWCA, 173

Zeidel, Al, 103